ILLUSTRATED ENVIRONMENTAL STUDIES

E. DEJARDIN

Collins *Educational*

An imprint of HarperCollins *Publishers*

Published 1991 by
CollinsEducational
An imprint of HarperCollins*Publishers*
77–85 Fulham Palace Road
Hammersmith
London W6 8JB

Reprinted 1989, 1991

Dejardin, Elizabeth
  Illustrated environmental studies.
  1. Human ecology
  I. Title
  333.7   GF43

  ISBN 0–00–322243–8

Cover design by Ken Cox
Typeset by MS Filmsetting Limited, Frome, Somerset
Printed in Great Britain by Bell and Bain Ltd., Glasgow.

Acknowledgements

The author would like to express her thanks to the following: Richard Kemp, Humanities advisor for Buckinghamshire County Council for his guidance and encouragement to write in the first place. Michael R Shorthouse for his patience and initial editing. Jonathan Wray, a very helpful editor. Mr M Nicholson for his time and marvellous tours around his pig farm. Simon Perry, Anthony Bandle and Roger Langley. Bryan Selley and colleagues at Bicester school. Alice Coleman (National Landuse Survey). Graham Fuller (Farmer's Weekly). Dr Steve Tilling of the Field Studies Council and Dr R A D Cameron (and associates) of the University of Birmingham. Colin W Plant, Assistant Curator of Passmore Edwards Museum. Case. I.H. The Nature Conservancy Council. The National Water Council. The National Trust. Friends of the Earth Trust Ltd. The Countryside Commission, and many other organisations concerned with the environment. British Petroleum Company plc for information taken from the 1986 B.P. Statistical Review of World Energy. Milton Keynes Development Corporation. Norwich City Council Planning. The Scottish Development Agency. The Bicester Advertiser, Daily Telegraph and Sunday Times for permission to reproduce the articles used in this book. Vince Driver for the illustrations. Ken Cox for the cover design.
Last but not least, Eleanor and Giles for tolerating a working mother.

To the Teacher

This is the book I desperately searched for when I set out to teach environmental studies at Bicester School, instead of working for years with pamphlets, collected snippets and 'homemade' worksheets. Pupils can really succeed in this subject. They may have shown interest in Geography, Biology or History but failed to grasp all the technical terms and details. Often hopeless at mathematics they suddenly find Environmental Studies a science they are good at! Encourage them to read around, to watch the news and collect cuttings from magazines and papers about environmental issues. Above all, persuade them to state the obvious when recording and answering questions and to use their common sense.

Now you have the text you can start environmental studies in your school. If your course is only one year as often happens with sixth formers, start immediately with the ecology and any individual project work involving ecology. (You will miss the best months for ecology, June to July.)

Individual projects are a problem. Some syllabusses ask the pupils to complete at least three. Sixth formers need a lot of guidance, let alone fourth years. Prepare in advance lists of project ideas from different sections of the syllabus which would work in your locality. Follow this up with basic outline plans of how to set about recording and collecting data. Make them write up a detailed account every step of the way, handing their work in frequently to be checked. Ideally a project should aim to answer one or more hypothetical questions. Conclusions are so important. They must be written and rewritten even when negative. Obviously for advanced pupils more detail on certain issues will still need to be presented by the teacher.

Geofile by Mary Glasgow Publications Ltd may be a useful source of data.

E J Dejardin

T = Teacher assistance necessary

Contents

1. Planet Earth

THE SOLAR SYSTEM

A **star** is a sphere of gases at extremely high temperature, giving out light. A **planet** orbits round a star. In the **solar system**, the sun is a star. It has nine cool planets which 'shine' by reflecting sunlight. The earth is one of them.

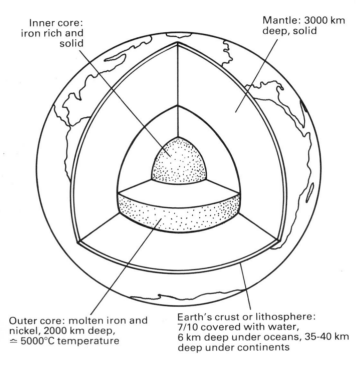

Inner core: iron rich and solid

Mantle: 3000 km deep, solid

Outer core: molten iron and nickel, 2000 km deep, ≃ 5000°C temperature

Earth's crust or lithosphere: 7/10 covered with water, 6 km deep under oceans, 35-40 km deep under continents

FIG. 1.1 THE INTERNAL STRUCTURE OF THE EARTH

All these planets rotate around the sun in elliptical **orbits**. The time taken for the earth to complete one orbit of the sun is called a year (365¼ days). Each planet also **revolves** on its own axis. The earth's axis is not vertical. It is tilted at an angle of 23.5°. As the earth revolves, the surface moves into and out of the light from the sun, giving day and night. Both of these movements lead to variations in the length of night and day during the year and also cause the changes of the seasons. They greatly affect the lives of living things on earth.

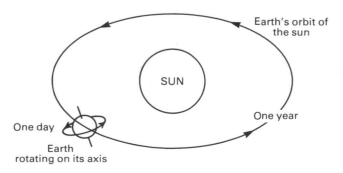

Earth's orbit of the sun

SUN

One day

One year

Earth rotating on its axis

FIG. 1.2 THE EARTH ROTATING ON ITS AXIS

Space exploration and astronomy have led scientists to believe that earth is the only planet to support life as we know it. It is the only one in the solar system to have the right combination of surface temperatures, water vapour, oxygen and the right density of atmosphere, giving sufficient protection from the harmful effects of the sun's radiation.

The moon is a natural satellite which orbits the earth every 27.3 days. The gravitational pull of the moon 'heaps up' the water of the seas to produce **tides**. When the pull of the sun and the moon act in the same direction this produces higher **spring tides**. When the pull in opposite directions this produces lower **neap tides**.

RADIATION

The sun emits radiant energy. It reaches the earth's surface in the form of **heat** and **light**. At night the earth itself loses heat by radiation. The temperature of the earth is controlled as follows:

- The earth only receives a small proportion of the sun's energy because of its great distance from the sun and its relatively small size.
- Due to the curvature of the earth's surface and the angle at which the rays strike it, the sun's energy is more concentrated in areas such as the equator and spread over a larger area nearer to the poles.
- The atmosphere absorbs 50% of the sun's energy before it reaches the earth's surface, and limits the amount of heat lost by the earth at night. (Clouds are particularly important at night as they form an insulating layer. Frosts may occur on still cloudless nights during the winter.)

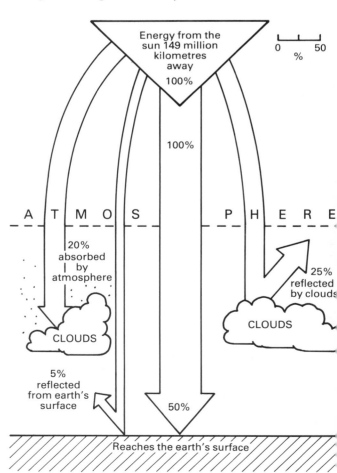

Energy from the sun 149 million kilometres away 100%

0   %   50

100%

ATMOSPHERE

20% absorbed by atmosphere

25% reflected by clouds

CLOUDS

CLOUDS

5% reflected from earth's surface

50%

Reaches the earth's surface

FIG. 1.3 THE EARTH'S HEAT BUDGET

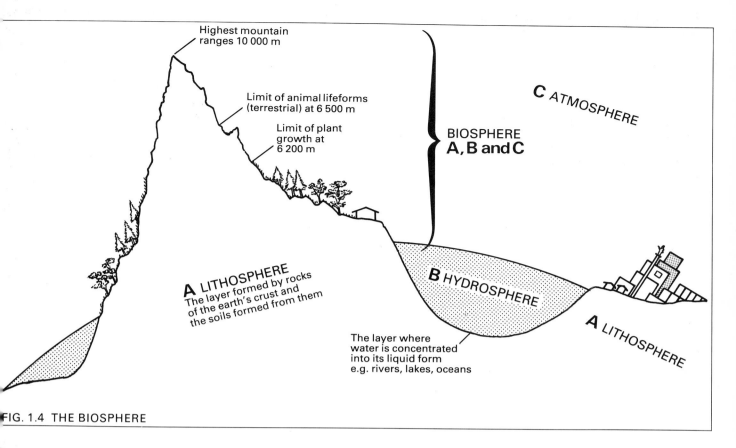

FIG. 1.4 THE BIOSPHERE

THE ATMOSPHERE

This is a gaseous covering, about 480 km thick, over the earth. It allows 50% of the sun's radiation to reach the earth and warm the rocks, soil and water. (see Fig. 1.3). Between 20 and 40 km above sea level is the layer containing ozone. This absorbs very short wave ultra-violet rays, known as 'burning rays'. They cause severe skin and dye damage, and would kill plants if they reached the earth's surface.

The atmosphere is made up of three layers. The weather occurs in the **troposphere**. Most of the water vapour is found in this layer. Higher up, the air becomes thinner (less oxygen), the air pressure lower and the temperature colder.

The **tropopause** marks the end of the troposphere and the upper limit of 'the weather'. It is lower over the poles (8 km) and higher over the equator (16 km). Above it, the **stratosphere** is composed of thin cloudless air with little water vapour or dust and the **ionosphere** has very thin air. It has electrically conducting layers that allow electromagnetic waves to be reflected. This property is used in radio transmission. Weather satellites orbit the earth in this layer.

Questions

1. Gravity prevents the gases of the atmosphere escaping. Apart from water vapour, the amounts of which vary, these are the approximate proportions of gas in the atmosphere:

Nitrogen	78%
Oxygen	21%
Argon	0.9%
Carbon dioxide	0.03%
Trace gases, e.g. neon, ozone, helium, methane	0.07%
Total	100%

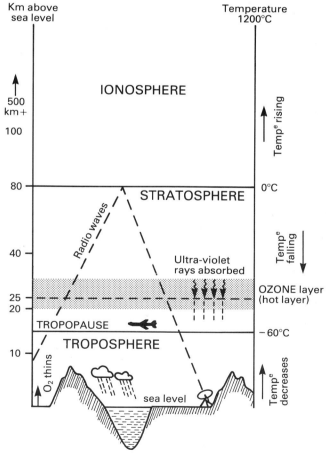

FIG. 1.5 THE ATMOSPHERE OF THE EARTH

Construct a pie chart of these figures.
Remember: $100\% = 360°$
$1\% = 3.6°$
$21\% = 3.6° \times 21 = 75.6°$

3

HOW ARE PEOPLE CHANGING THE WEATHER?

1. **By increasing the amount of carbon dioxide (CO_2) in the atmosphere?** CO_2 acts like the glass in Fig. 1.6. **Short wave radiation** from the sun passes through the CO_2 in the atmosphere to reach the earth. The earth reflects some of it out again as **long wave radiation** and CO_2 is thought to stop this escaping into outer space. The heat remains in the atmosphere. The fuels we burn add to the amount of CO_2 which is released into the atmosphere (see Fig. 1.7). Will this create a 'greenhouse effect' and increase the temperature at the earth's surface?

2. **By increasing the amount of particles in the air caused by pollution?** (See p. 81). Some of the sun's radiation is reflected back off these particles before reaching the earth's surface.

3. **By breaking down the ozone layer?** Man-made chemicals called **chlorofluorocarbons (CFCs)** eg freons are used to propel the products through the nozzle of aerosol sprays. They escape into the atmosphere and are thought to break down the gas ozone.

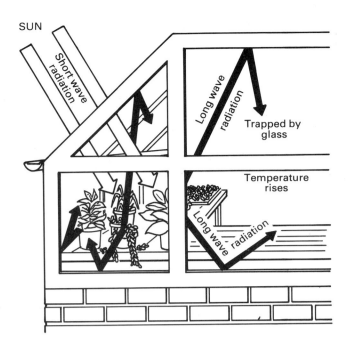

FIG. 1.6 THE 'GREENHOUSE EFFECT'

Questions

1. What might be the consequences of a steady rise in temperature caused by the 'greenhouse effect'? (Key words: polar ice caps, sea level)
2. How might atmospheric temperature be affected by an increase in airborne particles caused by pollution?
3. Explain why you shouldn't leave a child or animal locked in a car without a window open on a hot summer's day.
4. Explain the carbon cycle using Fig. 1.7.

5. Collect together all the aerosols used in your house.
   (a) What sorts of products are packed in aerosol containers?
   (b) Could they be packed in another way or form?
   (c) What effect could the breaking down of the ozone layer have on life on earth?
6. What important part do the clouds and dust play in the **heat budget** for the earth and its atmosphere? (See Fig. 1.3).

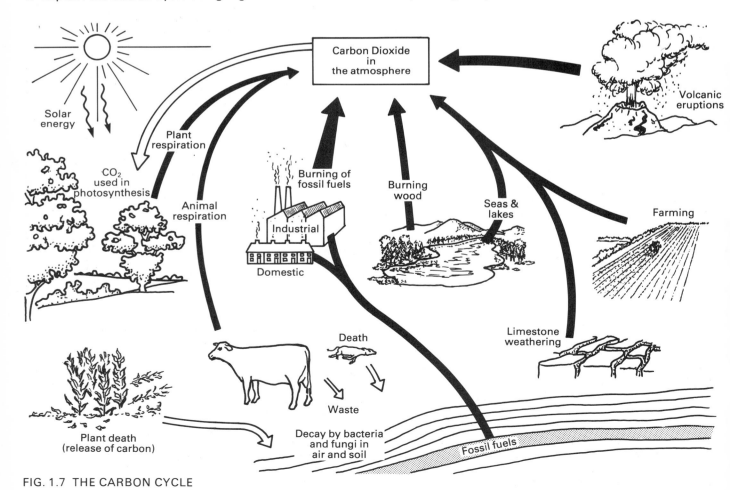

FIG. 1.7 THE CARBON CYCLE

4

2. The Land

Land is a scarce and precious resource. It cannot be increased appreciably but it can be used more productively (see p. 37) or reclaimed (see p. 75). People need land to build homes, factories, schools and shops; to grow food, forests and to have open spaces. There is great competition for the 24 million hectares of land in the densely populated land that makes up Great Britain. Therefore land values have risen dramatically. The Second Land Use Survey of Britain, directed by Alice Coleman, produced a series of maps to show exactly how the land is used.

FIELDWORK

Carry out a simplified land use survey

LAND USE	FIELD SYMBOL	COLOUR
GRASSLAND	G	GREEN
ARABLE	SUITABLE LETTERS, eg. C for Cereals	BROWN
HORTICULTURE	SUITABLE LETTERS	MAUVE
ORCHARDS	🗄🗄🗄 or O	MAUVE
WOODS	♣♣♣ ♧♧♧	DARK GREEN
HEATH, ROUGH PASTURE	Φ	YELLOW
WATER, MARSH	⚘	BLUE
DERELICT LAND	░	WHITE
UNVEGETATED	✖	WHITE
PUBLIC OPEN SPACE	OS	LIME GREEN
TRANSPORT	T	ORANGE
INDUSTRY	I	RED
SETTLEMENT	▨▨	GREY

TABLE 2.1

1. Use a base map provided by your teacher. (Scale 1:10 000 or 1:25 000 to show up the field boundaries.) Decide the line of your transect – perhaps along a road or footpath.
2. Take a copy of the symbols of the **simplified** scheme in Table 2.1.
3. Walk through, or view from high vantage points, the selected area, recording on your base map, **in pencil**, the field symbols of the various land uses. An example is done for you in Fig. 2.1.
4. Back in the classroom, use the correct colours to complete your map. Record the date and place of the survey. Add a title and key.
5. Ask yourself some questions about the results. For example: How has the relief (lie of the land) affected the land use along your transect? What percentage of the land would you consider to be barren or unproductive?
6. Complete the work by writing **at least ten statements** about your results. For example: The area is dominated by cereal crops such as . . . . There was little evidence of . . . due to . . . . There is very little derelict land. This is because . . . .

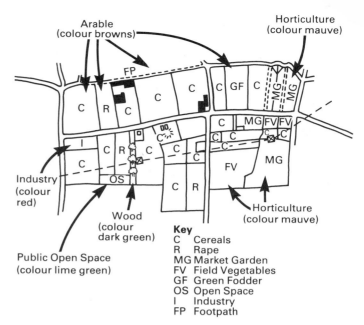

FIG. 2.1 EXAMPLE OF FIELDWORK USING SIMPLIFIED LAND-USE SYMBOLS. (Add colour back in the classroom)

VARIATIONS ON A THEME

● Use a clinometer on the survey to measure the angle of slope.
● Take soil tests for acidity/alkalinity (see p. 22) at intervals.
● Examine a geological map of the area.
● Use the survey techniques to study the land use on **one** farm. Identify **each** crop. Use your results to answer some questions, for example: Is there any connection between
   – distance from the farm and land use?
   – height/angle of slope and farming type?
   – soil acidity/alkalinity and crop type? etc.

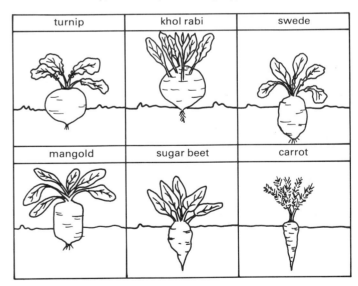

FIG. 2.2 IDENTIFYING ROOT CROPS

Questions

Use a land use sheet provided by your teacher to carry out the following:
1. Choose a short transect line, e.g. along a road or a river. Describe the land use along it in detail.
2. Describe people's use of the land in three contrasting squares selected by your teacher.

T Try the Great Yarmouth Land Use sheet 486.

5

...he **shape** of the physical landscape using ...nce Survey maps. This is known as the **relief**. ...y be hilly, mountainous, undulating (rolling or ...nded), low lying or flat. The variation in height of the land's surface is shown by **contours**. These are continuous lines which join up places of the same height above sea level. They are spaced at **regular vertical intervals**, every 10 m on a Series 2 1:50 000 O.S. map. Their interpretation can help you understand different landforms, such as hills and valleys.

The human landscape is a result of people's activities on the physical landscape: how they have used, incorporated or avoided such landforms as valleys, river basins, gaps and hills when developing villages, towns, industries and communications.

USEFUL TERMINOLOGY

Plain. A flat area of low lying land.
Plateau. A flat area of high land.
Ridge. A long, narrow area of high land.
Spur. A long, narrow projection of high land into lower land.
Knoll. A low detached hill.
Col (or **saddle**). A dip between two hills.
Gap (or **pass**). An easy route through high land, often used by communication links, i.e. road or rail, or maybe a whole town, e.g. Dorking.
Concave slope. Steeper at the top than at the bottom. (Think of a cave!)
Convex slope. Steeper at the bottom than at the top.
Valley. A depression, usually occupied by a river.
River basin. The area drained by a river and its tributaries.
Watershed. A area of high land which divides the streams flowing into one river basin from the streams flowing into another.
Estuary. A wide tidal river mouth.
Ria. A drowned river estuary.
Bay. A large coastal inlet.
Promontory or headland. Resistant rock forming high land with cliffs, jutting out to sea.

CROSS SECTIONS

1. Check the highest and lowest points on the section.
2. Place a piece of paper along line A–B.
3. Mark where the contours 'cut' the paper. Note their heights; mark on features such as rivers.
4. Draw a base line the same length as A–B on the same or separate paper. Work out a vertical height scale and draw faint guidelines.
5. Transfer your recorded heights by putting tiny crosses at the correct height and spacing on the section.
6. With a smooth line join up the crosses. Rub out guidelines and name features.
7. DESCRIBE the shape of the relief in the cross section.
   DESCRIBE the slopes C–D and E–F.
   DESCRIBE the feature found at G.
   PREPARE your own sections as advised by your teacher.

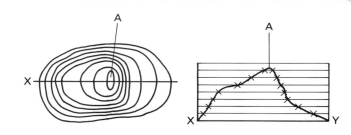

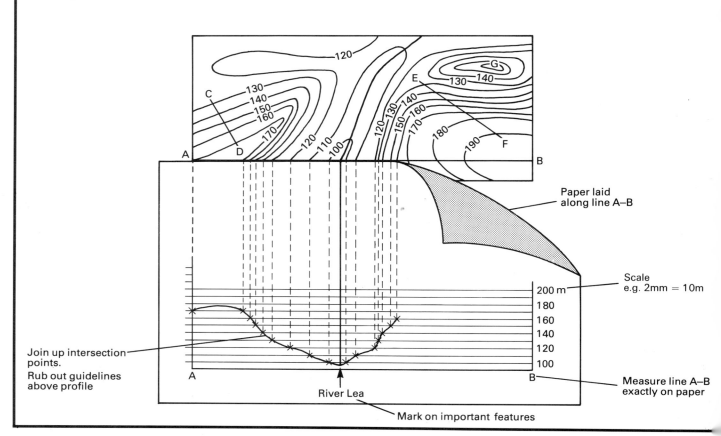

Paper laid along line A–B

Scale e.g. 2mm = 10m

Join up intersection points. Rub out guidelines above profile

Measure line A–B exactly on paper

River Lea

Mark on important features

3. Landforms and Mapwork

FIG. 3.1 ERODING RIVERS

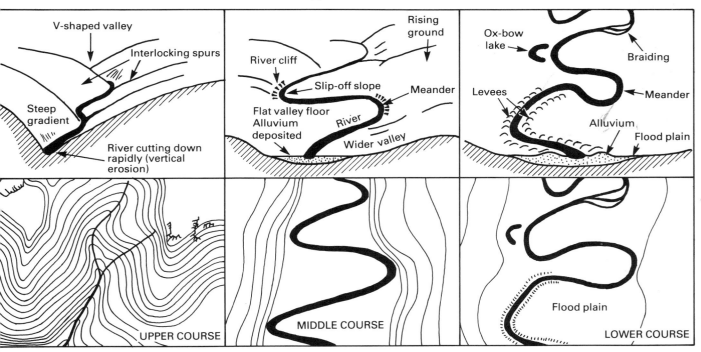

V-shaped valley · **Interlocking spurs** · **Steep gradient** · **River cutting down rapidly (vertical erosion)**

Rising ground · **River cliff** · **Slip-off slope** · **Meander** · **Flat valley floor Alluvium deposited** · **River** · **Wider valley**

Ox-bow lake · **Braiding** · **Meander** · **Levees** · **Alluvium** · **Flood plain**

UPPER COURSE · MIDDLE COURSE · Flood plain · LOWER COURSE

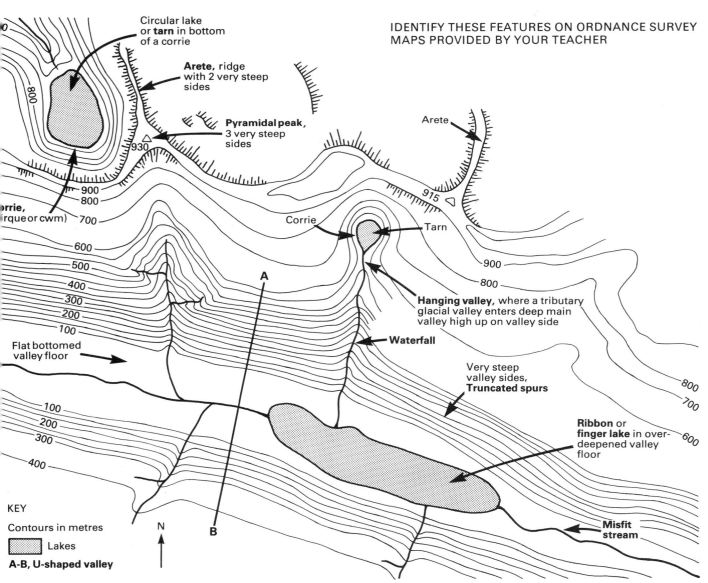

IDENTIFY THESE FEATURES ON ORDNANCE SURVEY MAPS PROVIDED BY YOUR TEACHER

Circular lake or **tarn** in bottom of a corrie

Arete, ridge with 2 very steep sides

Pyramidal peak, 3 very steep sides

Arete

930

915

orrie, irque or cwm)

Corrie

Tarn

Hanging valley, where a tributary glacial valley enters deep main valley high up on valley side

Waterfall

Very steep valley sides, **Truncated spurs**

Ribbon or **finger lake** in over-deepened valley floor

Flat bottomed valley floor

Misfit stream

800 900 800 700 600 500 400 300 200 100

100 200 300 400

900 800 800 700 600

KEY

Contours in metres

Lakes

A-B, U-shaped valley

N

A

B

G. 3.2 CONTOUR MAP OF A GLACIATED LANDSCAPE

7

ROCK TYPE. AREA EXAMPLE.	P/IMP.	CLUES FOR MAPWORK.
CARBONIFEROUS LIMESTONE. Ingleborough. Derbyshire. Mendips. South Wales.	P	**Pot holes. Swallow holes** Underground water – **caves** Bare rock outcrops. Limestone pavement (clints and grikes) Dry valleys with associated potholes. **Dry gorges** e.g. Cheddar gorge.
JURASSIC LIMESTONE. North Yorkshire. Midlands. Portland Bill. Lincoln Edge. Scunthorpe, Lincs. Corby, Northants.	P	More surface drainage. Some dry valleys. Some escarpments e.g. Cotswolds. Often associated with bands of clay and ironstone. Good **arable farmland.** Open cast **iron ore mining.**
CHALK. North and South Downs. Chilterns.	P	Rock is weak, rarely find caves. No potholes. May be 'sinks'. Typical are **dry valleys** and **escarpments** with steep scarp face, coombs and gentle back dip. **Springs** at base of scarp slope. **Rounded low hills,** undulating. Sheep, pastureland. Cement works. Tumuli. White Horses.
CLAYS. Oxfordshire. Bedfordshire clay vales. Thames Valley.	IMP	Heavy soils, **may need drainage.** Straightened water courses, straight blue lines. (Don't confuse with alluvium of river banks and estuaries.) Easily worn down. **Vales,** with **major river systems.** Patches of deciduous woodland – remnants of once forested vales. **Brickyards. Claypits.**
SANDSTONES. Pennines (Millstone grit). Scotland (Old red sandstone).	IMP	Wet boggy **moorland.** Rocks often coincide with high rainfall areas. Much surface water. **'Gills' 'Becks' 'Cloughs'.** Reservoirs. **Steep sided valleys.** Waterfalls, rapids at harder outcrops. Quarries. Dry stone walls.
Weald of Kent (Greensands). Breckland of Norfolk.	P	**Sandpits.** Acid soils support **heathland** vegetation and coniferous trees.
IGNEOUS. METAMORPHIC. Western Britain. Dartmoor. Bodmin Moor (Granite). Lake District (Slates).	IMP	Often coincide with high rainfall areas. Frost shattered pinnacles, **plateaus, mountains. Quarries. Mining** for **tin, kaolin** (china clay).

PERMEABLE. (P) Rocks which allow water to pass quickly through them to underground water systems due to their:
- **porosity.** There are large spaces between the mineral particles, e.g. sandstone.
- **solubility.** Where the chemical nature of the rock, e.g. calcium carbonate content, allows it to dissolve in rainwater e.g. chalk.
- **joints and fissures.** Where the rock is broken by joints and fissures and allows water to travel along them, e.g. limestone.

Look for a dry landscape with few surface streams.

IMPERMEABLE (IMP) Rocks which don't allow water to pass through them, due to:
- the closeness or absence of joints and fissures.
- the nature of the rock minerals which have minute pore spaces that fill with water and stop more water passing through, e.g. clay.

Look for many surface streams and rivers and sometimes poorly drained land.

There are three main types of rock:

SEDIMENTARY ROCKS

These are usually layered rocks, e.g. limestone and sandstone. They consist of deposited material that has been 'cemented' together under water and laid down in bedding planes which may be later folded and faulted. They are easily broken down into soils.

IGNEOUS ROCKS

These are formed by volcanic activity. When molten magma cools it forms rocks such as quartz, granite and lava. These are very hard rocks, resistant to weathering and erosion.

METAMORPHIC ROCKS

These are rocks that have been changed by either great heat or pressure or both. For instance, limestone is changed to marble and shale is changed to slate.

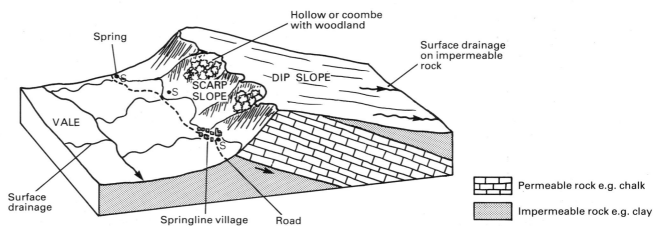

FIG. 3.3 FEATURES OF AN ESCARPMENT

4. Resources

FIG. 4.1 WORLD RESERVES OF NATURAL GAS

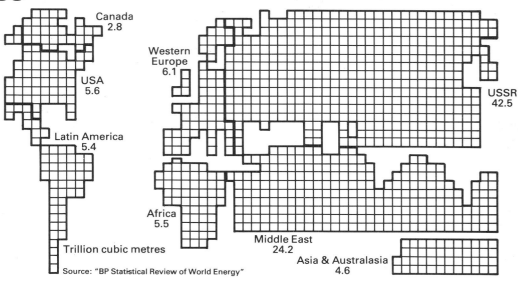

The conventional world map has been redrawn to highlight the world distribution of natural gas. The continents appear in proportion to their reserves at the end of 1985. The figures are in trillion cubic metres of natural gas. (from British Petroleum, see Acknowledgements.)

Canada 2.8
Western Europe 6.1
USA 5.6
USSR 42.5
Latin America 5.4
Trillion cubic metres
Africa 5.5
Middle East 24.2
Asia & Australasia 4.6
Source: "BP Statistical Review of World Energy"

The earth and its atmosphere have only a limited supply of useful materials which we call resources, such as air, fresh water, soil, minerals and fossil fuels. The larger and more wasteful the population, the sooner these resources will be used up unless more effort is made to conserve them. There are two main kinds of resources:
Renewable. These resources can, theoretically, be renewed or replaced within a person's lifetime, i.e. approximately 70–80 years. For example, water, forests and food. The chances of them being renewed may be spoiled by soil exhaustion or erosion (see p. 23) and pollution (see p. 81 and p. 84).
Non-renewable. These resources take millions of years to be replaced once they have been used. For example, metal ores, fossil fuels.
All resources can be **conserved** to some extent so that future generations will also be able to use them.
Recycling (p. 78) is one answer.
Unfortunately, not all resources are evenly distributed across the earth (see Figs. 4.1 and 4.2). Even solar energy would be better harnessed in some areas rather than others.

Consider the following points:
● Some resources are found in difficult locations, for example, under water or in sparsely populated hot or cold barren lands, e.g. diamonds in Namibia.
● Some resources cannot be 'tapped' until the technology for extracting or using them has been improved, e.g. Alaskan oil.
● Some resources are of high quality or grade and some are of inferior quality or grade.
● Some resources are known about but remain 'untapped' due to the difficulty of access (Siberian coal and iron ore).
● Some poorer developing countries may have been exploited by richer developed countries who want their resources. These resources are often exported as primary products which are less valuable in their raw state, e.g. rubber, coffee and tobacco.
● Some resources might become political weapons of the future (uranium).

Questions

1. For each point given above, suggest one or two known examples from anywhere in the world, and also suggest the possible consequences resulting from each point.
2. Choose either Alaska or the North Sea. Carry out your own research on how commonsense and technology have been used to profitably extract oil and/or natural gas.
3. Study Fig. 4.2. Where would you concentrate the development of solar power in the U.S.A. and why?
4. Here is a varied list of resources.
   Air, water, land, soil, food from plants, food from animals, coal, oil, natural gas, geothermal energy, solar energy, wind and wave energy, H.E.P., iron ore, bauxite, uranium, gold, timber and whales.
   (a) Explain why each one is either renewable or non-renewable.
   (b) Can it be recycled? (See p. 78.)
   (c) Can it be conserved? Should it be conserved? (See p. 88.)

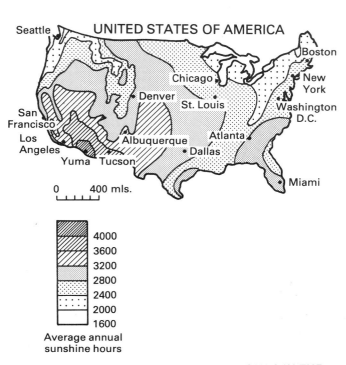

UNITED STATES OF AMERICA

Seattle
Boston
Chicago
New York
Denver
St. Louis
Washington D.C.
San Francisco
Albuquerque
Atlanta
Los Angeles
Dallas
Yuma Tucson
Miami

0   400 mls.

4000
3600
3200
2800
2400
2000
1600
Average annual sunshine hours

FIG. 4.2 AVERAGE ANNUAL SUNSHINE HOURS IN THE U.S.A.

IRON

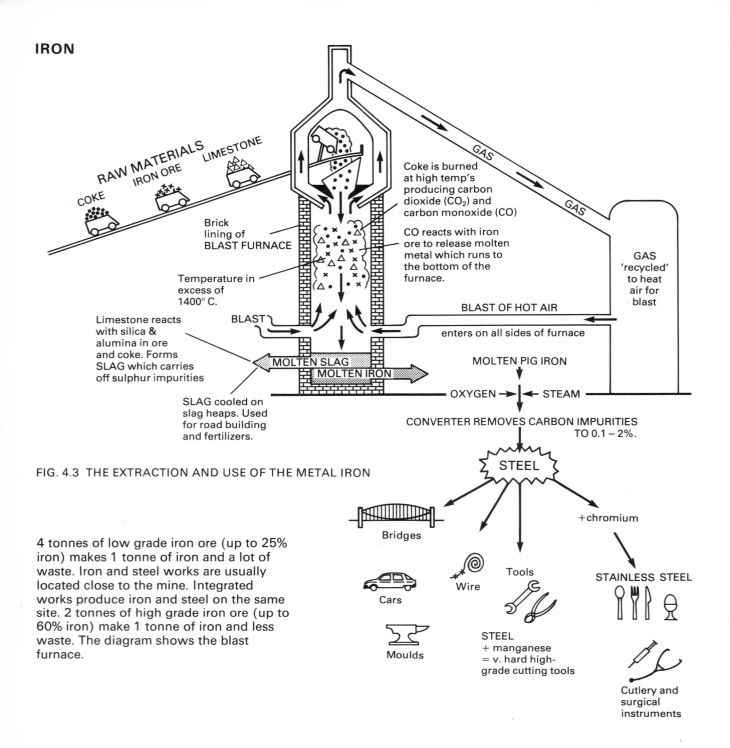

FIG. 4.3 THE EXTRACTION AND USE OF THE METAL IRON

4 tonnes of low grade iron ore (up to 25% iron) makes 1 tonne of iron and a lot of waste. Iron and steel works are usually located close to the mine. Integrated works produce iron and steel on the same site. 2 tonnes of high grade iron ore (up to 60% iron) make 1 tonne of iron and less waste. The diagram shows the blast furnace.

Iron accounts for 90% of the weight of all metals used in the world. A modern blast furnace can operate continuously producing approximately 2000 tonnes per day.

Iron ores such as magnetite (Fe_3O_4) and haematite (Fe_2O_3) are found in igneous rock, e.g. in USSR and Sweden. Lower grade ores are usually found in sedimentary rocks, e.g. in Lincolnshire, Northamptonshire, England, Lorraine and France.

ALUMINIUM

This is a versatile non-rusting metal. It is ideal for aeroplane construction because it is very **strong** but also very **light**. Other uses include window frames, saucepans, kitchen foil and the all-aluminium drinks can. Aluminium oxide (Al_2O_3) occurs naturally in

deposits of the mineral ore **bauxite**. One third of the world's supply is produced by the United States followed by the U.S.S.R., Japan, West Germany and Canada.

Smelting aluminium needs huge amounts of electricity. Recycling would therefore be uneconomic unless done on a large scale. Estimates shown that at the current annual growth rate of consumption (6%) reserves may only last 30 years.

1. Compare the properties and uses of iron, steel and aluminium. Explain how life would differ if we have to live without them.
2. Choose one metal resource. Working in small groups of 3 or 4 students, research its origins, extraction, production and uses. With the use of display aids, prepare a lecture to give to the rest of the class.

5. Energy Resources

Fuel which has come from once-living plant and animal material originally received its energy from the sun. The energy is trapped by green plants in the process known as **photosynthesis**:

$$\text{Carbon dioxide} + \text{Water} \xrightarrow[\text{Chlorophyll}]{\text{Light energy}} \text{Carbohydrates} + \text{Oxygen}.$$

The fossil fuels, oil, coal and natural gas, are all examples. Also wood, which is, perhaps, one of the most important domestic fuels used today. In developing countries almost one third of the working day may be spent looking for wood to use for cooking and heating. It is estimated that 2300 million tonnes are burnt each year and very little is being renewed in the countries where it is most needed.

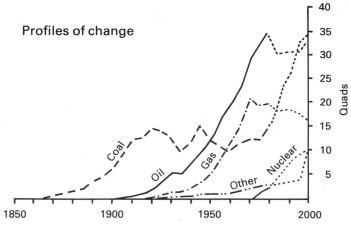

Profiles of change

FIG. 5.1 CHANGES IN ENERGY USE

COAL

Coal was formed some 300 million years ago from the woody parts (cellulose) of trees and other vegetation. The trees fell into swamps where decomposition changed the vegetation into peat which then became buried and compressed. These carbon deposits are now found in **seams** of various thicknesses amongst sedimentary rocks. **Lignite** is the soft 'brown' coal sometimes burned in power stations. **Anthracite** is 'hard' coal with a high carbon content, more often used in the home. **Coke** is a man-made smokeless fuel formed by heating coal in the absence of air. It is very important in the production of iron and steel.

Coal still meets 25% of the world's energy needs even though its production has declined with the popularity of oil and gas. World reserves are estimated at 400 billion tonnes (oil equivalent) which can be economically mined and recovered. Even if production increased to meet one third of our energy needs it is estimated that these reserves may only last for 100–300 years.

Coal is often considered difficult to produce, transport and use, causing greater environmental problems e.g. air pollution, than other forms of energy. By-products of coal are similar to those produced from oil, e.g. paint, pesticides, explosives, sulphuric acid and other chemicals, fertilisers, plastics, man-made fibres. One of its most important uses is for generating electricity.

TABLE 5.1

Fuel resource	Proved world reserves 1979 (Quads of energy)	% of energy used in Britain today	Estimated depletion at present rate of production & known reserves
Coal	16 480	25%	300 yrs
Natural Gas	2650	25%	20 yrs
Oil	3720	45%	30 yrs
Uranium	850	3½%	300 yrs†
H.E.P.	—	½%	Renewable

*Quad – A quadrillion British thermal units.

†If the **fast reactor** is adopted uranium could be used far more efficiently than in a thermal reactor and therefore resources would last as long as recoverable coal reserves.

FIG. 5.2 WORLD RESERVES OF COAL AT END OF 1985
(from British Petroleum, see Acknowledgements)

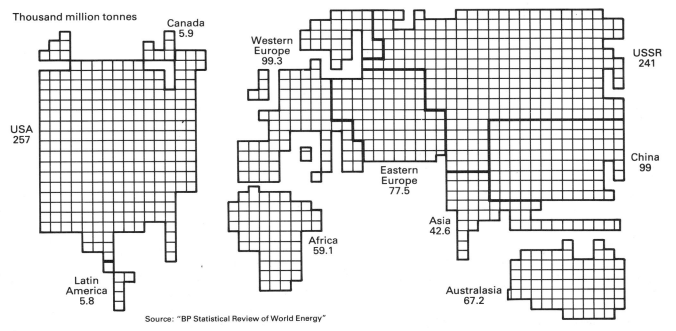

Thousand million tonnes

Canada 5.9
Western Europe 99.3
USSR 241
USA 257
China 99
Eastern Europe 77.5
Africa 59.1
Asia 42.6
Latin America 5.8
Australasia 67.2

Source: "BP Statistical Review of World Energy"

OIL

Oil was formed some 400 million years ago by the decomposition of millions of soft-bodied animals and plants living in the sea. They died and were buried under mud. Bacteria working without oxygen acted upon them. With gradual change over time and under the pressure of layer upon layer of deposits, crude oil was formed. It accumulated in **porous** sedimentary rocks such as sandstone, sandwiched between **impermeable** rocks, such as clay. (See Fig. 5.4) This is known as a **'trap'**. A typical trap occurs where beds of rock have been forced into the shape of an arch or **anticline**. If the 'cap' rock is punctured by drilling (1000–5000m on average) the oil (and gas) usually rise up to the surface under their own pressure.

Oil became very popular in the 1960s when cheap Middle Eastern oil flooded the market. The supply seemed inexhaustible. Oil is easy to transport by pipeline, ship, rail or road. It has a high energy density, i.e. oil produces a lot of power per litre. The world has used up 25% of the known oil reserves. Transport is heavily dependent on oil and so is a huge petrochemical industry producing plastics, drugs, detergents, man-made fibres, varnishes, cosmetics, sulphuric acid and fertilisers etc. Oil accounts for 50% of the world's energy consumption each year. At the present rate of production and use, world reserves, estimated at 88–90 billion tonnes, are not expected to last much beyond the end of the century. (This includes North Sea oil.) The 1973–4 oil crisis made people think about their dependence on oil and all other energy resources. OPEC, the Organisation of Petroleum Exporting Countries, was formed in 1961. In 1973 OPEC began increasing the price of oil to the oil companies. The OPEC countries used some of the profits to improve their people's standards of living and to develop their own industries. The world price of oil is still strongly influenced by OPEC: it increased dramatically in the ten years 1973–83, but has started to fall since new sources have been discovered and supply now exceeds demand.

NATURAL GAS

Only 30 years ago most gas consumed in the home and by industry was **town gas** produced by heating coal in the absence of air at the local gas works. In the last 20 years, natural gas (**methane**), usually found in association with deposits of oil, has provided a fifth of the world's energy needs (Fig. 5.4). World reserves are estimated at 60 billion tonnes (oil equivalent). At the present rate of production these are not expected to last much longer than the end of the century. Efforts must be made to conserve present resources. For example, 'flaring' has been used to burn off waste gas on oil fields. It is estimated that the total gas flared in the

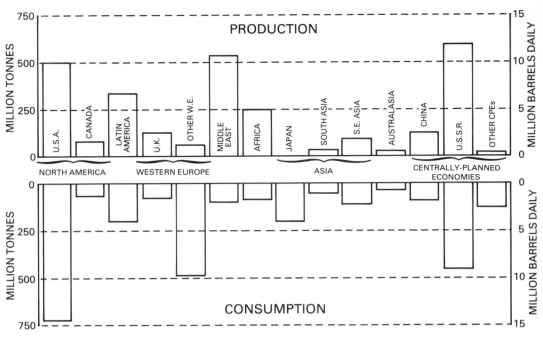

FIG. 5.3 WORLD OIL PRODUCTION AND CONSUMPTION 1985 (from British Petroleum Statistical Review of World Energy, 1986)

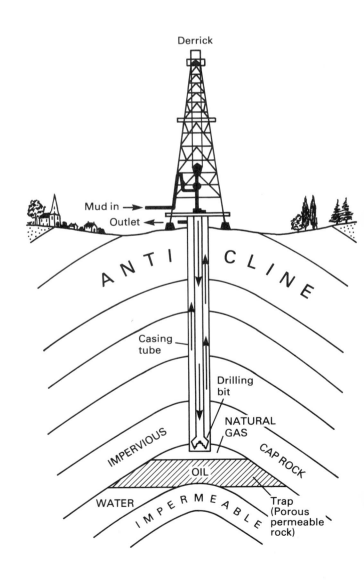

FIG. 5.4 DRILLING FOR OIL AND NATURAL GAS

Middle East in 1978 would have supplied half the total EEC requirement, i.e. all the gas produced by the Netherlands in that year.

Natural gas is a high grade quality fuel. It is used in **premium** markets, i.e. where it can be used to the best advantage, in the home and in selective industries such as chemical and glass making, and is not used for generating electricity. It can be piped underground over long distances. It can be liquefied (L.N.G.) at −160°C for storage and long distance transportation overseas, although this is still expensive at present. It requires little treatment, often being produced in a nearly pure state. (The 'gas smell' even has to be added for safety!) It is clean to use. Research and manufacture is now being carried out to produce substitute natural gas (S.N.G.) from coal and heavy oil.

Questions

1. Coal, oil and natural gas are all fossil fuels. What do you understand by this term? (See glossary.)

2. Comment on the distribution of world reserves and the production of coal, natural gas and oil (Figs. 4.1, 5.2 and 5.3), particularly between the northern and southern hemispheres and the developed and developing nations. Compare this to the distribution of population. (Fig. 11.2, p. 30.)

3. Examine Table 5.1 and Fig. 5.1. By the year 2000 which particular fuels might we need to have found alternatives for, or make more effort to conserve? Which fuels will remain important or increase in importance by the year 2000?

4. Draw an enlarged copy of the flow diagram below.

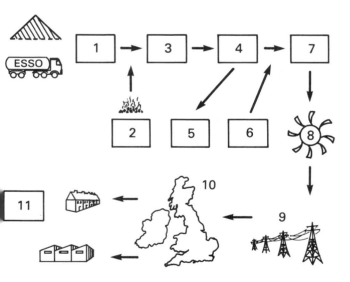

Replace the numbers with the following labels in the correct order: H.E.P. National Grid System. Steam. Fossil fuels. Electricity. Homes and factories. Combustion. Generator. $\frac{1}{3}$ potential energy loss due to poor conversion. Turbines.

5. List the forms of **primary energy**. Electricity is a form of **secondary energy**. Explain why this is so.

6. How many different methods are used to transport gas, oil, electricity and coal about a country? In terms of these methods which of the four fuels has least impact visually on the environment? Explain your answer.

7. By 1985 two million cars in Brazil were running on **sugar alcohol** called Alcool at the filling station. The cars are cheaper to buy, do not require a road tax and will be able to get alcohol at weekends when petrol is not for sale.

Imagine you are a new Minister for Transport. Your aim in your new transport policy is to:
● reduce the dependence on oil as a transport fuel.
● reduce the total consumption of oil, in your country.

Write a report on how you would try to do this. Here are some ideas to help you. Alternative forms of energy, car size, road usage, tax and licences, advertising; alternative forms of transport, for example, rail, canal; public transport (buses, trams). (Use this as a theme for an open day display.)

8. The members of **OPEC** are Iran, Iraq, Kuwait, Saudi Arabia, Venezuela, Algeria, Ecuador, Gabon, Libya, Indonesia, Nigeria, Qatar and the United Arab Emirates.
   (a) Which of these countries are found in the Middle East?
   (b) Suggest at least four things that all these countries have in common.
   (c) Why are most of the members of OPEC developing countries? Why should decisions made by OPEC be of major concern to North America, Western Europe, the U.S.S.R. and Japan? See Fig. 5.3.
   (d) The U.S.A. was an early major producer of oil. Comment on its present level of production and consumption compared with the countries/regions in Fig. 5.3.
   (e) Which region of the world, and which country, produce most oil at the present time?

9. How much energy is used in the domestic sector? (See Fig. 5.5.) How does this compare with other users?

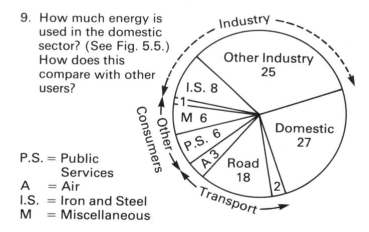

P.S. = Public Services
A = Air
I.S. = Iron and Steel
M = Miscellaneous

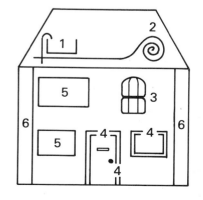

List the ways you could make energy savings in the home. Don't forget insulation (1–6), room temperatures, for example 18°C downstairs, 14°C upstairs, metering and different methods of heating.

FIG. 5.5 ENERGY USERS

6. Alternative Energy

WIND

New **aerogenerator** 'windmills' have been developed which can produce electricity from the wind. Wind is a renewable clean resource. It is plentiful and is at its greatest strength in coastal and mountainous areas. It can be particularly useful as an energy source in isolated areas such as highlands and islands. Although there is a problem with noise and in storing power for calm days, a new aerogenerator can be built in a short time, i.e. only two years as compared with perhaps 10 years to build a power station which uses fossil fuel. Estimates show that 20–48% of Great Britain's electricity could be generated by the wind by the 1990s, but this would require an active programme of building large groups of aerogenerators to begin now.

GEOTHERMAL

Countries such as Iceland and New Zealand already harness the steam and hot water which are found naturally where molten rock occurs close to the earth's surface. This may be used directly to provide domestic and industrial heating or to generate electricity. In Great Britain, water-bearing rocks such as limestone and sandstone at depths of more than 1800 metres could provide hot water at 60–80°C. Research is being carried out at Bath, where there are hot springs, and by the River Test near Southampton. The Department of Energy also suggests that if technology advances so that we are able to tap the upper 10 km of the earth's crust beneath Britain this could provide us with heat energy equivalent to 50 thousand million million tonnes of coal. To tap only one millionth of this would be as much as Britain's estimated recoverable coal reserves.

WATER

1. Wave

Floating or moored devices such as Salter's Ducks or Cockerell's Rafts (see Fig. 6.2) have been invented which could harness wave action to generate electricity. Again, choice of sites would be limited but the west coast of Great Britain is considered suitable. Major problems would be the **cost, anchoring** the devices, **transmitting** the electricity onshore, and the effect on marine and shore habitats.

Reading University, Dept of Engineering

FIG. 6.1 MUSGROVE AEROGENERATOR

Questions

1. What types of machinery have been successfully powered by the wind other than electricity generators?
2. Imagine 100 Musgrove aerogenerators (see Fig. 6.1) in a shallow offshore coastal area. White down the arguments for and against their siting and use which might be put forward by local environmentalists.

SALTER'S DUCKS
(bob up and down like ducks)

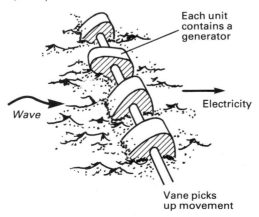

Each unit contains a generator

Wave

Electricity

Vane picks up movement

COCKERELL'S RAFTS

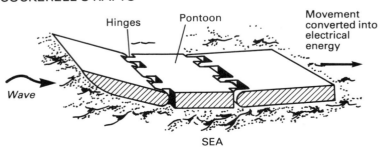

Hinges

Pontoon

Movement converted into electrical energy

Wave

SEA

FIG. 6.2 DEVICES TO HARNESS WAVE ENERGY AND GENERATE ELECTRICITY

3. Imagine a 100 km stretch of generators in the Atlantic Ocean. (This is the estimated number needed to meet half of Great Britain's electricity needs.) Bad weather conditions in the North Sea have made drilling and operating oil wells very difficult. Why are weather conditions in the Atlantic Ocean usually harsher than the North Sea?
4. What problems would this pose for harnessing wave energy?
5. Consider the alternatives to tidal power in Britain and the facts given on this page. Do you think the Severn Barrage project would be justified in terms of cost, production and environment? Write about the problems and advantages which might be caused by its presence.

Other facts for the first phase:–
Barrage length, 17 km. Extra road.
£20–£45 million for further research.
£5700 million for construction, taking 12 + years.
Would only supply 6% Britain's electricity needs.
Would destroy some natural habitats, e.g. for waders.
Effect of locks and gates on estuary traffic and port of Bristol.
Without the second phase, a coal or nuclear power station would be needed to meet the gap in energy needs.

6. Why do you think that H.E.P. only contributes 2% of Great Britain's electricity production?
7. Many developing countries have the potential for producing H.E.P. but continue to import expensive oil. Suggest reasons for this.
8. Find out more details about **one** H.E.P. scheme, i.e. location, cost, problems, benefits.

IG. 6.3 HOOVER DAM, U.S.A.

2. H.E.P. Hydroelectric power
Many countries have already harnessed their rivers to turn turbines and so generate electricity. Normally this requires either fast flowing water discharged regularly throughout the year or the creation of reservoirs (see Fig. 10.5) to balance irregular or seasonal flow of water in the river. Reservoirs are formed by building dams and flooding suitable valleys. They vary considerably in size. Lake Volta in Ghana occupies over 7500 km². Marchlyn Mawr in Great Britain occupies 0.27 km².
Some countries have a great potential than others for the production of H.E.P. Norway can produce 90% of her electricity needs in this way.
Initial capital outlay is often very high, but once established, running costs are low, the method clean and the resource renewable. Dams and reservoirs may even form part of a multi-purpose water development scheme, providing flood control and irrigation in addition to electricity.

Pumped storage
At night, when the demand for electricity is low, electricity is used to pump water back to a high reservoir, such as Marchlyn Mawr at Dinorwig, North Wales. When demand is high during the day, water is allowed to return to a low reservoir in a steady flow over turbines in the electricity station, which is situated between the two reservoirs. This in turn generates more electricity.

3. Tidal
Tidal energy can be harnessed by building a **barrage** with associated power station across an estuary which has a large tidal range, i.e. a large difference between low and high tide. The cost of construction is very high and the choice of sites few. The only working example is on the Rance estuary, in France.
The Severn estuary has a large tidal range with a rise and fall difference of 12 m at the peak of the lunar cycle. Research has shown that a barrage could be constructed in two phases, the first to form an inner basin between Lavernock and Brean and the second to form an outer basin between Minehead and Aberthaw. The former would generate power on average only six hours a day on the ebb tide, as water flows back out to sea over the turbines. The latter would use the flood tide (advancing and rising) to give a continuous source of power.

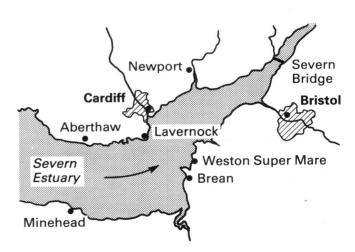

FIG. 6.4 PROPOSALS FOR SEVERN BARRAGE

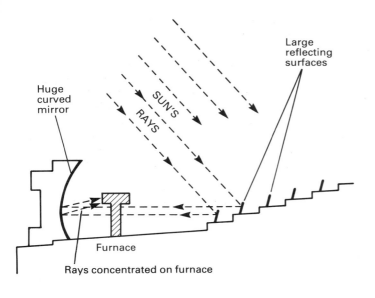

Huge curved mirror

SUN'S RAYS

Large reflecting surfaces

Furnace

Rays concentrated on furnace

FIG. 6.5 SOLAR FURNACE

SOLAR

Solar energy is the energy reaching the earth from the sun. It is already used by green plants in photosynthesis and is 'locked into' fossil fuels as they are formed from living plants and animals once dependent on the sun's energy. Many people see this as the main, cheap, non-polluting renewable energy source of the future.
Solar energy is already being used in a variety of forms. For example:

1. **Solar heat absorbers**. These are fitted on roofs to collect the sun's energy and use it to provide hot water and operate central heating systems.
2. **Solar furnaces**. Reflecting surfaces are used to reflect the sun's rays, as it moves across the sky, onto a huge curved mirror. This in turn focuses the rays onto the furnace, creating enough heat (over 538°C) to produce steam for generating electricity.
3. **Solar cells**. These are made from wafer-thin pure silicon crystals with a tiny amount of boron impurity. When light falls on them, an electric current starts to flow. Satellites in space are already powered by them. Scientists dream of building solar power stations in space with huge 9.5 km by 13.5 km solar panels, composed of solar cells! The electricity produced would be beamed to earth as microwaves

FIG. 6.6 SOLAR POWERED HOUSE

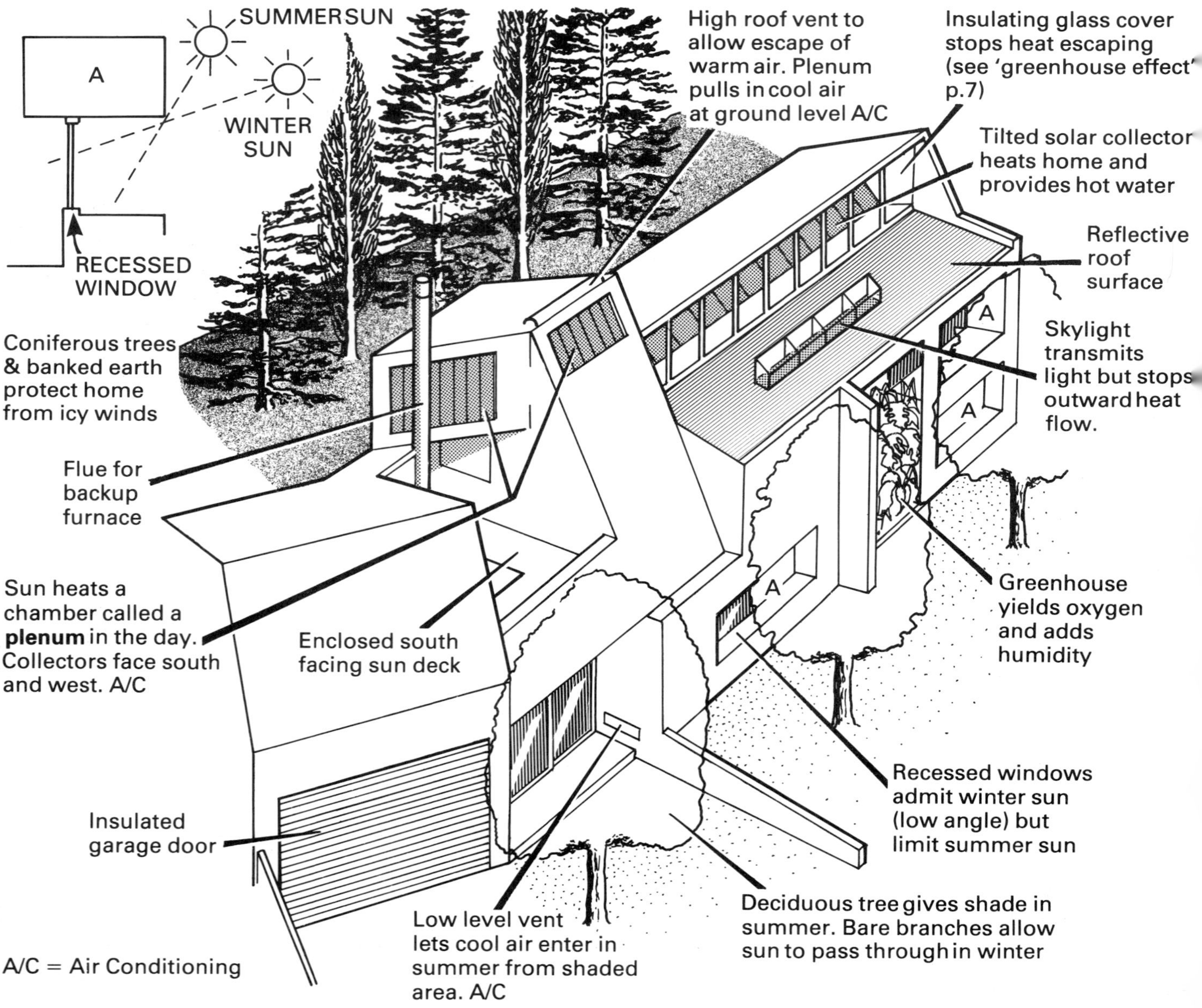

A

SUMMER SUN

WINTER SUN

RECESSED WINDOW

High roof vent to allow escape of warm air. Plenum pulls in cool air at ground level A/C

Insulating glass cover stops heat escaping (see 'greenhouse effect' p.7)

Tilted solar collector heats home and provides hot water

Reflective roof surface

Skylight transmits light but stops outward heat flow.

Coniferous trees & banked earth protect home from icy winds

Flue for backup furnace

Sun heats a chamber called a **plenum** in the day. Collectors face south and west. A/C

Enclosed south facing sun deck

Greenhouse yields oxygen and adds humidity

Recessed windows admit winter sun (low angle) but limit summer sun

Insulated garage door

Low level vent lets cool air enter in summer from shaded area. A/C

Deciduous tree gives shade in summer. Bare branches allow sun to pass through in winter

A/C = Air Conditioning

16

and then turned back into electricity. The station would have the advantage of remaining in sunlight for all of its life in orbit, except during an eclipse. NASA's Skylab was run on solar cells.

There are two main problems for harnessing solar energy: the difference in sunlight hours (see Fig. 4.2, p. 9) according to the time of day, year and the location of the country; also the present cost of equipment such as aluminium, glass, and of research.

Questions

1. If high-rise buildings in cites became dependent on solar energy, why might laws have to be passed about sun rights?

2. Why would solar power stations have to be **built** in space?
   Examine Fig. 6.6 of a model solar powered house. Describe how it has been adapted to benefit fully from solar energy.
   In what ways have aspect and vegetation contributed to the use and conservation of energy in this house?
   Why would you need a back-up furnace?
   Why might you have to consider air conditioning as well as heating?

3. Describe simply how electricity is generated from a nuclear reactor. See Fig. 6.10.

NUCLEAR

Splitting the atom

Each atom of an element consists of a **central core** or **nucleus** around which are arranged particles called **electrons**. In all chemical reactions the nucleus remains unchanged but the outer arrangement of electrons is changed. In a nuclear reaction it is the nucleus which undergoes changes. The nucleus consists of two types of particle, **protons** and **neutrons**. If the nucleus is split, some of the neutrons are set free along with enormous amounts of energy. The free neutrons can bombard more nuclei at high speed and split them, causing a chain reaction (see Fig. 6.7).

Nuclear fission and nuclear fusion

In nature some nuclei can split spontaneously. This is known as **radioactive decay** and can continue until a stable nucleus is formed. However, the rate at which this occurs is not high enough for us to use as a source of energy. But, if many heavy nuclei can be encouraged to become very unstable and split by bombarding them with neutrons, then large amounts of energy can be released. This is what is done in a **nuclear reactor** at a nuclear power station, and is known as **nuclear fission**. New research is being centred around the opposite process, i.e. the **fusion** of the light nuclei of atoms such as deuterium and lithium. (There are plentiful sources of these in water and rocks.) This process is known as **nuclear fusion**.

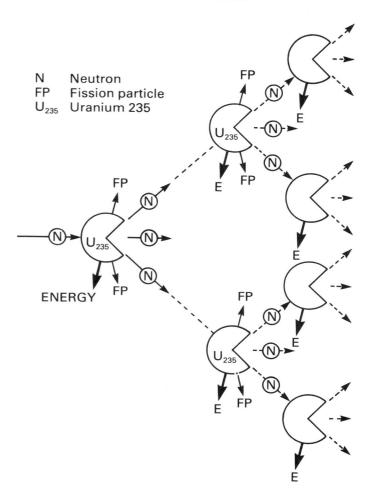

N   Neutron
FP   Fission particle
U_{235} Uranium 235

FIG. 6.7 NUCLEAR FISSION CHAIN REACTION

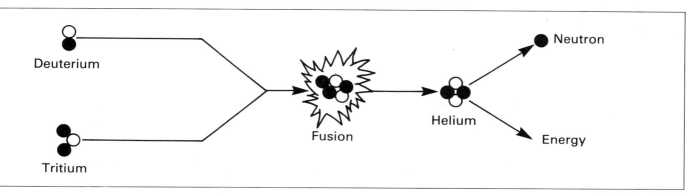

FIG. 6.8 NUCLEAR FUSION

Nuclear fuel

Natural **uranium** consists of a mixture of two main types or isotopes of the element, which differ in the mass of their nuclei. There is about 1% of **uranium-235** which is unstable and easily releases energy of its nucleus is split. It is said to be **fissile**. The other 99% is **uranium-238** which is non-fissile but fertile, i.e. it can be converted into fissile material such as **plutonium-239** in a nuclear reactor. 'Enriched uranium' is natural uranium processed to increase the proportion of uranium-235 to make it more fissile. These are the fuels used in present-day nuclear reactors.

The fast breeder reactor

There are many designs of nuclear reactor from gas cooled to fast breeder. The first prototype of the latter in Great Britain is at Dounreay, Scotland. It is different because it is capable of converting uranium-238 into plutonium more rapidly than it uses or 'burns' plutonium to generate electricity, so the initial stock of plutonium grows or breeds! It uses uranium 50 times more efficiently than before. This means that resources will last longer and also produce more fissile material which can be used to fuel other reactors.

Reprocessing

Nuclear fuel is reprocessed at intervals because impurities build up which stop the reaction working efficiently. The used fuel is transported in heavily shielded containers to a reprocessing plant where it is separated into unstable fuel and the unwanted remainder, which is still highly radioactive and has to be kept in safe storage (see p. 87). It is far too dangerous to be released directly into the environment. Great

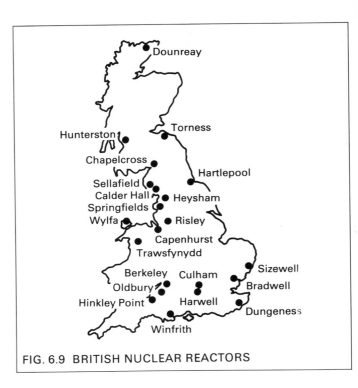

FIG. 6.9 BRITISH NUCLEAR REACTORS

Britain reprocesses and disposes of nuclear waste from other countries, an industry worth £2½ billion to the British economy, at **Sellafield** (Windscale), Cumbria. This site is becoming known as the world's 'nuclear laundry'. Dounreay may be chosen as the new site for reprocessing plutonium if fast breeders are adopted in Europe. There is no planning permission for Dounreay as yet and the C.E.E.B. may not adopt a fast breeder for twenty five years.

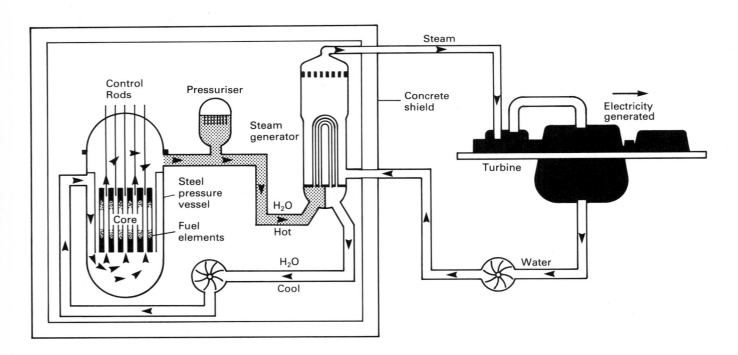

Pressurised water reactor (PWR)

Fuel	Enriched uranium oxide
Coolant	Water
Moderator	Water

FIG. 6.10 PRESSURISED WATER REACTOR (PWR)

7. The Farmers' Weather

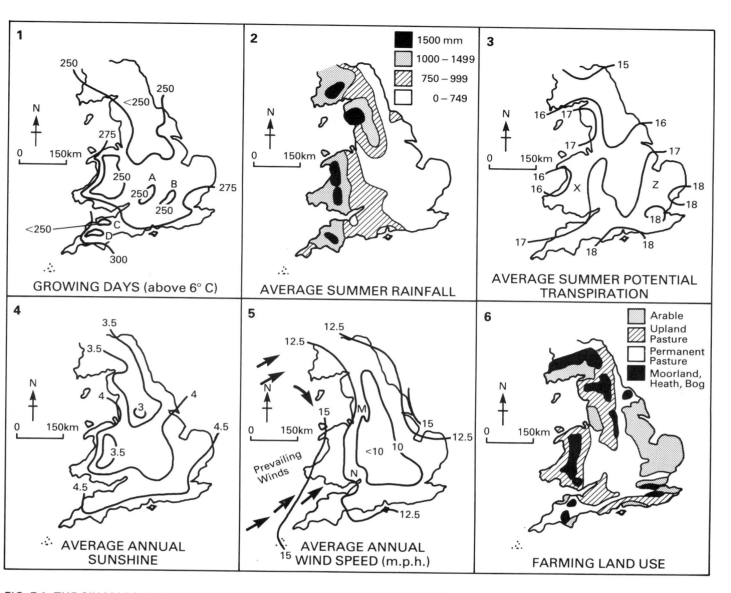

FIG. 7.1 THE SIX MAPS SHOW WEATHER FACTORS AFFECTING FARMING IN ENGLAND

How the land is used for farming is very dependent on the weather, including **local variations** for each individual farmer. England and Wales are chosen for study here.

Altitude

● The temperature generally decreases with height. The growing season, therefore, may decrease by 4 or 5 days for every 30 m rise in altitude.

● Rainfall increases, particularly on the western slopes in Great Britain.

● The amount and speed of wind may increase.

Latitude

Hours of sunshine decrease with increasing latitude.

Aspect

A field tilted towards the south receives more sunshine to warm the soil and the crops. (See Fig. 7.3.)

Topography

The shape of the surrounding land can be important. Fig. 7.4 shows that on a **cold cloudless calm night** the lowest temperatures are often found, not on the hillsides, but in the valleys where the risk of **frost** is

much higher. The site of a fruit orchard or vineyard must be carefully chosen.

Soil type (See p. 21)

Have available a relief map of England and Wales in an atlas, showing the highland and lowland.

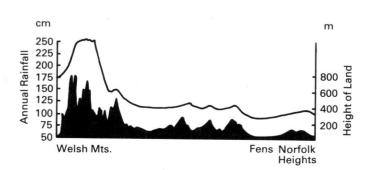

FIG. 7.2 THE EFFECT OF ALTITUDE ON RAINFALL

19

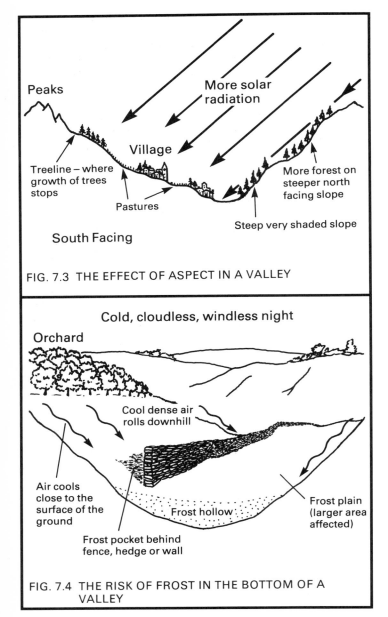

Peaks

More solar radiation

Village

Treeline – where growth of trees stops

Pastures

South Facing

More forest on steeper north facing slope

Steep very shaded slope

FIG. 7.3 THE EFFECT OF ASPECT IN A VALLEY

Cold, cloudless, windless night

Orchard

Cool dense air rolls downhill

Air cools close to the surface of the ground

Frost hollow

Frost pocket behind fence, hedge or wall

Frost plain (larger area affected)

FIG. 7.4 THE RISK OF FROST IN THE BOTTOM OF A VALLEY

Questions

1. Map 1 shows the length of the growing season based on temperature in a typical year. Spring growth doesn't usually start until the mean daily temperature reaches **6.1°C** and is maintained daily.
   (a) What have the areas with less than 250 days growing season got in common? Name A, B, C and D.
   (b) Comment on the growing season in most of lowland England and Wales.
   (c) Which area of the country has the benefit of 300 growing days or more?
   (d) If winter is defined as the non-growing season, approximately how many days would it last in Cornwall and the Pennines?
   (e) Which one particular area would be good for growing early varieties of vegetables?

2. Summer rainfall and the rate at which plants use the moisture in the soil during transpiration are very important in the farming year. Maps 2 and 3. (Potential transpiration, i.e. how much moisture might be transpired, can be calculated from recorded measurements of temperature, humidity, wind and sunshine.) Along with relief, these two factors

greatly affect the farming types found from west to east across England and Wales.
   (a) In general, where is the rainfall greatest and where is it lowest? Use Map 2 and Fig. 7.2.
   (b) What effect does high land have on the rainfall figures? Give two named examples from Fig. 7.2.
   (c) Copy and complete the following table. Use Map 6.

Area	Summer Rainfall	Potential Transpiration (mm)	+/− Diff.	Moisture Conditions	Farming Type
X	605			WET	Rough pasture Moorland
Y			−76		
Z		457			

   (d) Match these statements up to X, Y and Z.
   ● The best grasslands for livestock grow where it is neither too wet nor too dry.
   ● Deep rooted crops are better suited to dry conditions.
   ● Summer input of rain exceeds transpiration output. Soils are leached and infertile.

3. Sunshine varies on average from about 7 out of 16 possible hours in summer to about 1 out of 8 in winter. See Map 4. The hours of sunshine are quite low in England and Wales.
   (a) In general, where are the sunniest areas?
   (b) Why might one expect local variations near large towns and in hills?
   (c) At what time of the farming year is more sunshine, rather than a higher temperature, important?

4. Wind. See Map 5.
   (a) From which direction are the **prevailing** winds?
   (b) How true is it to say that the areas with most sunshine generally have most wind?
   (c) Ireland offers mainland England and Wales some protection from wind. Comment on what happens at M and N.

5. Mixed farming combines both crops and livestock but in certain areas one of the other is more important. See Map 6.
   (a) The main arable crops in Britain are the cereals wheat and barley. Where is cereal growing most concentrated?
   (b) Hardy breeds of sheep may be kept on the **upland pastures**. Using Maps 1–5 as well, write down what sort of conditions they will have to tolerate.
   (c) Draw an outline map to the same scale as Map 6 on tracing paper. Use an atlas to mark on the highland and lowland. Lay it over Map 6. Comment on the effect of **relief** on the patterns of farming.
   (d) Comment on the location of the **permanent pastures** and the relief of the land.

8. Soil

Soil is formed over thousands of years from a raw or **parent** material such as igneous, metamorphic or sedimentary **rock** (see p. 11), through the process of **weathering**. There are three main types of weathering.

Physical weathering. The parent rock is broken up by the action of frost-shattering or other changes in the temperature which cause the rock to expand and contract.

Chemical weathering. Rainwater combines with carbon dioxide to form weak carbonic acid which dissolves rocks such as limestone.

Biological weathering. Rock is broken down by the action of living organisms such as plant roots, animal burrows and bacteria.

Agents such as running water, wind, moving ice and waves all **erode** the parent rock, helping to reduce it to smaller and smaller pieces. This material is **deposited** to form soil
Over a period of time **soil erosion** may take place. This can be very slow or very rapid process and results in the stripping away of **topsoil** before new soil has had the chance to form.

SOIL COMPOSITION

Soils are always changing. They vary considerably according to their origin, age and the amount and combination of the following substances.

1. **Inorganic or mineral particles**. These are the minute pieces of parent rock such as sand and clay. A large clay content may produce a heavy, poorly drained, cold soil which is difficult to work. A high sand content may produce a soil which is warmer and easily worked but which loses water and minerals easily.
2. **Air** fills minute spaces. Oxygen is needed by plant roots and soil organisms, such as bacteria and earthworms, for respiration.
3. **Water** spreads over all the particles in a thin film, or remains between the particles.
4. **Humus** is a dark fibrous substance formed from the decay of plant and animal (organic) remains in the soil. It helps to form a crumb structure of the soil by holding particles together. It is important for retaining moisture and a reservoir of mineral salts such as nitrates which are gradually released back into the soil.
5. **Mineral salts** such as calcium, potassium and phosphates are dissolved out of the rock particles or humus by the soil water. They are essential for plant growth.
6. **Bacteria and other living soil organisms**. Especially important are those which break down organic matter and release mineral salts which can be taken up by plant roots.

SOIL PROFILE

The interaction of origin, age, climate, composition and lack of disturbance results in the formation of horizontal layers or **horizons** in the soil. Each horizon has its own characteristics. A **loam soil** has a good balance between humus, larger sand and smaller clay particles. It is very productive in agriculture.

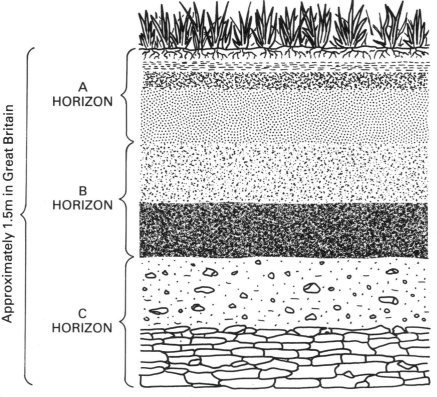

A00 Undecomposed living organic material.

A0 Decomposing organic material. Humus.

A1 Dark coloured, fairly rich in humus. Deeper in areas of low rainfall.

A2 Lighter coloured ash grey layer. Leached. (Rain water washes away mineral salts to lower horizons).

B1 Upper layer where mineral salts may begin to accumulate, e.g. iron, aluminium.

B2 Main layer for deposited mineral salts washed down from A horizon. Iron hardpan may form.

C Weathered parent material. SUBSOIL.

Parent rock showing signs of weathering at upper levels.

Approximately 1.5m in Great Britain

A HORIZON

B HORIZON

C HORIZON

FIG. 8.1 TYPICAL SOIL PROFILE OF AN UNDISTURBED SOIL

A **peat soil** develops from the slow rotting and regrowth of water-tolerant plants in shallow lakes over hundreds of years. The lack of air caused by waterlogging results in only partial decay and the build-up of deep layers of peat. Peat bogs support a very different and interesting plant and animal community but much has been lost to farmland. The Fenlands of East Anglia have been drained, improved with fertilisers, mixed with clay and river silt and farmed intensively for many years. However, reclamation of the unique and fertile Somerset Levels has been largely halted by the Nature Conservancy Council and farming conservationalists themselves.

1	**acid** orange-red
2	
3	
4	
5	
6	
7	**neutral** yellow-green
8	
9	
10	
11	
12	
13	**alkaline** green-blue
14	

Soil auger

20cm deep

Pipette

Distilled water

3-5 drops universal indicator

Soil and barium sulphate

Flocculated soil

tap the tube shake

The pH of the soil tells you whether it is **acidic, alkaline** or **neutral**. Most plants and animals prefer neutral conditions that lie in the middle of the pH range.

Questions

1. Carry out a pH test on a small sample of fresh peat. (Fig. 8.2.) Find out what sort of wild plants can tolerate this pH and make a list.

2. Weigh a small sample of peat and then let it dry out in a warm oven. Re-weigh it. What do you notice about the texture and the weight?

3. Keep this sample in an open petri dish in a safe place for a few weeks. Has the exposure to the air made any difference to the texture of the peat? (Hint – bacteria.)

4. Use the results from your experiments to explain what might happen if peat soil is drained extensively.

5. Give at least three reasons why the Fenlands have suffered from major soil erosion. (See p. 23.)

6. Why would mixing with clay make peat soil more stable and productive?

7. Why are fertiliser manufacturers and machines as seen on p. 38 a threat to peat bog habitats?

8. How might livestock rather than arable farming (as in the Fens) prevent soil erosion?

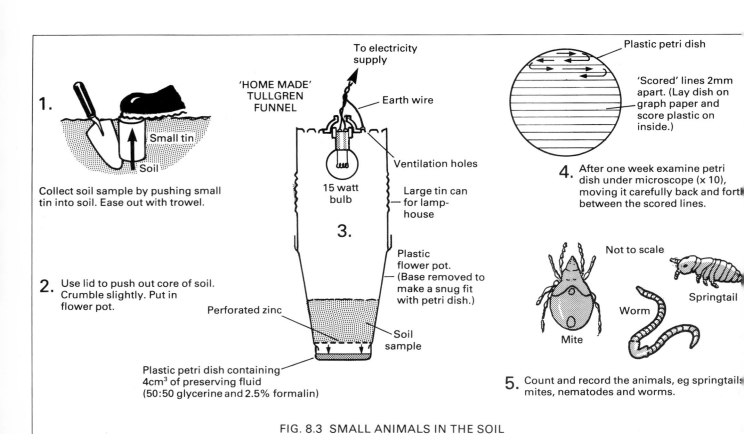

1. Collect soil sample by pushing small tin into soil. Ease out with trowel.

   Small tin
   Soil

2. Use lid to push out core of soil. Crumble slightly. Put in flower pot.

'HOME MADE' TULLGREN FUNNEL

To electricity supply

Earth wire

Ventilation holes

15 watt bulb

Large tin can for lamp-house

3.

Plastic flower pot. (Base removed to make a snug fit with petri dish.)

Perforated zinc

Soil sample

Plastic petri dish containing 4cm³ of preserving fluid (50:50 glycerine and 2.5% formalin)

Plastic petri dish

'Scored' lines 2mm apart. (Lay dish on graph paper and score plastic on inside.)

4. After one week examine petri dish under microscope (x 10), moving it carefully back and forth between the scored lines.

Not to scale

Mite   Worm   Springtail

5. Count and record the animals, eg springtails, mites, nematodes and worms.

FIG. 8.3 SMALL ANIMALS IN THE SOIL

22

9. Soil Erosion

The surface soil (topsoil) is removed, along with valuable seed and fertilisers in some cases, by agents such as wind and water. This leaves the subsoil which is not as fertile or as easy to cultivate.

CONDITIONS WHICH ENCOURAGE SOIL EROSION

- When there is little or no vegetation cover, leaving exposed bare earth.
- When rain or wind is able to reach the soil.
- When rain is not able to penetrate the soil, causing more run-off over the surface carrying away soil particles.
- When soil is very dry, light and friable. (Fine particles are often the most fertile.)
- Where there are steep slopes which encourage faster water run-off. This running water can carry a greater load of soil particles.

FIG. 9.1 DAMAGE BY WATER

REASONS FOR THE INCREASE IN SOIL EROSION

During the twentieth century the increase in soil erosion has been largely due to how the land has been managed or mismanaged by people. For example:
1. Poor forest management, especially the complete removal of every tree by quick and efficient machinery on steep slopes, e.g. in North America.
2. Trying to produce more food for a growing population by cultivating new areas or increasing yields from old areas.
   (a) By overgrazing. There is a limit to the number of animals a pasture will support. When the rate at which the grass is eaten is faster than regrowth then the grass will die leaving bare soil.
   (b) By removing hedgerows, which leaves large, often flat, open plains.

REASONS FOR REMOVING HEDGEROWS

1. They take up valuable space. More crops can be grown on the land released by their removal. More hectares can be put under cultivation.
2. Hedges are expensive to maintain, in time, money, and labour.
3. Monoculture farming: farmers specialising in one main crop require large fields and larger machines to make it economically worthwhile.

Questions

1. During the 1930s poor land management in the western prairies of the U.S.A. resulted in the 'Dust Bowl'. Find out more about this disaster.
2. Farmers removed hedgerows, especially in Lincolnshire and East Anglia in the late 1960s and early 1970s. Carry out your own research on this either by field work, newspaper reports, farming magazines or other written accounts. Investigate what the Nature Conservancy Council think about the value of hedgerows, especially as habitats. Organise a debate in your class. Some students should represent the views of the Nature Conservancy Council. Some should represent the views of the National Farmers' Union. A suitable debating title could be:
   'Hedgerows are a vital part of the rural environment.'

FIG. 9.2 A SOIL BLIZZARD

Ideas for Reducing Soil Erosion

This is used where slopes are gentle and erosion slight. Ploughing *up* and *down* slopes leaves ridges and depressions for water to run down and enlarge into **rills** and **gullies**. Ploughing *along* the side of the slope following the contours (land of the same height) builds up level ridges of earth running along the slope and reduces erosion by water. (See Fig. 9.3.) On steeper slopes contour ploughing is used with **terraces**. When heavy rain falls, water naturally flows downhill but only travels a short distance before being trapped by these larger ridges of earth known as terraces. Water then tends to soak in and not run away completely.

This is ideal for land where the soil is exposed, light, dry and friable, especially an area of open plains where there are few hedges or barriers and which is prone to strong winds. The worst effects of erosion can be overcome by planting crops (two at least) in wide **rows** or **strips** at right angles to the direction of the prevailing wind. Any blown soil may be caught in the next furrows or trapped by the next strip of crop which is harvested at a different time.

FIG. 9.3 CONTOUR PLOUGHING AND TERRACES

FIG. 9.5 SOYBEAN CROP GROWING THROUGH WHEAT STRAW

DIRECT DRILLING

Ploughing is kept to a minimum in this method. By leaving last year's crop remains in the ground (roots, stalks and stubble) erosion can be greatly reduced. Planting is finished in one pass across the field. A coulter carves a narrow slit which an opener enlarges. The seed drops in and a press wheel closes the slit. No furrow is made. There are of course disadvantages. Initially, crop yields are reduced until the new process is learnt. New equipment is very expensive. Powerful herbicides are needed to kill off the remains of last year's growth before planting.

USDA – Soil Conservation Service

FIG. 9.4 CONTOUR STRIP CROPPING

10. Water

WATER SUPPLY

We depend on a continuous supply of water from the water (hydrological) cycle. (See Fig. 10.2) Since 1974, ten regional water authorities have been responsible for the supply of water in England and Wales. The government decided to privatise the water industry in 1989.

The authorities extract water from a number of sources such as rivers, lakes, reservoirs and aquifers. They are responsible for:

● water control and management,

● water supply and quality,

● water conservation,

● sewage treatment,

● river management,

● recreation.

As standards of living improve, so water usage increases. In Great Britain a conservative estimate might be 300 litres per head per day. Surprisingly in the U.S.A. a figure of 220 litres/head per day is more realistic, due to American toilets using only nine gallon (40.50 litre) flushes. If the demands of industry and agriculture are also taken into consideration, the average consumption would be over 4000 litres/head per day.

Industry and agriculture consume huge quantities of water. For example, 182 litres of water are needed to grow enough hen feed to produce one egg; 70 litres of water are needed to refine one litre of petrol; 4.5 litres of water are needed to produce each newspaper we read. An industry may need to be located near a large water supply for processing, cooling or disposing of waste water (**effluent**). Illegal disposal of effluent may carry poisonous acids and chemicals into rivers. Warm water may affect fish and increase the growth of algae. This is known as **thermal pollution**.

PROBLEMS FOR THE WATER AUTHORITIES

1. Water isn't always found where it is needed. (See Fig. 7.1.) The heaviest rainfall in Great Britain falls in the north and west of the country, especially in the highland areas where the density of population is low. The lowest rainfall falls in the east and southeast, where the highest density of population is found.

2. It is costly to distribute water from areas of surplus to areas of deficit.

3. New reservoirs can be formed by damming and flooding valleys, often in upland areas. There is often a public outcry because:

(a) good farmland, buildings and even villages are drowned,

(b) ecological habitats and rare species may be lost,

(c) the scenic value changes,

(d) the water is piped to supply populations many miles away from the reservoir. For example, Wales supplies Liverpool and Birmingham, and the Lake District supplies Manchester 170 km away.

Questions

1. Use the information in the table below to draw a pie chart to show how one person's daily consumption of water is divided.

AVERAGE HOUSEHOLD WATER USE

Water use 140 litres/head per day	Litres	%	Degrees (× 3.6)
WC flushing	35	25	90
Baths/Showers	30	21	77
Washing machine	25	18	64
Luxury appliances	15	11	40
Outside use	5	4	14
Miscellaneous	30	21	75
Total	140	100	360

2. What would be the total annual consumption for one person?

3. How else might water be used in the home which has contributed to the large percentage for 'miscellaneous'?

4. In 1975 the EEC introduced a 'bathing directive' allowing 10 years for member nations to comply with certain criteria if they wished their beaches to be recognised as **Eurobeaches**. (Bathing water should not contain more than 10 000 coliform bacteria or 2000 faecal coliforms per 100 ml.) Of 600 beaches in Britain only 27 were submitted which reaches these standards. Some important ones were missing from the list, for example Blackpool, Brighton and Ramsgate.

(a) Where do the sewage bacteria come from to make the water so polluted?

(b) What remedies might you suggest? Who would pay for the cost?

(c) How do you think British beaches compare with the heavily criticised Mediterranean beaches? Why are the dangers greater in summer? Why might it be safer to paddle rather than swim in the water?

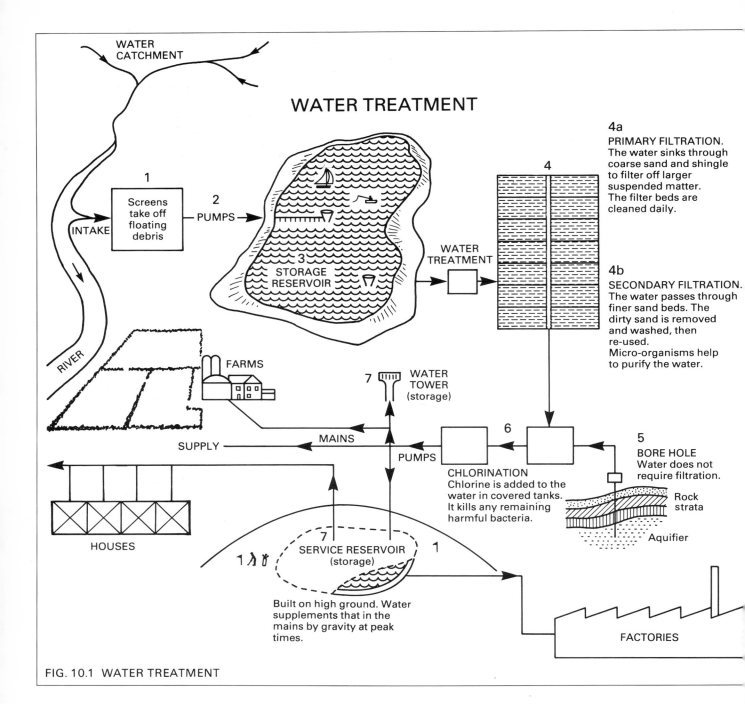

WATER TREATMENT

1 Screens take off floating debris

2 PUMPS

INTAKE

RIVER

WATER CATCHMENT

3 STORAGE RESERVOIR

WATER TREATMENT

4a PRIMARY FILTRATION. The water sinks through coarse sand and shingle to filter off larger suspended matter. The filter beds are cleaned daily.

4

4b SECONDARY FILTRATION. The water passes through finer sand beds. The dirty sand is removed and washed, then re-used. Micro-organisms help to purify the water.

FARMS

7 WATER TOWER (storage)

SUPPLY

MAINS

PUMPS

6 CHLORINATION Chlorine is added to the water in covered tanks. It kills any remaining harmful bacteria.

5 BORE HOLE Water does not require filtration.

Rock strata

Aquifer

HOUSES

7 SERVICE RESERVOIR (storage)

1

Built on high ground. Water supplements that in the mains by gravity at peak times.

FACTORIES

FIG. 10.1 WATER TREATMENT

PROVIDING MORE WATER FOR THE FUTURE

These are ways in which more water might be made available to meet increasing demands.

1. Flooding more valleys for reservoirs (see p. 27).
2. Desalination plants. These remove salt from sea water. The water would be more expensive to produce and may encourage more industry and pollution on the coast.
3. Making better use of our present supply.
   - By metering supplies. It has been proved that water consumption goes down by nearly half if people pay by the litre!
   - By reducing waste, e.g. dripping taps, using hoses on cars, etc.
   - By having different grades of water. Pure water for drinking and cooking. Less pure or 'grey' water for flushing toilets and industry. But, this would probably prove too costly and impractical a change.
   - By adapting houses to catch and use their own rainwater as 'grey water'.
   - By reducing losses in the distribution of water. This is often caused by old and badly worn pipes.
4. Increasing the use of underground water by pumps and wells or diverting water from rivers with a surplus to deficit areas.

Questions

1. Use any diagrams and information here to write an account of how less water could be used in the home, whether it be because of a shortage or not.
2. Investigate and record what recreational facilities are available on or near water such as rivers, canals and reservoirs.
3. Write in your own words an account of how water is purified and supplied to the home (use Fig. 10.1).

The Fluoride Issue

Did you know?

1. Fluoride is a poison. Above 20 mg daily can cause chronic poisoning. Fluorosis in cattle causes bones to bend and teeth to fall out. The cattle can't get up or feed and so die.
2. Research has found that a level of fluoride above 1 ppm (1 part to 1 million parts of water) in drinking water can cause a mottling effect on teeth, especially if it reaches 8 ppm.
3. Below, and up to 1 ppm, it can be helpful to the teeth causing less tooth decay, because the enamel of the tooth absorbs the fluoride and becomes more resistant to acid, formed by bacteria and food left on the teeth.
4. After the age of about 16, fluoride cannot be absorbed through the enamel, so brushing with a fluoride toothpaste becomes less effective.
5. Fluoride can be added (at great cost) to the drinking water by water authorities if it does not occur naturally in the area. It reaches the teeth by the blood system in the centre of each tooth.

In small groups, debate whether fluoride should be added to the drinking water to help solve problems of tooth decay.

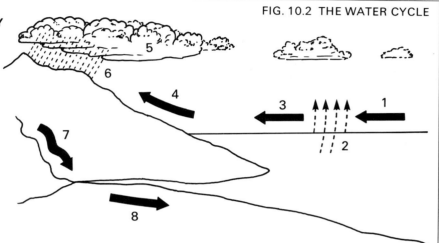

THE WATER CYCLE
IF YOU DON'T KNOW THE WATER CYCLE BY NOW YOU NEVER WILL!

Copy the diagram in Fig. 10.2.
Match these captions to the relevant letters.
River flows to sea.
Clouds form due to condensation.
Sea water evaporates.
Warm, moist air.
Droplets combine and fall as rain.
Moist air rises and cools.
Warm air blows over sea.
Rainfall drains into rivers.

What is evaporation?
What is condensation?
Write a paragraph account of what happens in the water cycle.

FIG. 10.2 THE WATER CYCLE

FIG. 10.3 HYDRO-ELECTRIC POWER STATION AT KERRY FALLS, SCOTLAND

Reservoirs

A reservoir is formed when a dam is built across a river, flooding the valley behind the dam. It is used to:

- store water for domestic and industrial uses. The water is treated before it is used as in Fig. 10.1.

- store water, especially in highland areas, to use in the production of electricity. (Hydro-electric power, H.E.P.) This requires not only a reservoir but a power station, which is sometimes built underground, a high dam and transmission lines to the major centres of population.

Britain's largest man-made reservoir is **Rutland Water** or Empingham Reservoir. It was opened in 1976 at a cost of £30 million, under its own Act of Parliament. It provides the expanding towns of Peterborough, Northampton, Daventry, Corby and Wellingborough with domestic and industrial water. This area is one of the driest regions in England. It has 147 mm of 'effective' annual rainfall compared with 487 mm in the rest of the country. The Anglian Water Authority, which is responsible for water supply in this area, estimated that they would be short of 225 000 m³ of water per day by 2001 if Rutland Water had not come into existence.

SITING A RESERVOIR

This is not an easy task, especially when 1600 ha. of good agricultural land will be lost in an area known for its high quality landscape. The following are the sort of criteria used for siting a reservoir:

1. In an area, usually highland, where the natural contours of the land would be capable of holding the required volume of water to be stored.
2. Close to main rivers to minimise pumping costs.
3. In a naturally watertight valley, i.e. one lined with clay.
4. Where there is enough local material to construct an earth dam and the underlying rock is strong enough to support the weight of the dam.
5. Close to centres of population which need water.

Only two out of 64 sites in Rutland (now part of Leicestershire) met with all these criteria. The Gwash Valley was chosen because it would be cheaper. The River Gwash, a tributary of the River Welland, only provides 5% of the reservoir's yield. Most of the water is pumped from the River Nene and Welland through 17 km of aqueduct. A quantity of 110 000 m³ is produced daily through a water treatment plant at Wing, only one third of the reservoir's capacity.

FIG. 10.4 RUTLAND WATER

Questions

1. £1.05 million was invested in landscaping the whole site of Rutland Water and developing recreational facilities. Using Fig. 10.4, write your own account of what the reservoir offers the public apart from a ready water supply.
2. New building has been avoided where possible, in favour of using existing buildings. Water skiing has been totally rejected and so has an idea for a self catering chalet complex. Choose 4 students from your class to act as spokesmen for the following.

Opposing the siting of the reservoir
    The County Council.
    The National Farmers' Union.
In favour of siting the reservoir
    Leicester and Rutland Trust for Nature
    Conservation
    The Anglian Water Authority.
Use the information on this page and your own ideas to have a debate for and against the siting of Rutland Water.

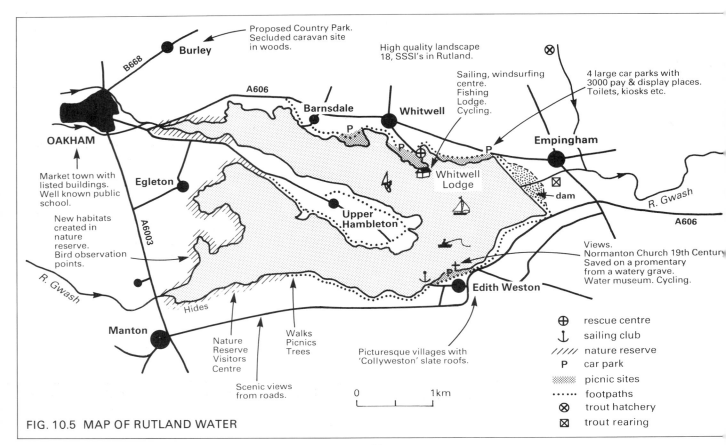

FIG. 10.5 MAP OF RUTLAND WATER

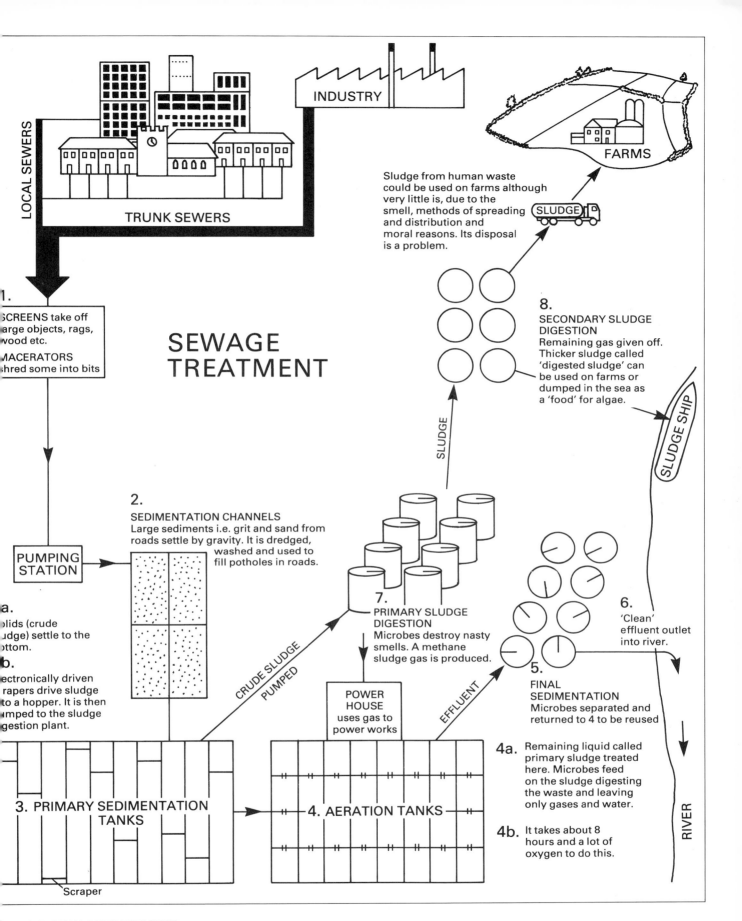

SEWAGE TREATMENT

LOCAL SEWERS

TRUNK SEWERS

INDUSTRY

FARMS

Sludge from human waste could be used on farms although very little is, due to the smell, methods of spreading and distribution and moral reasons. Its disposal is a problem.

SLUDGE

1.
SCREENS take off large objects, rags, wood etc.
MACERATORS shred some into bits

8.
SECONDARY SLUDGE DIGESTION
Remaining gas given off. Thicker sludge called 'digested sludge' can be used on farms or dumped in the sea as a 'food' for algae.

SLUDGE SHIP

2.
SEDIMENTATION CHANNELS
Large sediments i.e. grit and sand from roads settle by gravity. It is dredged, washed and used to fill potholes in roads.

PUMPING STATION

SLUDGE

a.
olids (crude ludge) settle to the ottom.

b.
ectronically driven rapers drive sludge to a hopper. It is then umped to the sludge gestion plant.

7.
PRIMARY SLUDGE DIGESTION
Microbes destroy nasty smells. A methane sludge gas is produced.

CRUDE SLUDGE PUMPED

POWER HOUSE
uses gas to power works

EFFLUENT

6.
'Clean' effluent outlet into river.

5.
FINAL SEDIMENTATION
Microbes separated and returned to 4 to be reused

3. PRIMARY SEDIMENTATION TANKS

Scraper

4. AERATION TANKS

4a. Remaining liquid called primary sludge treated here. Microbes feed on the sludge digesting the waste and leaving only gases and water.

4b. It takes about 8 hours and a lot of oxygen to do this.

RIVER

FIG. 10.6 SEWAGE TREATMENT

. Study Fig. 10.6. Write an account of how sewage is treated before the 'cleaned' effluent is returned to the rivers.

4. Why does returning effluent at the same outlet on the river cause problems for wildlife in the water and at the banks near the outlet? (See p. 45 'Eutrophication', and the glossary.)

11. Population

Population. The total number of a certain species in a given area is the population.

Birth rate. This is the average number of births for every 1000 individuals in a population each year.

Death rate. This is the average number of individuals who die each year for every 1000 in a population.

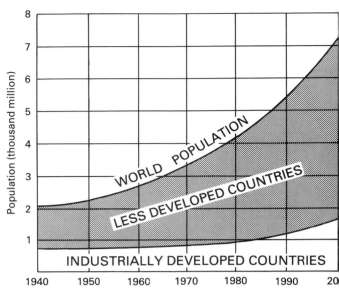

FIG. 11.1 GRAPHS TO SHOW POPULATION GROWTHS

To show that the world's human population first reached 1000m in 1830, took 100 years to add a further 1000m, and is now rising rapidly.

To show increases since 1940 and forecast up to 2000. Stresses ve rapid increase in population of less developed lands.

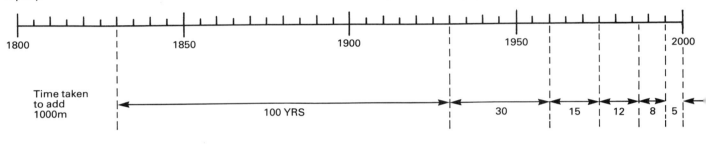

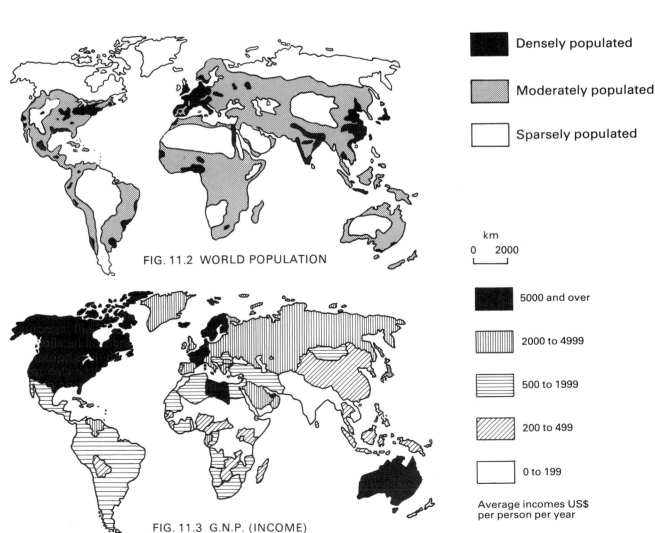

FIG. 11.2 WORLD POPULATION

Densely populated

Moderately populated

Sparsely populated

km
0   2000

FIG. 11.3 G.N.P. (INCOME)

5000 and over

2000 to 4999

500 to 1999

200 to 499

0 to 199

Average incomes US$ per person per year

30

POPULATION TRENDS

The world population in 1984 was 4.7 billion. Its growth has been **accelerating** by 200 000 daily. Such rapid growth is often referred to as the **population explosion**. (See Fig. 11.1.)

Here are some of the reasons why population growth 'took off' in Europe after 1780.

● Improvements in agriculture, machinery and mining which paved the way for the agricultural and industrial revolutions.

● Improved diet.

● Improvements in hygiene; efficient sewage disposal and the supply of purified water.

● Improvements in medicine and the health services. With a rise in the standard of living more children survived to adulthood, major killers such as cholera and diphtheria were kept under control and there was a reduction in the death rate.

THE CYCLE OF POPULATION CHANGE IN WESTERN EUROPE

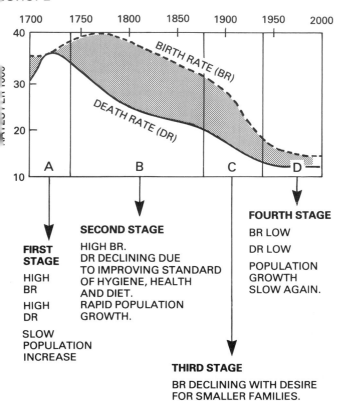

FIRST STAGE
HIGH BR
HIGH DR
SLOW POPULATION INCREASE

SECOND STAGE
HIGH BR.
DR DECLINING DUE TO IMPROVING STANDARD OF HYGIENE, HEALTH AND DIET.
RAPID POPULATION GROWTH.

THIRD STAGE
BR DECLINING WITH DESIRE FOR SMALLER FAMILIES.
BIRTH CONTROL.
DR DECLINES. POPULATION GROWTH STILL RAPID BUT STARTING TO SLOW DOWN.

FOURTH STAGE
BR LOW
DR LOW
POPULATION GROWTH SLOW AGAIN.

Most developed countries are at the 4th stage of population growth, i.e. very slow. Many developing countries are in the second stage with rapidly expanding populations. There is no guarantee that they will follow the same pattern as the developed countries.

FIG. 11.4 CYCLE OF POPULATION CHANGE IN W. EUROPE

For richer, for poorer

The population is growing most **rapidly** in the poorer, less industrialised, **developing countries** of the world, areas which do not have a sufficient share of the world's resources of food. In these countries, such as India and Bangladesh, a high birth rate used to be essential for the survival of a few. Since the 1940s and 1950s there has been a decline in the death rate due largely to the introduction of modern drugs and ideas on public health, for example, those used in the control of malaria and yellow fever. The continuing high birth rate then resulted in rapid population growth (see Fig. 11.1) and increased poverty. The majority of individuals suffer from **undernourishment**, meaning simply not enough to eat, and **malnutrition**, meaning that their diet, such as it is, is totally unbalanced, often devoid of any protein content. The birth rate in developing countries is now declining slowly (see Fig. 11.4), but it is still much greater than in the **developed** countries, such as those in North America and Europe. These countries are comparatively rich in resources and incomes. A developed country is often defined as one with a high **gross national product** per head of population (G.N.P.). This is the total value of all the goods and services produced by that country per annum divided by its population. Fig. 11.3 therefore gives one a good idea of which countries are considered to be developed or developing.

Questions

1. Study Fig. 11.1. Between 1830 and 1930 the world's human population increased by 1000 million. How soon did the population increase by a further 1000 m? Explain what is happening to the growth rate in the rest of the diagram.

2. Using an atlas, name and make a list of the most densely populated and sparsely populated areas of the world shown in Fig. 11.2. Compare these with areas of high and low incomes shown in Fig. 11.3. Which areas of the world will be very vulnerable to poverty?

3. Why is a rapid population growth rate in a developing country, such as India, a huge problem? Give some reasons why famine occurs.

4. Food, water, shelter and space usually limit the size of a natural animal or plant population. This population may increase until the **carrying capacity** is reached. Over this limit, the animals or plants may die in large numbers, for example, due to competition, starvation or disease, until a balance is regained. In human populations it is possible for **overpopulation** to occur. The carrying capacity may be reached, causing damage to the land and the whole environment, but the population still rises. (See Glossary.)

Explain some ways in which human populations overcome the sort of limiting factors which affect natural populations, causing overpopulation and a strain on resources.

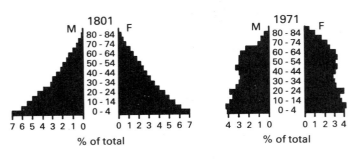

FIG. 11.5 DEMOGRAPHIC TRANSITION: ENGLAND AND WALES

POPULATION PYRAMIDS

The pyramid is used to show the **age** and **sex** structure of a human population. The population is divided into males, located on the left and females, located on the right of the graph. The data is further divided into age groups, starting at the bottom with births and finishing at the top with the aged. Each group is often shown as a percentage of the total population. Each group shows trends in births and deaths. The information they provide can be used when decisions have to be made about future social needs, for example, schools and housing. They are also used in the comparison of different countries or periods in history.

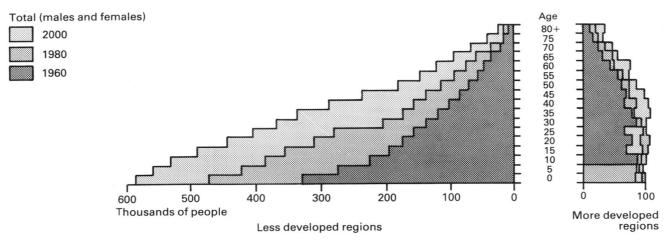

FIG. 11.6 POPULATION AGE PYRAMID, LESS AND MORE DEVELOPED REGIONS 1960–2000

Questions

Study Figs. 11.4, 11.5 and 11.6
1. In general, which die younger, males or females?
2. After the Second World War there was an increase in births, the 'post-war baby boom'. Identify this on Fig. 11.5. Explain your answer. List some reasons why this happened.
3. Fig. 11.6 is unusual because it compares the total population age structure in developed and developing countries.
   (a) Compare the birth rates in 1960, 1980 and those estimated for 2000 on both sides of the graph. Write down your observations.

(b) What is happening to the death rate in the developing countries over these 40 years? Give reasons why you think this is happening and what effect it will have on the total population in these countries.
(c) Compare the pyramid for England and Wales in 1801 with that of the developing countries in Fig. 11.6. Suggest reasons why there are similarities between them.
4. Write a description of the structure of the population in England and Wales in 1971.

BIRTH CONTROL

In a poor developing country a large family could ensure:
● a large work force to earn the family living,
● enough dependants, after **infant mortality**, to support the parents in old age, as there are no pension schemes.
The governments of such countries are trying to educate their people, by birth control campaigns, to understand that fewer offspring can mean:
● a better standard of living,
● a better share of resources for all.
To control the numbers of births each year means using some method of **family planning**, i.e. **contraception**. The pill, the coil and the sheath are some of the most popular and efficient methods when used properly. Fathers with 2 or more children are encouraged to have a vasectomy. (See glossary.)

The Communist Party in China are aiming at zero population growth by the year 2000. They actively encourage only one child per couple by a system of rewards, e.g. cash, free education, housing benefits, and punishments (none of these things). What do you think of this policy? What effect, if any, might it have on abortion rates and male and female ratios? Sketch the possible effect on the population pyramid by the year 2000.

Imagine a village in India, regularly cut off by the monsoons with a visiting medical team only twice a year. Which method of contraception would you encourage them to use and why? Which methods would seem unsuitable and why?

2. Increasing Food Production for a Growing Population

FOOD TRENDS

Scientists have estimated that enough food could be produced for everyone until the year 2000, but:

Food is costly. It goes to those who can afford it.

It is not evenly distributed throughout the world, nor is it likely to be in the future. Many developing countries do not produce enough now to feed all their people. The undernourished may increase from 600 million to 1300 million by the year 2000.

Some foods have increasing yields, e.g. cereals, but others are not keeping pace with population growth, e.g. beef and fish.

There are great losses of food due to it being contaminated at harvest, eaten by pests, badly stored and poorly distributed. Feeding grain to animals to convert it into meat also wastes food if the animal doesn't have a relatively good **food conversion rate.**

ALL CHANGE DOWN ON THE FARM

C18th ⟶ C20th

Better farming practice such as crop rotation.
Invention and increased use of **machinery**, for example the tractor and harvester.
Becoming less **labour intensive**, i.e. reducing the labour force who demand high wages.
Specialisation. Growing one or two crops on a **larger** farm, to make the maximum use of expensive machinery, chemicals etc.
Becoming more **capital intensive**. Huge sums of money are required for automatic machines electricity bills, animals shelter and chemicals.
Moving towards **intensive** rather than **extensive** farming systems, in an attempt to increase yields and profits. For example, battery or deep litter systems for poultry in controlled environment houses rather than free range systems.

NEWER and OLDER IDEAS in use today

1. Irrigation. p. 34
2. Drainage.
3. Fertilisers. p. 44
4. Pest control. p. 42
5. Crop rotation.
6. Improved animal and plant strains. p. 34.
7. Improved photosynthetic rate. (Importance of O_2/CO_2 balance.)
8. Efficient use of sunlight. Fig. 12.1.
9. Leaf proteins. Oil proteins.
10. Feeding high fibre foods to animals with a good food conversion rate. p. 121.
11. Hydroponics. p. 34.
12. More use of controlled environments. Glasshouses. Animal houses. p. 40.
13. Fresh- and salt-water food.
14. Making more use of the 'lower plant kingdom'. Fungi. Algae. Fig. 12.1.
15. New and improved farm machinery. p. 37.
16. Making more of known and 'untapped' sources. Soya bean. Fig. 12.2.

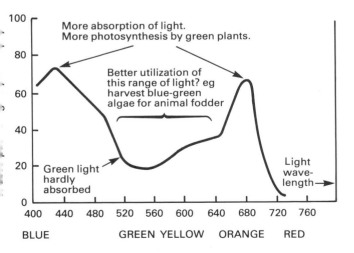

FIG. 12.1 MAKING USE OF THE DIFFERENT WAVELENGTHS OF LIGHT

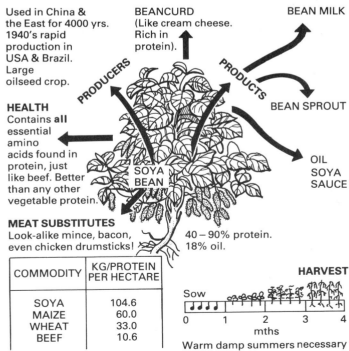

FIG. 12.2 MAKE MORE USE OF SOYA?

IRRIGATION

This means adding water to the land artificially to increase plant performance and yields.

● In wetter, humid climates the problem is one of **controlling** and **distributing** large quantities of water just at the right time in the growing season to increase yields by 10–50%. Methods such as sprinklers and subsurface perforated pipes are popular.

● In hot climates the problem is one of **water shortage**. Any rain often comes as heavy downpours causing 'flash floods'. Water is soon lost by high evaporation rates and run-off into rivers. Method may be ancient, such as shadufs and canal systems, or very sophisticated. Some of the richer arab countries grow salad crops under glass by hydroponics in the middle of deserts!

● **Drainage** may become a problem. Too much water may lead to the soil becoming **waterlogged**. Roots will die beause thay cannot get enough oxygen for respiration. Natural mineral salts may build up in the topsoil if water evaporates rapidly from the surface instead of being flushed down to below the root zone. Very salty or **saline** soil is toxic to plants. This process is known as **salinisation**.

IMPROVING PLANTS AND ANIMALS

Developing or improving new strains or breeds of plants and animals has helped to increase farm yields substantially in the last 50 years. Careful breeding programmes can result in a better performance from the offspring or progeny, for example, more flesh, more milk, more grain per ear etc. Some breeders believe that 75% of the variation in milk production between diary herds may be due to the environment and management but 25% is due to **genetic** differences, which an individual **inherits** from its parents.

HYDROPONICS

This is a method of growing plants in water without soil. A lightweight water-absorbent material such as sand, gravel or vermiculite is usually used on a small scale. On a larger scale a mat is placed in the bottom o a trough. A nutrient medium to which essential minera salts have been added is pumped through the trough. The plant roots grow directly into this medium.

Duntech Irrigation Services Ltd

FIG. 12.3 HYDROPONIC SYSTEM

Programme	Animal	Plant
Inbreeding	No new stock is brought in. Closely related animals are selected on their performance and mated, e.g. father and daughter.	The breeder takes out the 'best lines' each year and self pollinates the plants e.g. by putting plastic bags over the flower heads. (This method helps to produce pure-bred lines for cross-breeding.)
Crossbreeding or Outbreeding	Parents, which may be from different breeds of the same species, are selected for particular good characteristics and bred together.	Parent plants are selected for particular characteristics and cross pollinated, e.g. the two strains might be grown side by side in a polythene tunnel using insect pollinators to carry out the cross pollination. The 'wild type' is often used as one parent to increase resistance to disease.

TABLE 12.1

Questions

1. Choose **two** methods for increasing food for a growing population **not** covered in detail on these pages. Find out as much information as possible to report back to the rest of the class.

2. Graph and comment on the yields of the arable crops in this table.

Yields (Tonnes per hectare)

Great Britain	1939	1982
Wheat	2.2	4.4
Potatoes	17.5	28.5
Sugar beet	16.4	34.1

3. Write an account of progeny testing from Fig. 12.4. What is A.I.? What are the advantages of this system for the small dairy herd farmer?

4. Which breeding programme, inbreeding or outbreeding, would lead to more **variation** in the offspring? Which might lead to the development of inherited diseases? (Table 12.1.)

5. Imagine an apple, an egg, a beef calf, a wheat plant and a lettuce. Which characteristics might you want to select in each in order to
   (a) increase the yield,
   (b) make it easier to manage or harvest,
   (c) make it more appealing to the consumer?

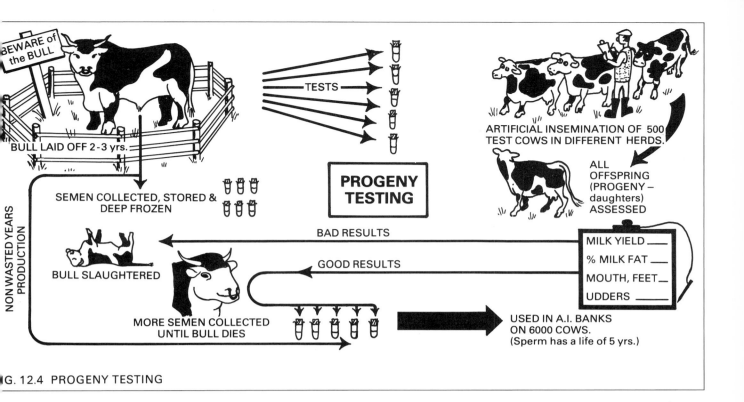

FIG. 12.4 PROGENY TESTING

FOOD STORAGE, PROCESSING AND HANDLING

PROCESS	TECHNIQUE	EFFECT	OTHER COMMENTS
Canning	All air expressed from tin by heating. Sealed. Sterilised by heating to high temperatures.	Bacteria and enzymes destroyed. Keeps well. Vitamins/flavour not too impaired.	Do within 48 hours of being picked. 'Blown' tins due to decomposition inside.
Quick Freezing	Reduce to −18°C as rapidly as possible.	Bacteria and enzymes destroyed or growth slowed right down. Long storage time. Good taste and nutritional value.	Slow freezing causes large ice crystals to form. Flavour and goodness lost in cooking. Possibility of food poisoning, e.g. chicken not thawed properly.
Dehydration	Removal of moisture. Reconstitute by adding water again.	Quick drying methods retain vitamins and flavour. Less bulk and weight.	Does not kill bacteria. Slow drying may destroy some vitamins, e.g. Vitamin C.
Chemicals Salting or Curing	Addition of salt.	Water is drawn away from food to dissolve salt/sugar.	
Jam making	Addition of sugar.	None for bacteria or enzymes.	
Pickling	Addition of acetic acid (vinegar).	Acidity too high (pH too low) for bacteria/enzymes.	Distinct flavour and taste.
Smoking	Food exposed to 'wood' smoke after salting.	Outer layers have antiseptic effect. Bacteria may be killed.	Distinct flavour and taste.
Irradiation	Food exposed to radiation.	Bacteria destroyed.	Expensive. Flavour and texture altered.

TABLE 12.2 THE MAIN METHODS OF FOOD PRESERVATION

Food is wasted daily. Here are some reasons why.

1. Storage facilities need to be **cool** and **dry** with **free air movement**. Large stocks of food in warm humid conditions are ideal places for moulds, bacteria and pests such as rats, mice, termites and weevils to feed, grow and breed in.

2. There are problems concerning certain foods. Fats and oils can spoil by chemical decomposition. Fruit needs very gentle handling. Individual fruits may need separation and a controlled environment in which carbon dioxide and temperature are carefully monitored. Warmth and physical damage such as bruising encourage enzyme action. This results in the breakdown of the cells causing premature ripening and decay which can spread from fruit to fruit if they are in close contact. Spontaneous combustion (fire) may damage hay and silage.

3. Developing countries suffer more because:
   ● Storing, processing and refining large quantities of food is costly.
   ● Controlled drying facilities are few. (In tropical countries this may be seen as an energy efficient advantage, i.e. to dry crops such as coffee beans out in the sun.)
   ● Drought may mean that seed stored for next year's growth has to be eaten.
   ● Poverty may mean that crops have to be harvested prematurely. Unripe sugar cane, for instance, will have a lower sugar, oil and starch content.
   ● A poor communications system doesn't allow food to be easily distributed in, out or around the country.

Experiments

Carry out these simple experiments. They should be put in an undisturbed place for 1–2 weeks, with your initials labelled on them.

1. **Fast freeze** a brussel sprout, i.e. freeze it quickly to its centre, below −18°C. (Speak nicely to the home economics teacher to use the deep freeze!)
   Slow freeze another sprout in the ice department of an ordinary fridge.
   Leave a third sprout in the laboratory.
   Record the appearance of all three after one week. Cook all the fast freeze sprouts for the class in a beaker of water for 5–10 mins. Cook all the slow freeze sprouts in the same amount of water in another beaker. Examine and record the final sprout colour, texture and water colour.
2. Cover a slice of peeled apple, pear or peach in a beaker with **strong sugar** solution.
   Cover a similar slice in the same amount of **water** in another beaker as a control.
3. Cover a pickling onion or some red cabbage with **vinegar** in a beaker.
   Cover another with the same amount of **water** as a control. Test the vinegar with universal indicator paper. Record the pH.
4. Leave a 4 cm² slice of **dry** bread wrapped in a piece of paper in the laboratory.
   Leave a 4 cm² slice of bread **soaked** in 5 ml of water in a petri dish, covered with a lid to keep in the moisture.

5. Obtain a sample of **fresh untreated milk** from a farm.
   Heat 250 ml to 71–73°C for 10 to 15 secs. Cool, cover and place in a refrigerator.
   Heat another 250 ml to 100°C for 10–15 secs. Cool, cover and place in a refrigerator.
   Place a third 250 ml of covered untreated milk in the refrigerator. Check all three **daily** for smell and appearance.

Record all the results. Include comments on freshness, appearance, presence of mould etc. **Do not touch or inhale mould or bacteria**.

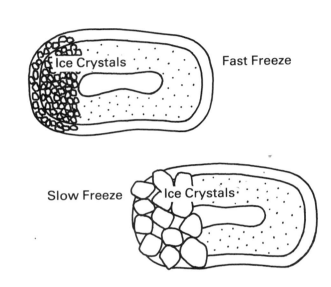

FIG. 12.5 THE EFFECT OF FREEZING ON PLANT CELLS

Questions

1. Study Fig. 12.5. Which method of freezing reduces the loss of important minerals and vitamins during cooking? (This may be judged by the loss of the green pigment chlorophyll in Expt. 1.) Why is this so?
2. Has any mould formed on top of the sugar solution in Expt. 2? How does the process of canning prevent this? Why should food be treated as fresh once a can is open?
3. The presence of microscopic **bacteria** and **moulds** causes the perishing of food. Find out how large concentrations of salt or sugar prevent the food in bottling and canning from perishing.
4. **Enzyme action** within the food also causes it to rot. How does temperature and acidity affect enzyme activity? (Experiments 1 & 3).
5. Find out more about the pasteurisation and sterilisation of milk. Which method helps to preserve the milk for the longest? Why is pasteurised milk generally preferred in Britain? How may the invasion of 'long life' milk from other EEC countries affect milk production in Britain?
6. What do you conclude about the conditions needed for the growth of bacteria and moulds and enzyme activity from these experiments and Table 12.2?

3. Mechanisation

...fficient and versatile machines are largely responsible ...or the decline in the workforce on our farms. (See Fig. 3.1.) The tractor remains the most important machine ...n the farm. The combine harvester has had a ...gnificant impact in the last 20 years and may continue ...o do so along with the other machines shown on these ...ages.

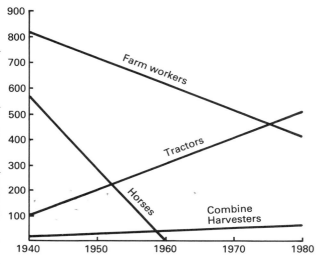

FIG. 13.1 CHANGES IN WORKING METHODS SINCE THE 1940s

Grass crops are important in Great Britain. New technology is speeding up the field drying process while the harvest is being gathered. This combination mower with **conditioner** cuts drying time by 55%. The conditioner is made up of nylon brushes which scratch the stem and leaf, without breaking or bruising them, to remove a lot of the wax. A light fluffy swath of hay is deposited on the field which wilts and dries out much faster than before.

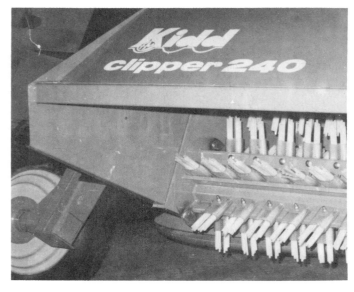

FIG. 13.2 KIDD MOWER CONDITIONER

Crop ➡ Grain ➡ Straw ◀▶ Chaff ⟱

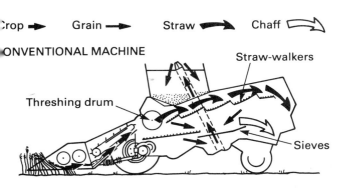

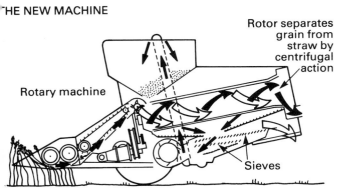

FIG. 13.3 TWO TYPES OF COMBINE HARVESTER

THE AXIAL FLOW COMBINE HARVESTER

This machine is already popular in the U.S.A. and France. Between 1980 and 1986 an estimated 230 000 hectares of wheat, barley, oats, rye, grass seed, oilseed rape, beans and peas have been harvested with this new type of combine in Great Britain. The main difference in design is that one huge fast turning **rotary drum** replaces 16 other moving parts such as chains, pulleys, belts and **strawwalkers** which are used in the conventional harvester. The drum threshes the corn **several** times in one single operation. It has a gentle rubbing action which does little damage to the grain. Augers move the grain to the cleaning sieves and eventually to the grain tank.
Fanned air removes dust and chaff.
The main advantages appear to be that:
● There are fewer moving machine parts to break down.
● The crop is gathered quickly.
● The machine is versatile, many different crops can be gathered by changing the concaves.
● It can work on slopes, wet or laid crops.
● There is less waste.
● It discharges a full tank of grain in 90 secs.
● The operation is smooth and very quiet.
● The whole harvest can be accomplished in a two man operation.
The main disadvantages appear to be:
● The cost of the machine.
● The production of poorer quality straw (broken and shorter) more suitable for burning.

THE ROUND BALER

 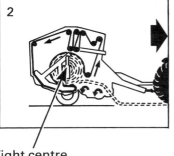 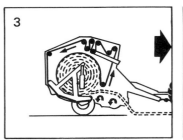 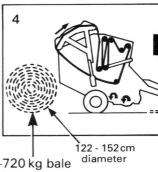

Tight centre

540–720 kg bale

122 - 152 cm diameter

FIG. 13.4 HOW THE ROUND BALER WORKS

The round baler machine has almost revolutionised the field handling of hay, silage and straw. It involves far less field work than the smaller conventional (rectangular) baler. One man can clear 4–5 acres in half an hour. The bales are tight, neat and waterproof. (They are rolled tight, right from the start. Air trapped in the centre may prevent good fermentation of, for instance, silage.) Now each bale can be wrapped in an open plastic 'stocking' net. This keeps the shape of the bale and makes handling easier. Silage may be baled into black plastic bags straight away – a new eyesore on the English landscape!

Fisons plc, Horticultural Division

Peat is traditionally 'hand cut' which is a slow hard process but conserves peat resources.

Neil M Godsman Peat Machinery

FIG. 13.5 PEAT CUTTING BY HAND AND 'ROUND' PEAT CUTTER

Questions
1. List the advantages and disadvantages of the new and old systems.
2. What might be the consequences if a similar machine were used, for example, in the Somerset Levels? See p. 22.

THE CONTROLLED DROPLET SPRAYER

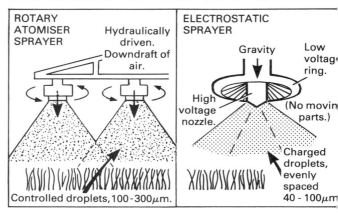

FIG. 13.6 CONTROLLED DROPLET SPRAYER

Research has shown that 'large' droplets of sprayed chemicals, such as pesticides, over 300 microns (μm) in size bounce off leaves onto the ground. Sizes between 100–300 μm are much more favourable. Very small droplets may drift away from their target.

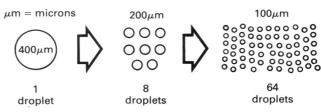

One 'large' droplet can be broken up into many smaller more useful droplets. This means that the actual amount of pesticide used could be reduced. Two new developments may become important.

1. The hydraulic driven **rotary atomisers**. These use a downdraft of air to carry the spray to the target. The size of the droplet can be controlled to 100–300 μm. The manufacturers claim that the foliage is disturbed enough to allow complete penetration of most dense crops.
2. **Electrostatic sprayers. Evenly sized** droplets in the range between 40–200 μm are electrically charged so that they repel fellow droplets and are all **evenly spaced** in the spray. They are physically attracted to the plants in a 'wrap around' way. So far they have been successfully used on newly planted or less dense crops but do not penetrate dense crops well.

4. A Production System

BREEDING

The farmer breeds his own pigs for fattening (follow the diagrams 2–7) but he buys in, at some expense, the original parent stock from specialist **pig breeding companies**. These companies isolate and test different breeds of pig on a large scale in **multiplier farms**. They carry out performance testing. (See p. 34.) Desirable qualities in a breed for bacon production might be long backs, lean meat, a relatively good food conversion rate (see glossary) and resistance to disease. The farmer will want some reassurance from the company that the parent stock he is buying are known to have an inherited potential for these characteristics. It has been found that the offspring or progeny from crossbred gilts (dams) are more robust than the offspring from purebred dams. So, in this case the Camborough gilt is used. She is a hybrid. This means she is a first cross (offspring from a mating) between a purebred Landrace pig and a purebred Large White pig. She is then mated with a purebred Landrace, or a purebred Large White boar. (See Fig. 14.1.)

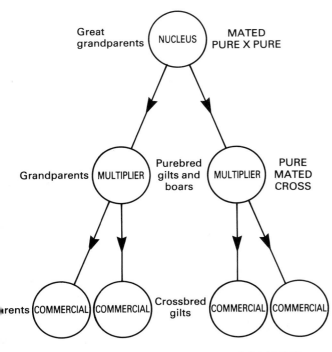

FIG. 14.1 A BREEDING IMPROVEMENT PROGRAMME

ENVIRONMENT

All animals need to breathe in **oxygen** and breathe out **carbon dioxide** to allow them to carry out respiration. A good ventilation system gives this flow of air and exchange of gases. It should also keep the pig as near as possible to its **lower critical temperature**, i.e. the temperature at which the pig performs well. If the temperature is not maintained the pig will need to eat extra food to keep up its body temperature. This in turn will cost the farmer more money! (The critical temperature will also be affected by the number of pigs in the pen, the type of floor surface, amount of insulation and bedding.) Good ventilation should also prevent a high relative humidity. Above 50% relative humidity usually results in a poor performance. Fig 14.2 shows some of the main ventilation systems used in pig housing.

Questions

1. The production system shown on p. 40 and p. 41 is an intensive system. The photograph here shows an extensive free range system of rearing pigs. In what obvious ways does it differ from the Manor Farm system?
2. List the ways in which Farmer Nicholson has intensified his system. For example,
   (a) Weaning at 3 weeks instead of 5 weeks old.
   (b) ...
3. Write an account of the whole production system using the numbers as a guide. You should include references to controlled environments or housing (heating, temperature, insulation, ventilation, feeding, automation, slurry removal) breeding stock, costs, life cycle, markets etc.

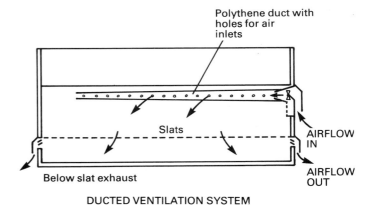

DUCTED VENTILATION SYSTEM

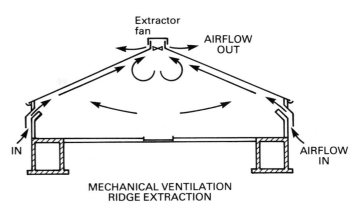

MECHANICAL VENTILATION
RIDGE EXTRACTION

FIG. 14.2 TWO MAIN VENTILATION SYSTEMS USED IN PIG HOUSING

PIG PRODUCTION SYSTEM

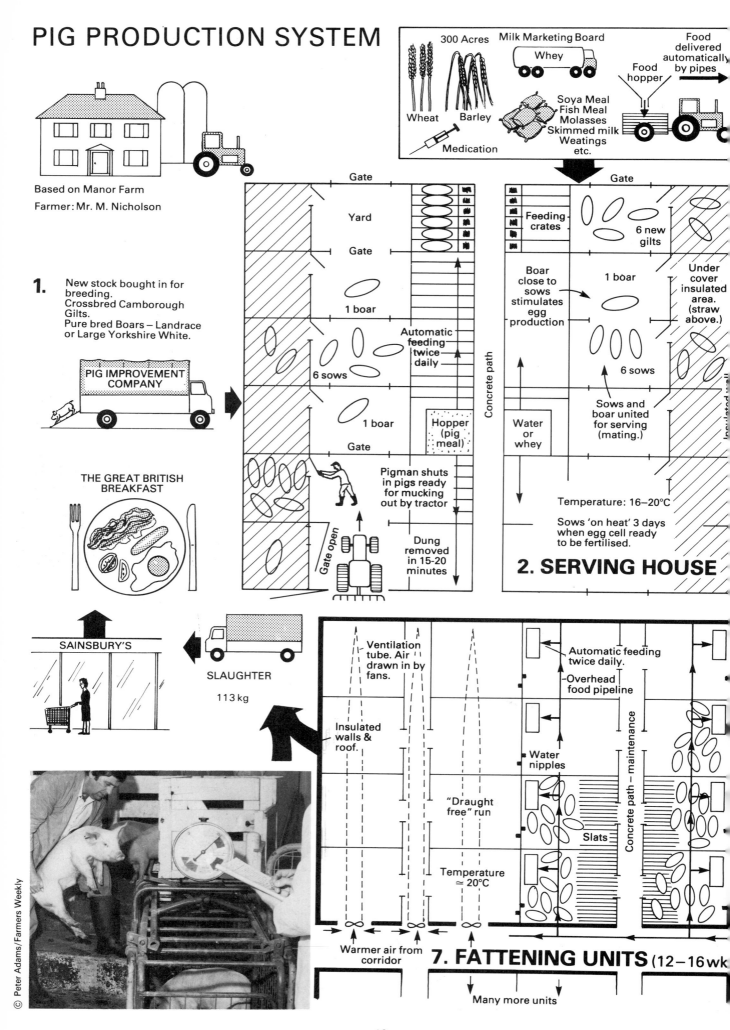

300 Acres
Milk Marketing Board
Whey

Wheat Barley

Soya Meal
Fish Meal
Molasses
Skimmed milk
Weatings
etc.

Medication

Food hopper

Food delivered automatically by pipes

Based on Manor Farm
Farmer: Mr. M. Nicholson

1. New stock bought in for breeding.
Crossbred Camborough Gilts.
Pure bred Boars – Landrace or Large Yorkshire White.

PIG IMPROVEMENT COMPANY

THE GREAT BRITISH BREAKFAST

SAINSBURY'S

SLAUGHTER

113 kg

Gate

Yard

Gate

1 boar

Automatic feeding twice daily

6 sows

1 boar

Gate

Hopper (pig meal)

Gate open

Pigman shuts in pigs ready for mucking out by tractor

Dung removed in 15-20 minutes

Concrete path

Gate

Feeding crates

6 new gilts

Boar close to sows stimulates egg production

1 boar

Under cover insulated area. (straw above.)

6 sows

Sows and boar united for serving (mating.)

Water or whey

Temperature: 16–20°C

Sows 'on heat' 3 days when egg cell ready to be fertilised.

2. SERVING HOUSE

Ventilation tube. Air drawn in by fans.

Automatic feeding twice daily.

Overhead food pipeline

Insulated walls & roof.

Water nipples

"Draught free" run

Concrete path – maintenance

Slats

Temperature ≈ 20°C

Warmer air from corridor

7. FATTENING UNITS (12–16 wk

Many more units

40

3. DRY SOW HOUSE (All gilts & sows in pig.)

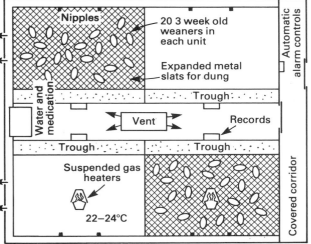

Feed

Feeding troughs

Automatic feeding twice daily and water

Concrete path

54 sows (in crates) in pig

Keep warm by body heat (food) & insulated housing (varies)

Tractor access

Slats

Dung pumped away twice weekly

Temperature not below 18°C

SOWS ARE IN PIG FOR **16 WEEKS** INDIVIDUAL RECORDS KEPT. MOVED TO FARROWING HOUSE WHEN BIRTHS DUE.

AVERAGE SIZE OF LITTER **9**

LITTER WEANED AT 3 WEEKS. SOW GOES BACK TO THE SERVING HOUSE (2)

5. FLAT DECK HOUSES
Weaners 3 – 5/6 wks old.

Nipples

20 3 week old weaners in each unit

Expanded metal slats for dung

Automatic alarm controls

Water and medication

Trough

Vent

Records

Trough

Trough

Suspended gas heaters

22–24°C

Covered corridor

Heating and ventilation thermostatically controlled. Alarm link to farmhouse.

© Peter Allen/Farmers Weekly

6. VERANDAH HOUSE, in section.
5/6 wks old (11kg) → 10 wks (30kg)

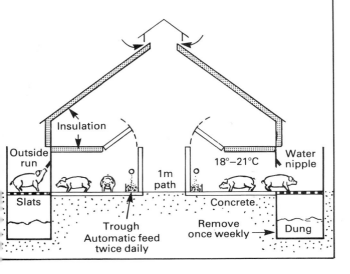

Insulation

Outside run

1m path

18°–21°C

Water nipple

Slats

Concrete

Trough
Automatic feed twice daily

Remove once weekly →

Dung

4. FARROWING HOUSE (3 wks)

Young

Water pipe
Food pipe
Insulation
Trough

Crate

Crate

Path

Slats

Nipple for young

Infrared lamp

Crate

Automatic feed twice daily and water

Air

Dung pumped out twice weekly

Temperature
18°C for sow
26–29°C for litter in 1st 48hrs
Under lamps
21–24°C up to 3 wks

41

15. Pesticides

A **pest** is anything destructive or detrimental to man.

A **pesticide** kills pests. This may be on a domestic scale in the home or garden, or on a large scale in agriculture or industry.

Selective pesticides have been developed to work specifically on one or a small number of species rather than killing everything.

Insecticides kill insects. Some insects like ladybirds and honey bees which are beneficial to man are killed accidentally.

Herbicides kill weeds. Weeds are plants which grow where man doesn't want them. For example, among crops where they compete for space, water and mineral salts.

Fungicides kill fungi. Particularly those which are parasitic on cereal crops and fruit trees such as rusts, smuts and mildew.

ADVANTAGES OF PESTICIDES

1. They increase world food supplies by protecting crops and so helping to achieve large yields per hectare of land.
2. They save stored crops from being destroyed by pests.
3. They save labour in tasks such as weeding and harrowing between crops, and therefore save time and money.
4. They help to preserve property, for example, timber and wool.

DISADVANTAGES OF PESTICIDES

1. They are extremely harmful and need to be handled carefully.
2. Man, domestic animals, all species of wild-life and their habits can be adversely affected.
3. Some are cumulative poisons. (See Figs. 15.1 and 15.2.) The total effects of one spray might take months or years to be realised.
4. Scientists are still learning the full extent of their side effects on living things. Certain defoliants used to clear vegetation in the Vietnam War are now known to have caused miscarriages.
5. Pests may become resistant to them, so new expensive substitutes have to be found.

DDT – A Cumulative Poison

DDT was first used effectively during the 2nd World War. It killed body lice, which were responsible for spreading disease, on soldiers. Later it was also used in swamplands to kill malaria spreading mosquitoes. The disastrous side effects of this 'marvellous' insecticide were found out later. The following tells one tale. The elm trees on a university campus in North America were suffering from Dutch elm disease. A

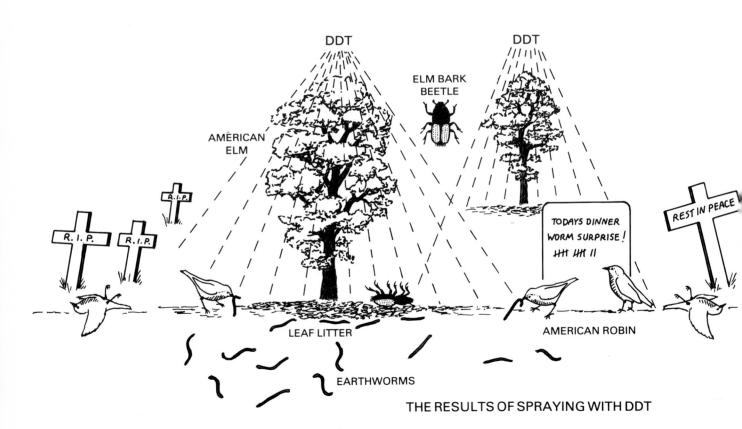

THE RESULTS OF SPRAYING WITH DDT

FIG. 15.1 DDT – A CUMULATIVE POISON

programme of spraying the beetle (which carries the fungus causing the disease) with DDT was started to save the elms. Birds began to lose their balance, have convulsions and die. Nearly 90% of the local American robin population died. A further 63 species of dead birds were found and no young were being reared in the nests. The use of DDT is now very restricted.

THERE ARE TWO MAIN GROUPS OF CHEMICAL INSECTICIDES:

ORGANOCHLORINES

(Chlorinated hydrocarbons)
1. Poisonous to man and other animals.
2. Slow to break down.
3. Last a season so don't have to be applied very often. Are persistant in soil and body tissues and may build up in the food chain.
5. Kill by direct contact or by entrance into the digestive system. Attack nervous system and cause paralysis. Stop exchange of gases.
   Examples: DDT, DDD, BHC (Lindane), Aldrin and Dieldrin.

ORGANOPHOSPHORUS COMPOUNDS

1. Poisonous to man and other animals.
2. Breakdown is rapid, maybe only a few days.
3. Crops may be harvested relatively soon after spraying e.g. two weeks.
4. May cost more as more than one application may be needed in a season.
5. Cause nervous spasms and paralysis. Many are systemic. They are absorbed through the roots into the sap. Aphids may suck the sap and die.
   Examples: Parathion, Malathion, Dichlorvos.

OTHER ALTERNATIVES

1. THE USE OF NATURAL PREDATORS
   Encarsia formosa is a small parasitic wasp which lays its eggs in the pupa case of the greenhouse whitefly, a real pest to horticulturalists in recent years. The pupa case turns black and a new wasp emerges instead of a whitefly. The wasp needs temperatures of 24–27°C to breed rapidly. The use of all insecticides must be stopped or the wasp would be killed as well.

2. STERILISATION
   A known pest is bred in captivity. All the captives are sterilised, for example by radiation. They are then released. Being sterile they cannot produce offspring after mating so the population falls next season.

3. TRAP CROPS
   A crop which may be known to be a favourite of a particular pest is grown alongside other arable crops. When the pests congregate in the trap crop an insecticide can be applied just to that strip.

4. PHEROMONES
   These are chemical messengers, produced by many animals, which affect their behaviour. Chemists can extract them or make them synthetically. They are **species specific**, i.e. only work on one species. They can be used in minute quantities, e.g. to attract the opposite sex away and therefore stop a population increase in the pest or to collect the pests in one area to kill with a pesticide.

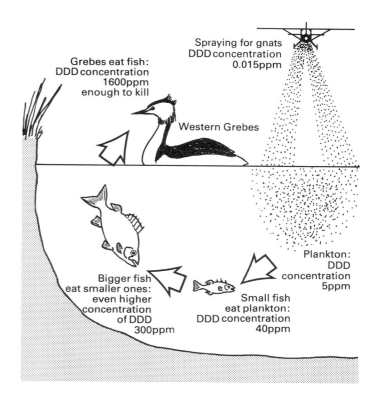

FIG. 15.2 POLLUTION IN CLEAR LAKE

Questions

1. Write out the food chains (see p. 103) found in Figs. 15.1 and 15.2.

2. Study Figs. 15.1 and 15.2. What do you understand by a cumulative poison?

3. Explain why the birds died after spraying the trees with DDT to kill beetles.

4. A similar problem was experienced in Clear Lake, California (See Fig. 15.2.) The first treatments with DDD were only 0.015 ppm or less. However, accumulations of 1600 ppm were found in the fat tissues of the dead western grebes. Use Fig. 15.2 to help you explain how this happened.

5. Read 'The Silent Spring' by Rachel Carson (1962).

6. What is meant by a pesticide? With the use of examples discuss four ways in which they are helpful to people and four ways in which they are harmful to the environment.

7. Find out from a local farmer how many times in one growing season his crop of wheat or barley was treated with chemicals, i.e. pesticides or fertilisers. For what purpose was each treatment made, and with what degree of success or failure? Explain the possible side effects on the local environment of that farm. (Look for ponds, streams, hedgerows, copses etc.) Were any of these side effects evident?

8. *Since the pink bollworm moved into California's cotton fields from Arizona the cotton production had dropped by $\frac{1}{3}$ and pesticide costs have doubled. Thousands of sterile bollworms are being dropped over the fields. (The Guardian March 1970.)* If a sterile bollworm mates with a non-sterile bollworm what would be the result? What must you know about the size of the pest population first? Why is it best if the worms only exchange sperm once?

16. Fertilisers

Fertilisers add richness to the soil, in the form of mineral salts, and are absorbed by the plants' roots. The most important of these are nitrogen (N), phosphorus (P) and potassium (K). These can be seen in Table 16.1 which also shows how they are used by the plant and the results of deficiency.

Fertilisers may be added to the soil:
● as a coating on the seed itself,
● when the seed is sown, as a powder or in pellet form,
● as a top dressing in the soil at the relevant growing time.

The Nitrogen Cycle

Nitrogen in the form of soluble nitrates is vitally important to green plants. It is used to build plant proteins which form a large part of every plant cell. If man interferes with the nitrogen cycle by cropping the plants, the nitrates in the soil may have to be replenished by the addition of a fertiliser or by careful rotation of crops.

Organic fertilisers. These are fertilisers derived from plants or animals, e.g. ground **hoof and horn** (NP), **bone meal** (NP), **ground compost** (NPK) and **manure** (NPK). Manure and garden compost have beneficial side effects.

1. They help to retain moisture in the soil.
2. They increase the bacteria which help the rotting down process, releasing mineral salts into the soil.
3. They help to improve soil texture.

Inorganic fertilisers. These fertilisers are either manufactured, quarried and/or processed, such as **Sulphate of ammonia** (N), **sodium nitrate** (N), **basic slag** (P), **rock phosphate** (P) and **sulphate of potash** (K). A fertiliser containing two or three of the principal elements (N, P and K) is known as a **compound fertiliser**, for example "Growmore".

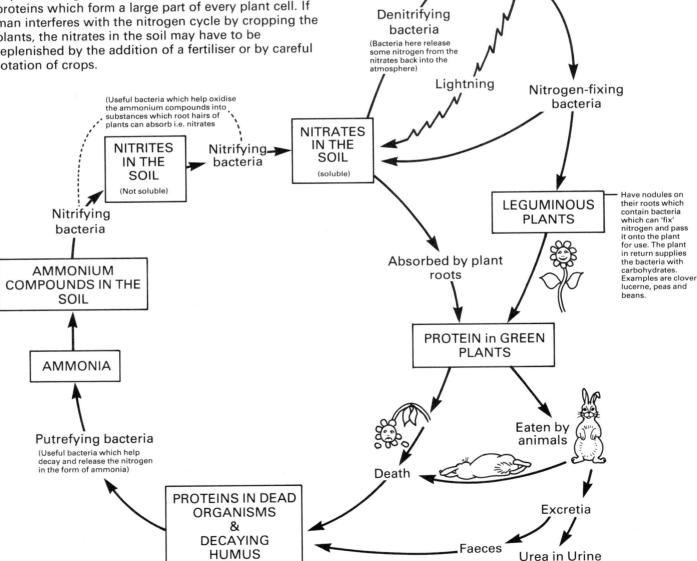

FIG. 16.1 THE NITROGEN CYCLE

44

ELEMENT	EFFECT OF DEFICIENCY	USE TO A GREEN PLANT
Nitrogen (absorbed as nitrates) N	Very little growth	Built into amino acid molecules which are in turn built into *proteins*. It may account for as much as 4% of the dry weight of a plant (see Nitrogen Cycle). Increases green colour of the leaves. Increases size by making protoplasm in new cells and improves yield. Increases the rate of growth and extends grazing time due to lush growth.
Phosphorus P	Thin weak shoots. Poor root development.	It is important for root crops as it encourages root development, early maturity and the nodules on leguminous plants (see Nitrogen Cycle). It helps the early ripening of a crop, especially cereals. Growth is generally slow and restricted without phosphates.
Potassium K	Poor growth. Leaves turn yellow.	A lack of potassium during the growing season may cause the older parts of the plant to die back. This means less food produced for fruit and seed. It plays an important part in the uptake and use of water and helps a crop's resistance to drought and extremes of temperature. It is concerned with the manufacture of sugars and starches and is essential for cell division. Growth may be poor without it.
Calcium	Growth stunted in root and shoot.	The amount of green pigment, *chlorophyll*, in the leaves is reduced, which in turn reduces the production of food and the growth rate. The calcium helps to bind cell walls together during growth.
Iron	Yellow leaves. Poor growth.	Iron is necessary for the formation of chlorophyll (see Calcium).
Sulphur	Poor growth. Pale leaves.	An element built into many proteins.
Magnesium	Poor growth. Yellow leaves.	This is essential to the formation of the chlorophyll molecule. Fewer seeds of poorer quality are produced without it.
Copper, Boron, Manganese, Zinc	Poor growth.	These elements are needed in such minute quantities that they are called *trace elements*, but they are still very important. For example, without boron, calcium cannot be absorbed efficiently by green plants.

TABLE 16.1 ELEMENTS ESSENTIAL FOR PLANT GROWTH

A PROBLEM OF FERTILISERS – EUTROPHICATION

Fertilisers are often used in excess or lost from the soil during downpours when water runs off the surface into ditches, rivers and lakes. This results in lush plant growth, algae in the lakes and increased bankside vegetation. Overcrowding causes the plants to rot and die. Bacteria, using huge amounts of oxygen, help them to decay. The water becomes depleted of oxygen. As a result, fish and other aquatic animals die and a foul layer builds up on the river or lake bed. This process is called **eutrophication**. The problem may be lessened by not adding the fertilisers in the autumn or at the time of planting as this gives rain water more time to wash the fertiliser away. It is better to add them just before the period of most rapid growth. It is unlikely that farmers would do this, as it would be difficult to apply the fertilisers without damaging the growing crops, e.g. by 'burning' the leaves or crushing the plants.

17. Forestry

Angela Johnston

THE FORESTRY COMMISSION

Until this century Britain's trees were felled without replacement. The Forestry Commission was set up in 1919 to restore the depleted timber resources after the First World War. It now manages 1 115 000 ha (1986) in Great Britain.
The commission has many aims and functions. These are:
1. To run the national forests.

2. To control and support the owners of 1 million hectares of private woods through grants, research and felling licenses.
3. To control timber pests and diseases and carry out research on them.
4. To advise on safety and training in forestry management and practise.
5. To increase the production of wood for existing industries.
6. To stimulate the economy and provide jobs in remote and possibly depopulated areas.
7. To protect and improve the environment by landscaping and nature conservation.
8. To provide 'reservoirs' for wildlife and recreational facilities, for example, in the National forest parks and forest nature reserves. These provide tourists with nature trails, viewpoints, car parks, picnic and camp sites, holiday cabins, information centres, pony trekking, orienteering and many other sporting facilities.

AFFORESTATION

Deciduous forests of oak and beech (on chalk) were once the climax of vegetaton when Britain was heavily wooded. Now over 60% of the trees are coniferous **softwoods** e.g. Sitka spruce and Scot's pine and only 40% are broad leaved **hardwoods**, e.g. oak and birch. The latter may take 120 years to reach maturity while coniferous trees will mature in 40–80 years.
Here is an 8 point plan for an afforestation programme.
1. The new area is ploughed and then allowed to drain.
2. If nutrients are lacking, fertiliser is added.
3. Seedlings from nurseries, such as pine, spruce and larch are transplanted in straight lines in the ploughed furrows.
4. These are thinned out after 20 years, i.e. some are removed at even intervals to allow the others to grow to full maturity. This timber is not wasted!
5. After about 50 years, felling takes place.
6. The logs are transported over hills, bogs and tree stumps to roadsides.
7. They are then transported to saw mills (for cut timber) or paper mills (small pieces).
8. The felled area is replanted after preparation of the soil

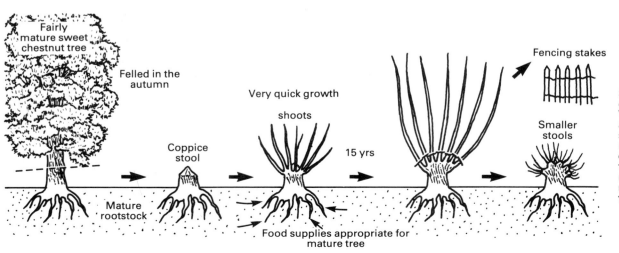

FIG. 17.1 COPPICING

46

Questions

1. People need forests. Use the information on these two pages to make a list of reasons why people need forests. Here are some ideas:
   - Wood is an important building material.
   - It is the raw material for the —— industry.
   - It is used in the manufacture of ————.
   - Forests offer peace and quiet.

2. What is **coppicing**? (See Fig. 17.1.) Describe how this system of managing woodland is useful to us.

3. How much of Britain's timber is imported?

4. Why should some animals not become too numerous in forests? Which animals are these?

5. Carry out your own research on the following: Plantations. Virgin forests. The Amazon Rain Forest. The effect of acid rain on forests (page 83). Make your own notes on them.

6. Write an essay on **Dutch Elm Disease** using the diagram below. Cover the following points: cause, signs, cycle, control.

DUTCH ELM DISEASE

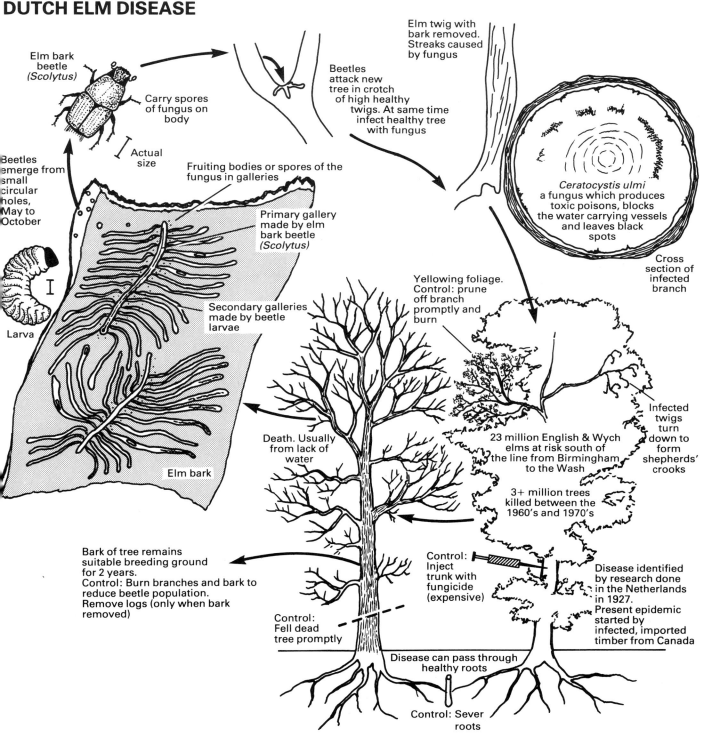

FIG. 17.2 THE WORK OF THE *SCOLYTUS* BEETLE ON BRITISH ELM TREES

18. Settlement

EARLY SETTLEMENT IN GREAT BRITAIN

Imagine the land covered in oak–ash forest (or beech forest on chalk). This is what early settlers would have found. The earliest known settlers were the **Celts** or Britons from about 4300 B.C. to 43 A.D. (See Table 18.1.) Some of their isolated farmsteads and hamlets might have been continuously occupied up to the present day in Zennor Parish, Cornwall. The Celts were pushed west and north by successive invaders onto the poorer soils of the higher ground.

The first invaders were the **Romans**. They crossed the Channel from Gaul (France) in 43 A.D. and rapidly gained control of southern England by defeating the Iron Age settlers who tried unsuccessfully to find refuge in their earthen hill forts. As the Romans forced the Celts into the hills and mountains of Wales and Scotland they constructed roads and forts to control the countryside. Towns, such as London, Lincoln, York and Winchester grew and villas (country house estates) were built. Many towns dating from the Roman occupation end in the words *'chester'* or *'caester'* which means fort. Roman settlements became less important during the fifth century A.D. when the Roman legions were recalled to Rome.

The **Saxons** and **Angles** (Anglo-Saxons) were the next settlers invading from what is now known as Holland and Germany (450 A.D.–1066 A.D.). They were farmers. They followed the river valleys especially in the south and east of the country. They cleared woodland with axes and the use of fire. England became a land of villages.

The next invaders were from Scandinavia, the **Danes** from what is now Denmark, the **Vikings** from Norway and Sweden. They settled where they could in the north of England on land left by the English (Anglo-Saxons) and unoccupied land. The Norwegians concentrated on the north west and the lake District. The Swedes and Danes settled in the north east and east midlands. Often they took over existing villages and renamed them. Popular place name endings were *'thorp(e)'* and *'thwaite'*. The Scandinavians appeared to like the farming methods of the English and adopted them.

William of Normandy invaded in 1066 A.D. The **Normans** organised the Domesday survey of 1086. Except for some of the industrial villages of the north and midlands, it is thought that 'nearly every village we know today had appeared on the scene by 1086'. (W G Hoskins, *The Making of the English Landscape*.) It has been estimated that at this time there was a population of some 1.25 million with approximately 10 people per km². The town had made its appearance or reappearance since Roman occupation times. Of over 1000 **boroughs** (towns) recorded in the Domesday

book only 5 (London Norwich, York, Lincoln and Winchester) had more than 1000 **burgesses** (freemen or citizens) in 1086.

At this point one must remember that the landscape was still largely one of forest, moor, heath, marsh and fen. It was underpopulated. Between 1086 and 1348 the population trebled to about 4 million and rapid changes took place.

● New boroughs were created. (These are often referred to now as **'planted towns'**.)

● More land was claimed for cultivation as the population grew. More forests were cleared. Some fens and marshes were drained.

But, in 1348 the 'Black Death' (bubonic plague) struck the country. The population was reduced by between one third to one half. There was no longer a hunger for new land, in fact settlers retreated from the **marginal lands** (see glossary p.121) of the moors, fens and marsh and landowners went looking for tenants. Many village sites at this time were deserted or relocated on a new, often better, site. (Look for isolated Parish churches!) Over 2000 deserted villages are known at present.

TIME SPAN	PREHISTORIC PEOPLES	PRESENT DAY EVIDENCE
c.4300–2400BC	Neolithic	Megalithic tombs. Long barrows.
c.2400–700BC	Bronze Age	Round barrows. Stone circles.
c.700BC–43AD	Iron Age	Hill forts. Farmsteads. Celtic fields, small, irregular shapes.

TABLE 18.1–PREHISTORIC SETTLEMENT IN GREAT BRITAIN

Questions

1. Trace a copy of the base map Fig. 18.1 *Note to the teacher: this exercise would work well using overlay (tracing paper) sheets.*

2. Celtic languages today include Welsh, Irish, Gaelic, Cornish and Manx. In black writing mark on your map the words CELTS in the appropriate places.

3. Label Hadrian's Wall on your map and on your key. The thin solid line represents the extent of Roman villas in lowland Britain. Shade the area with small dots on your map. Add to your map a similarly shaded bold arrow showing where the Romans invaded.

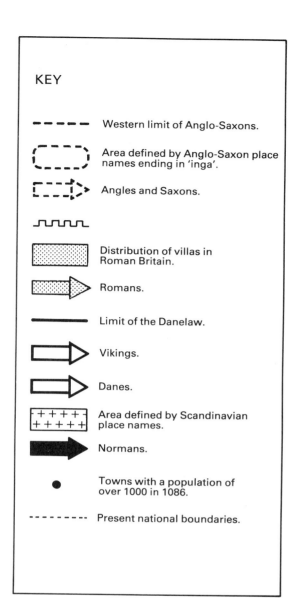

KEY

- – – – – Western limit of Anglo-Saxons.
- Area defined by Anglo-Saxon place names ending in 'inga'.
- Angles and Saxons.
- Distribution of villas in Roman Britain.
- Romans.
- Limit of the Danelaw.
- Vikings.
- Danes.
- +++++ Area defined by Scandinavian place names.
- Normans.
- • Towns with a population of over 1000 in 1086.
- - - - - - Present national boundaries.

FIG. 18.1 EARLY SETTLEMENT OF GREAT BRITAIN, 1086

4. The bold broken line represents the limits of the Anglo-Saxon (English) settlements based on the place name ending 'inga' which means 'the following of'. Shade the areas to the east of this line in a pale colour. Use similar coloured bold arrows to show where the Anglo-Saxons arrived.

5. The thick solid line shows the limit of the **Danelaw**, a recognised boundary between the Scandinavians and the Saxons. Label and colour the bold arrows showing the major invasions of the Vikings and Danes.
Shade the area from the present Welsh border and the Danelaw up to the present Scottish border with little crosses. This shows the main area settled by the Scandinavians.

6. Label the correct arrow for the Norman invasion. Mark on the label the following towns: London, York, Lincoln, Norwich and Winchester.

7. Make sure you have completed a key for all the colours, types of shading, arrows and lines you have used. Has your map got a title and scale?

8. Using the text and your composite map answer the following questions:

WERE there any areas particularly well settled?

WERE there any areas rather sparsely settled? Can you suggest reasons for this?

WHAT was the Danelaw?

WHAT is the Domesday book?

GIVE at least two reasons why the south and east of England were easily settled.

CHOOSING A SITE FOR A SETTLEMENT

1. A, B and C are three possible sites for early settlers to develop. (See Fig. 18.2.)

2. Fieldwork has already been carried out in the area to find good water points, suitable grazing land etc. Study Fig. 18.2. Which site would you favour initially and why?
Make a copy of Table 18.2. Work out the distances from all sites to the resources.

3. Some resources are of more immediate importance, for example, water. Others are of more long term importance, such as grazing land. Give each resource a 'weighting' on a scale from 1 to 10 according to how important you think it is. For example, if you consider that fuel is very important you might give it 9 or 10 points. A resource of little importance might be given 3 or 4 points. Fill in the fourth column of the table.

4. Complete the last columns of the table. The first example is completed for you.

5. Complete the totals for each site.

6. The site with the **lowest total** is the one which is thought to be the **most efficient** for the village. Which site did you find to be most efficient on this system? Compare your answer with others in the class. (Your opinions may well differ according to your weighting.) Does this answer agree with your initial decision?

7. Give a detailed written argument in favour of your final decision. (Include reasons against the development of the other sites).

8. Are any of the sites easier to defend than the others in your estimation? Explain why.

9. Select a town or city which is built on a good defensive site. Write a detailed account of it complete with a sketch map.

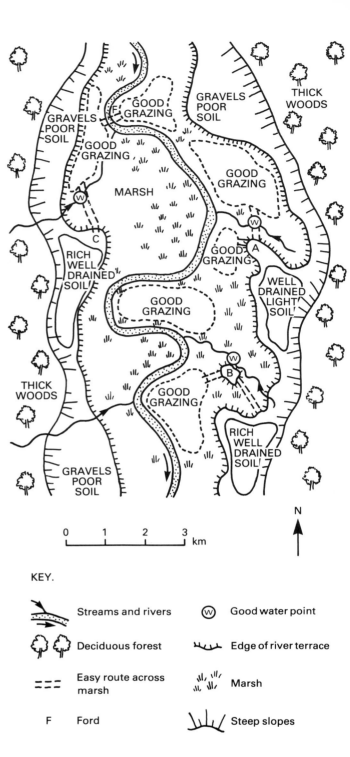

FIG. 18.2 THREE POSSIBLE VILLAGE SITES AND THEIR RESOURCES

KEY.

Streams and rivers		Good water point	
Deciduous forest		Edge of river terrace	
Easy route across marsh		Marsh	
F Ford		Steep slopes	

RESOURCE	DISTANCE FROM A	DISTANCE FROM B	DISTANCE FROM C	WEIGHTING (1–10)	DIST. × WEIGHTING A.	B.	C.
Water	0.3 km	0.1 km		eg. 10	3	1	
Arable							
Grazing		0.5 km					
Fuel							
Building Material							
				Totals			

TABLE 18.2 THREE POSSIBLE VILLAGE SITES AND THEIR RESOURCES.

19. Place Names

So that people could tell the difference between one place and another they gave them names. Studying place names can be fascinating. They tell us much about the settlement of Great Britain.

Some place names mean exactly what they say, for example, 'Nettlebed' means a place overgrown with nettles! In general it is the endings of place names which tell us most about their origins. The table shows some of the more common ones. Very often the first part of the place name relates to an individual or group of people. Here are some examples:

Egham	'Ecga's ham', meaning Ecga's homestead.
Scunthorpe	'Skúma's thorp', meaning the people of Skúma's settlement.
Felixstowe	St Felix's place.
Trumpington	The tun or homestead of 'Trump(a)'s' people.
Arncott	'Earn's cot', meaning the cottage or shelter of Earn's people.

Some place names are very individual, for example, 'Looe' in Cornwall means an inlet of water, a pool. (Is this were we get the word loo today?!) Others are easier to break up into elements we understand. Examine the place name 'Stratford'. 'Strat' comes from the Old English word 'Streat' which was probably a slightly altered version of the latin word 'strata'. It means a paved way or Roman road. 'Ford' is as it sounds, a crossing point on a river. In conclusion, we have:
'Stratford'   'A ford by which a Roman road crossed a river.'
(See The Concise Oxford Dictionary of English Place Names by Eilert Erkwell.)

Questions

1. Avon is a Celtic word meaning river. Stony might mean a stony site. Write down the meanings of these place names:
   Stratford upon Avon
   Stony Stratford
2. Using the list in the table, try these. Write them out and put their meanings alongside.

Swindon	Chesterford
Kirton	Eston
Stow-on-the-Wold	Osmondthorpe
Avenbury	Milton
Atherington	Monkleigh
Blethingley	Northam
Chippinghurst	Oxford

3. Make up some suitable place names for the following using the list in the table.
   (a) The homestead of Whippa's people.
   (b) A white cliff.
   (c) A trading place in the north.
   (d) A clearing or meadow near oak trees.
   (e) A cottage on a heath.
   (f) The mouth of the river Dovey.

TABLE 19.1 COMMON PLACE NAME ELEMENTS, THEIR MEANINGS AND THEIR ORIGINS

-barrow, borough, -burgh (from beorg), a hill or mound.	O.E.
-borough, -burgh, brough, bury (from burg), a fortified place.	O.E.
-beck, a stream.	S.
-by, a village or farm.	S.
-caster, -cester, caester, chester (from astra), a fort or camp, later a Roman town.	R.
-combe, crumb, a deep valley.	O.E.
-cot, -cote, an outlying hill or cottage.	O.E.
-croft, a small enclosure.	O.E.
-dale, a wide valley.	S.
-dean, -dene, -den, a small valley.	O.E.
-don, -down, a hill	C.
-ey, -y, an island.	O.E.
-fall, where trees have been felled.	O.E.
-fell, -how, a hill or mound.	S.
-field, an open field.	O.E.
-fos(s), a ditch.	R.
-gate, a road.	S.
-gill, a ravine or valley.	S.
-ham, a homestead or farmstead.	I.E.
-holm, a flat topped island.	S.
-holt, a thick wood	O.E.
-hurst, -hirst, a wooded hill	O.E.
-ings, a marsh or meadow.	S.
-ing, -inga(s), the followers of a tribal group.	O.E.
-ing, -ingham, -ington, a homestead or farmstead.	O.E.
-kirk, a church.	S.
-leigh, -ley, -lea, -lee, a clearing in a forest or wood sometimes pastureland or meadow.	O.E.
llan-, church.	W.
-mere, -mer, a lake.	O.E.
-ness, a cape.	O.E./S.
-port, port.	R.
-porth, port.	C.
-riding, -rod, cleared land.	O.E.
-stead, -sted, a place.	O.E.
-stoke, a daughter settlement, a small village.	O.E.
-stow, a holy place, a meeting place.	O.E.
-street (from strata), a paved way.	R.
-tarn, a lake.	S.
-thorp(e), a daughter settlement.	S.
-thwaite, a forest clearing or meadow, enclosed land.	S.
-ton, -tun, a homestead or farmstead.	O.E.
-toft, a homestead.	S.
-tre, a harbour.	C.
-weald, -wold, a high woodland or wasteland.	O.E.
-wood, a wood	O.E.
-worthy, -worth, a farm or enclosed land.	O.E.
-wick, -wich, an outlying inhabited farm, a brading place.	O.E.

Key C–Celtic, R–Roman, O.E.–Old English (Anglo-Saxon), S–Scandinavian, W–Welsh.

20. Site, Form, Function

SITE. The first settlers had to choose a place to build their homes. All the resources in Table 18.2 might be called **site factors**. Others which could be added to the list include:

● a sheltered position, for example, in a valley bottom or on a south facing slope,
● an accessible position easy for trading, for example, near a ford or where two roads cross,
● an easily defended site, for example, by a river meander or on a hill top,
● on land that will not flood,
● pure chance.

The site may have controlled the present development and shape of the settlement. When describing the site it is important to describe the lie of the land. Is it flat? Does it rise steeply on one side? Which side?

FORM. The form of a settlement is its **shape**. Some shapes are compact. The farms and houses are grouped closely together, often around a central core or nucleus. These are known as **nucleated** settlements. Some forms are **dispersed**, loose or fragmented. The dwellings have little relationship to one another or to a visible nucleus. They are spread out in a haphazard way. Another form which is quite common is the **linear** or **ribbon** settlement which has developed in a long and often narrow shape.

FUNCTION. The function of a village is its **purpose**. Many villages were and still are just simple farming communities with a few basic services such as a church, public house and village shop. Others grew up because of a particular function such as mining, weaving or fishing.

Questions

1. Describe in detail the site of Arncliffe.

2. If you have access to the OS map or a very detailed atlas, find Arncliffe in Littondale (near Wharfedale) Yorkshire. Describe the situation of Arncliffe.

3. What might be the function(s) of this village?

4. Match up the photographs A, B and C on the opposite page to the three major settlement forms, nucleated, dispersed or linear.

5. Look at the settlement in Fig. 20.2. Which common form is it? Match up this diagram with the correct photograph, A, B or C.

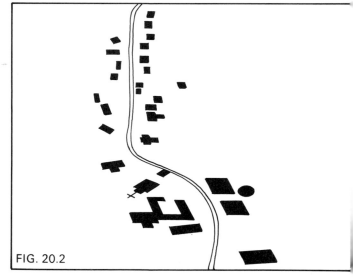

FIG. 20.2

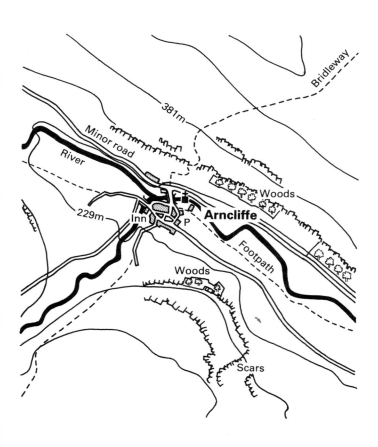

FIG. 20.1 SKETCH MAP BASED ON ARNCLIFFE, YORKSHIRE

6. Which of the site factors named on p. 50 would be most likely to encourage the growth of a settlement? Explain why.

7. Which site factors might lead to the early decline of a settlement especially if they were easily exhausted?

8. How many of the site factors named on this page and the next would be important today for the siting of a new settlement? Give reasons with your answers.

9. Find out what a dormitory village is.

10. How have these modern influences affected village life: the car, commuting, improved agricultural technology and an increased population?

52

TABLE 20.1 SOME FACTORS WHICH HAVE CONTRIBUTED TO THE MAJOR SETTLEMENT FORMS	NUCLEATED	LINEAR	DISPERSED

	Village greens
	Road junctions
	Medieval field system
	Defense sites
	Dry sites, away from marsh or bog
	Spring or well sites (water supply)
	Better soils
	Lowland
		Following some other linear formation, e.g.
		  a road
		  a valley side
		  one side of a river
		  an escarpment
		  a springline
		  a railway line
			Plenty of water
			Specialised farming, e.g.
			  market gardening
			  livestock farming
			Low densities of population
			Poor soils
			Highland

© Aerofilms Library

© Aerofilms Library

© West Air Photography/Barnaby's Picture Library

THE VILLAGE GREEN

The dwellings form a compact block facing into a green. In medieval times the green may have provided a safe place at night for livestock. Sheep drovers might stop the night and the villagers would charge a toll. Recently greens have been used for markets, fairs, sports etc. They are now protected open spaces for the public to enjoy under the 1968 act of parliament.

Christo

FIG. 20.3 THE VILLAGE GREEN, WALBERSWICK, SUFFOLK

53

21. Farming in a Medieval Village

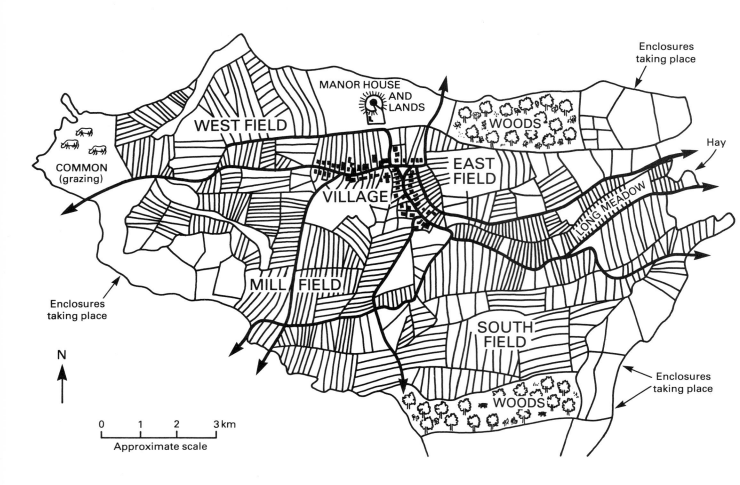

FIG. 21.1 OPEN FIELD SYSTEM (BASED ON LAXTON, NOTTINGHAMSHIRE)

Laxton, in Nottinghamshire, is one of the few surviving examples of a medieval **open field system**. (See Fig. 21.1.) Imagine a landscape full of such villages, set a few kilometres apart in lowland Britain. The original woodland was often cleared by burning. (The name Brentwood means 'burnt wood'.) Many villages had three huge hedgeless open fields although there were others with 2 or 4. These had names such as East Field, West Field, North Field, South Field and Mill Field. One whole field might grow wheat, another barley and one would be left **fallow** to rest the soil and provide grazing. Each field was divided into long narrow **strips** approximately 20 m (22 yds) wide and 200 m (220 yds) long. Each peasant farmer worked a number of strips which were scattered amongst the 3 fields. Some of these would be on good soils and others on poor. The farmer would walk to his strips each day from the houses and barns in the streets of the compact village. The farmers often worked in co-operation. They pooled their oxen and ploughs to form teams. One strip was considered one day's work by one team of peasant farmers. The up and down ploughing with a certain kind of plough threw the soil towards the centre of the strip producing a **ridge**. It was separated by a double **furrow** from its neighbour. The furrows acted as drainage channels. **Ridge and furrow** can still be seen today. (See Figs. 21.2 and 21.3.) Each village also had rough pasture for grazing, meadows for hay and woodland for the swine, fuel and building materials.

FIG. 21.2 RIDGE AND FURROW

54

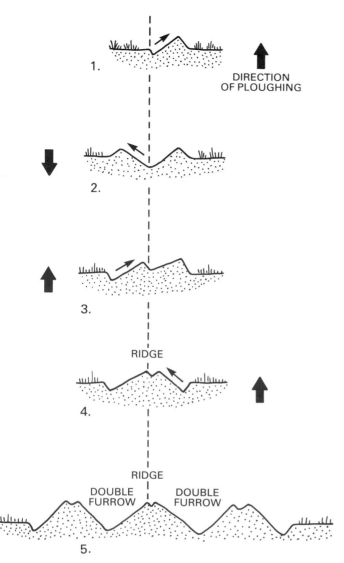

1.

DIRECTION
OF PLOUGHING

2.

3.

RIDGE

4.

RIDGE
DOUBLE
FURROW
DOUBLE
FURROW

5.

FIG. 21.3 DIAGRAM OF RIDGE AND FURROW

THE MEDIEVAL LANDSCAPE

The rural landscape of medieval Britain was one where the majority of peasants clustered in villages or townships, cultivating the surrounding ground on an **open field system** (p. 54). **Feudalism** was strong especially in lowland Britain. The king kept some royal estates and distributed the rest of his lands amongst his tenants-in-chief (barons and bishops). They in turn kept some estates or **manors** and distributed the rest amongst the under tenants or knights. They in turn kept some land or **demesne** and divided the rest between the labourers or peasants. The peasants were known as **villeins**. They were not free to do as they pleased. Each villein held his land in return for carrying out work on the demesne. The barons had to 'pay' the king by providing mounted Knights. This system of land in return for services rendered is known as feudalism. The manor was often a single village. Towards the north and south-west of England and across the Welsh border, large manors covered a number of different settlements. Here, relationships between lord and peasant were weaker and the peasant may have paid the lord in cash instead of services. In East Anglia one village may have had two or three manors.

THE ENCLOSURES

Between the 14th and 16th centuries the early enclosures started to take place. These were private agreements whereby a group of strips on the fringes of the open fields were blocked off together with a hedge to make an enclosure for one farmer or owner. They produced medium sized fields, fairly irregular in shape, with broad high hedges of hawthorn, privet and hazel. Later, in the 18th and 19th centuries came the **parliamentary enclosures**. Villages who still had large open fields or areas of common land applied for private acts of parliament to allow them to do away with the strips and redistribute the land amongst the landowners in compact plots. They produced larger fields, approximately 8 hectares in size, of more regular shapes. They had 1.25 m high neat hedges with an occasional tree of oak, elm or ash. The enclosures were responsible for the pattern of fields and hedgerows we have seen up to the present day.

SUMMARY

The changes which occurred in the system of land holding from the 16th to the late 19th century are known collectively as the **Agricultural** or **Agrarian Revolution**. This involved a shift from a feudal economy to a commercial or 'capitalist' system. Key features of the revolution were:

- Land became a valuable commodity in which to invest.
- Parcels of land were physical separated to create fields. These were known as the 'enclosures'.
- Common rights of use to the land were gradually eroded and replaced with individual ownership.
- New systems of farming emerged, new crops, e.g. clover and turnips, encouraging animals to be kept, along with new management techniques, e.g. the Norfolk four-course crop rotation.
- Much later new machinery was invented to save labour, e.g. Jethro Tull's seed drill.
- Tile drains were introduced in the 1830s to 1840s as were government loans to assist with costs.

Questions

1. Trace an outline map of Fig. 21.1 Simplify the number of strips. Mark on only 15 houses to represent 15 peasant farmers.

2. Colour the Lord of the Manor's house and grounds in red. Colour 25% of the strips in the same colour. These are worked for the Lord of the Manor.

3. Shade the common lands, meadows and woods in pencil grey.

4. Give each peasant farmer a different colour on the dwelling land plots. Using the same colours share out the rest of the strips between them, more to some than others and a mixture of possible good and poor land.

5. Add a key and title to your map.

6. Find out how the word 'furlong' came into being.

7. Write your own account of how you think ridge and furrow was formed, using the diagrams in Fig. 21.3.

8. Carry out your own research into the effect of early farm machinery on the landscape (see Graph on p. 37).

22. The Growth of a Settlement

Here are some reasons why one settlement might have grown faster, perhaps becoming a town or city while its neighbour remains a small village or hamlet.

1. The settlement had a **good site**, with plenty of open space for future development.
2. It's situation made it very **accessible** to the other surrounding settlements.
3. Because it was accessible, the people began to **trade** with each other. Tracks and paths, later becoming roads or other routeways, began to develop.

CARRY OUT THE FOLLOWING EXERCISE.

1. Study Fig. 22.1.

2. The lines represent tracks joining each settlement to its nearest neighbour. Some lines are completed for you. The continuous lines are correct. **The dotted lines show mistakes**. Don't draw a line
   (a) If it means crossing the river where there isn't a bridge, e.g. A–B.
   (b) If it means the track passes too close to another settlement, e.g. C–D.
   (c) If it means a track crosses another track, choose the shortest route, e.g. E–F.

3. Draw your own copy of Fig. 22.1. Complete the tracks without any mistakes. Use a pencil first! Keep the lines straight and direct.

4. If a settlement has 6 or more tracks leading to it, it might grow into a trade centre as it is very accessible. Ring any you have found with a bright colour. Mark this on your key.

5. If a settlement has 5 tracks leading to it it might grow into a large village or small town. Ring any you find with another colour, and mark it on your key.

6. If you have access to the OS Gainsborough sheet Scale 1 : 50,000 find the square grid reference 760820. Identify the name of the most accessible trade centre on the east bank of the River Trent.

7. Write a paragraph giving reasons why you think this settlement grew much larger than the others in this square.

8. Write another paragraph about the 5 track centres. Have you got any settlements which in your estimation should have grown and which have not? Give reasons why you think they didn't develop, e.g. Thonock, Knaith Park.

FIG. 22.1 WHICH SETTLEMENT WILL GROW?

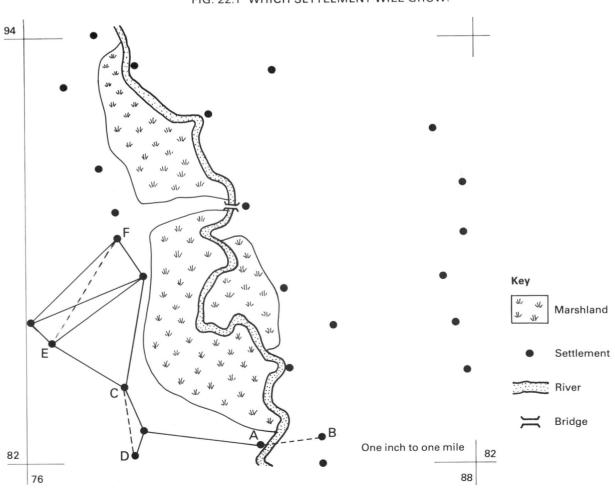

Key

Marshland

Settlement

River

Bridge

One inch to one mile

23. Towns

Many changes took place in Great Britain 200 years ago. Farming methods were using more and more efficient types of machinery. New factories were springing up in the towns.

RURAL-URBAN MIGRATION

The enclosures had pushed out the small landowners from the villages. Farm machinery had improved. One machine could do the jobs of many peasants. The jobless and landless peasants were attracted by the jobs in the factories of the towns. The population began to grow rapidly. At the turn of the 19th century most of the population was still rural but by 1891 the population of Great Britain had increase three times. Now, nearly half lived in the 185 towns of over 20 000. Within a century some places grew from hamlet status to cities of over 100 000, e.g. Middlesborough. London grew to 6.5 million.

It's no wonder that towns are often known as the most unplanned element in the landscape. Urban growth was so rapid that very often there was little thought for planning. Factories, houses and amenities were built on any suitable piece of land, resulting in **urban sprawl**. There are of course exceptions to this. See the aerial photograph of Newark.

Some towns also inherited the name of 'graves of mankind'. Housing standards varied considerably. There might be 'snobs row' for the wealthy which was often well planned **low density housing**, set out spaciously with gardens and such facilities as street lighting, pavements and piped water. The unskilled worker, however, lived in terrible conditions. Houses were packed in together (**high density housing**) back to back. They were arranged around an enclosed mud courtyard where refuse collected, the only entrance being a narrow tunnel. They had no piped water and no provision for sewerage removal. In some cases, before 1850, open fields (see p. 54) still existed beyond the town limits and further building outwards was not allowed. Rapid population growth meant that the working class areas soon became **slums**. Overcrowding, insanitary conditions and pollution from the factories and domestic fires lead to disease and the risk of early death. Various acts of parliament were brought in to improve housing conditions, especially to provide adequate water supply, drainage and sewerage provisions. Building land was sold in blocks so rows of improved high density terraced houses were built on a grid pattern of streets. They were so improved, with no courtyards, that the really poor couldn't afford them! Municipal or **council housing** actually began in 1869 in Liverpool but it was really only after 1900, particularly in the inter-war period that they were built in large numbers all over the country. The rents were subsidised by the town councils or corporations, i.e. very poor families were housed and were only expected to pay a minimal rent.

Questions

1. Suggest why people have moved to the towns.
2. Some students in your class might have better ideas than you. Pool your reasons by writing a list for the class on the blackboard. Discuss these reasons with your teacher.
3. Why might people want to move to towns in the present day? Explain your answers.
4. List the reasons why people might not want to live in towns in the present day.

FIG. 23.1 % OF POPULATION LIVING IN TOWNS AND CITIES OF AT LEAST 20 000

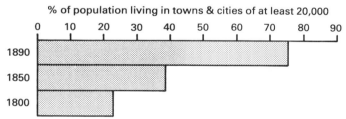

% of population living in towns & cities of at least 20,000

FIG. 23.2 HIGH DENSITY HOUSING IN 1909, PROVIDENCE PLACE, STEPNEY

FIG. 23.3
AERIAL VIEW
OF NEWARK

Questions

1. Use the *letters along the top* and the *numbers down the side* of the aerial photograph (Fig. 23.3) to locate the following features. The first example is completed for you:
   (a) The site of a castle.   D7
   (b) Medieval housing.
   (c) Back to back terrace housing, dating from the late 19th early 20th century.
   (d) The market square.
   (e) A bridging point on the river.
   (f) Industrial buildings.
   (g) A post war (1950's) housing estate, possibly council housing.
   (h) A very new housing estate. (Look for a more interesting layout.)
   (i) A park or recreation area.
   (j) A car park.
2. Can you locate any areas which suggest unplanned haphazard urban growth?
3. Can you locate any areas which show a modern carefully planned arrangement of houses, shops and other amenities?
4. Can you locate any areas which show a recent change in land use (see p. 5), either
   (a) carefully planned to be in keeping with the character of the town, or

   (b) for the convenience of providing a much needed facility, e.g. a car park?

FIG. 23.4 1950s SEMI-DETACHED COUNCIL HOUSES

58

ig. 23.5 WELWYN GARDEN CITY

Velwyn Garden City was a planned settlement
esigned by Ebenezer Howard at the end of the
Victorian era. In 1899 he conceived the Garden City
Association. Letchworth was built in 1903 and Welwyn
n 1919. Howard wanted a balance between town and
ountry, hence the parks and gardens. His ideas gave
irth to the idea of New Towns. (See p. 64.)

Questions

Jse the aerial photograph (Fig. 23.5) which shows part
f a formally planned Victorian settlement. Answer the
ollowing questions:

. Why do you think it was called a 'garden city'?

2. Why is it obvious that it was designed or planned
   where the roads, houses, amenities and even
   factories should be located?

3. Why is the industrial area isolated from the
   residential area?

4. Write a long paragraph comparing and contrasting
   with Newark. Here are some key words to help you:
   formal, informal, planned, unplanned, high density
   housing, low density housing, urban sprawl.

5. Which town most appeals to you? Give reasons for
   your answer.

The following pages are devoted to the influence of
transport on urban growth and the environment.

24. CBD

FIG. 24.1 PART OF A TYPICAL CBD

Questions

1. Study Fig. 24.1. Use tracing paper to draw your own sketch of this diagram. Using the information on this page and the following, write detailed labels for each of the letters A–I. C is completed for you.

2. Sometimes the CBD has been rebuilt or redeveloped. Is there any evidence of this in Fig. 24.1? Explain your answer.

3. What are these specialist streets known for? Broadway. Harley St. Fleet St. Wall St. Carnaby St. Regent St.

The centre of a town or city often contains the oldest buildings and street patterns. It is the place where most business and shopping is carried out, the core around which the rest of the town has developed. It is common to all the models of city structure (see p. 68) and is known as the **central business district** or **CBD**.

The following are some of the typical features of the CBD.

● It is the **focal point** of the transport network. It must be **accessible** to the public, many of whom have employment there.

It has the greatest volume of **traffic**, concentrated into what are often the oldest and narrowest streets. This causes **congestion**.

- It is the busiest part of the town, especially in the daytime. It has the greatest number of **pedestrians**. Pavements are often wide and some roads may have been pedestrianised. (See p. 72)
- It has more **shops**, especially large department stores, chain stores, shops selling a variety of goods and specialist shops e.g. books, jewellery. The shopper can easily make **comparisons** between similar goods offered by several shops.
- It has more **business** and therefore **offices**. It may house the head offices of a number of companies.
- There is great competition for the siting of shops and offices in order to get the most trade.
- The cost of renting and buying land is higher than anywhere else in the city.
- Few people actually live in the centre as it is too expensive.
- Due to the cost of land and the lack of space **high rise buildings** are often found. These may be **shared** by a number of different **users**. Services such as banks, cafés and shops may be found on the ground and first floors with commercial activities such as solicitors, architects and insurance brokers occupying the upper floors.
- There is a lack of manufacturing industry, mainly due to the cost of land and lack of room for expansion.
- Within the CBD there may be distinct areas where there are concentrations of particular activities such as banks and building societies.

CBD FIELDWORK

Preparation

1. Choose a town or city centre which you can easily reach for a day's fieldwork.
2. Work in small groups to ease the work load.
3. Choose one person in the group who can pace a metre (an elongated stride) consistently.
4. Your teacher will allocate one long street (both sides) or a number of small streets to your group.
5. Each person in the group should have lots of large sheets of lined or graph paper, a pencil, rubber and a clipboard covered with a sheet of polythene to protect the work from rain.
6. Each person in the group must record **all** the information. It should not be left to just one person. It takes hours to copy out someone else's information and wastes precious time.

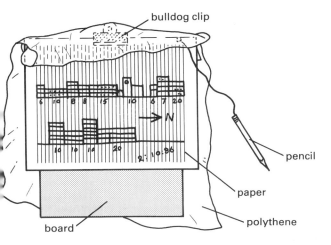

FIG. 24.2 WHAT YOU NEED TO RECORD YOUR INFORMATION

FIG. 24.3 HOW TO RECORD YOUR INFORMATION

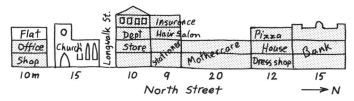

Recording

1. For **each building**:
   (a) **Pace the frontage and record its length** to the nearest metre.
   (b) **Record the number of storeys.**
   (c) **Record what each storey is used for** as accurately as possible.
2. Record the names of the streets, where north is and the date of the survey.
3. Continue to survey all your allocated area in the same way.
4. Back in the classroom, swap information about the areas your group didn't cover. An easy, but expensive way, is to photocopy the other rough recordings.
5. Using a huge sheet of full size graph paper map your results. (See Fig. 24.4.) It is best to total up the length of the longest street before you decide on a scale, so you can be sure your information will fit on one sheet, if possible.
6. Use this table to help you decide how to shade your diagram:

FUNCTIONS FOUND IN THE CBD	FUNCTIONS NOT USUALLY FOUND IN THE CBD
Retailing, i.e. department stores, chain Stores, specialist shops, supermarkets.	**Housing** **Industry** **Religious** **Educational** **Transport**, e.g. stations
Commercial, i.e. offices **Services**, e.g. banks, restaurants, hairdressers etc.	**Public services**, e.g. fire stations, hospitals. **Small food shops**
SHADE IN PINK	LEAVE UNSHADED

Conclusions

1. Complete your diagram with a title, date, key and north. Don't forget to name the streets.
2. Look for the areas where the pink shading peters out. (See Fig. 24.4.) Can you mark with a pencil the approximate edge of the CBD? Check this with your teacher and then go over the pencil line with a bold black line.
3. Write an account of how **exactly** you carried out this fieldwork. **State the obvious!**
4. Write an account about what you discovered. For example:

   The CBD extended from ... street in the north to ... street and ... in the ... and ..., covering an area of approx ... sq. km. All the well known functions were obvious. There were many shops, esp. concentrated in ... street and ... street including department stores such as Debenhams and Selfridges, chain stores such as Boots and .... Most of the buildings were 3/4 storeys high, each storey often being used for a different function, e.g. ... Offices ... Traffic ... Pedestrians .... There were signs of redevelopment .... No industry was ... but there were two churches at ....

There is so much you can say. **State the obvious!**

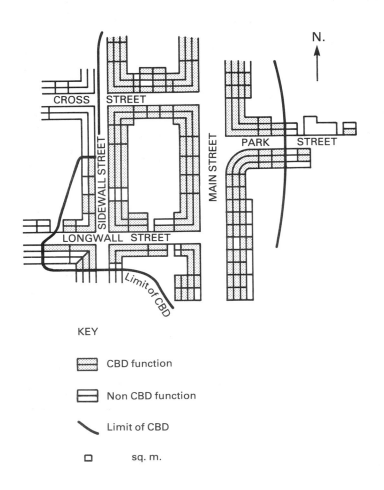

KEY

▨	CBD function
▭	Non CBD function
╲	Limit of CBD
▫	sq. m.

FIG. 24.4 DIAGRAM SHOWING HOW TO MAP FIELDWORK CARRIED OUT IN THE CBD.

FIG. 24.5 MANCHESTER CITY CENTRE

FIG. 24.6 AN EXAMPLE OF URBAN-RURAL FRINGE ON THE OUTSKIRTS OF CAMBRIDGE

THE URBAN-RURAL FRINGE

The uncontrolled and unplanned sprawl of many urban areas during the 19th and 20th centuries has not always resulted in the most desirable developments. The present planning laws have restricted this type of growth. Councils work within **structure plans** which control the size and shape of their cities or towns. At the edge of the built up area, urban land use gives way to the countryside. This area is known as the **urban-rural fringe**, where town meets countryside.

Arrange yourselves into small groups to carry out fieldwork in this area.

FIELDWORK

Preparation
1. Sort out a list an colour scheme of the sorts of land use you would expect to see. Here is an example: Residential (housing), grey. Derelict land, black. Shops, yellow. Water, blue. Industry, red. Pasture, green. Transport, orange. Arable, brown. Heath, moor, rough pasture, purple. Open public spaces, bright green. Mkt. gardening, mauve. Woodland, dark green. You may wish to add to this list.
2. With your teacher decide **where** you will start to record on all the major roads leading out of your chosen town or city.

Method

Either walk or take a bus ride out to the first local village. Work in pairs. Sit on opposite sides of the bus. Using rough **lined** paper turned sideways record the land use continuously when you get to your chosen point. (See Fig. 24.8.) Look, record, look, record! This takes a lot of concentration. No time for gossiping! Check your findings on the return journey. Record the date.

Results

Quickly go over your roughs marking on which colour each land use should have. Now copy up your results neatly. Don't forget a title, key, date and north. Mark your map not to scale. (You should estimate the distance covered.)

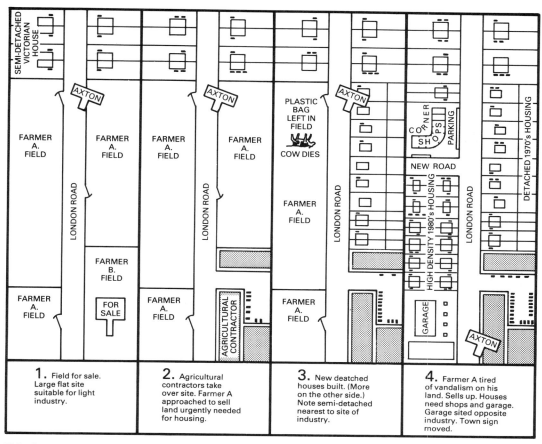

1. **Field for sale.** Large flat site suitable for light industry.

2. **Agricultural contractors take over site. Farmer A approached to sell land urgently needed for housing.**

3. **New deatched houses built. (More on the other side.) Note semi-detached nearest to site of industry.**

4. **Farmer A tired of vandalism on his land. Sells up. Houses need shops and garage. Garage sited opposite industry. Town sign moved.**

FIG. 24.7 DIAGRAM TO SHOW INFILLING ON THE URBAN-RURAL FRINGE OF THE IMAGINARY TOWN 'AXTON'.

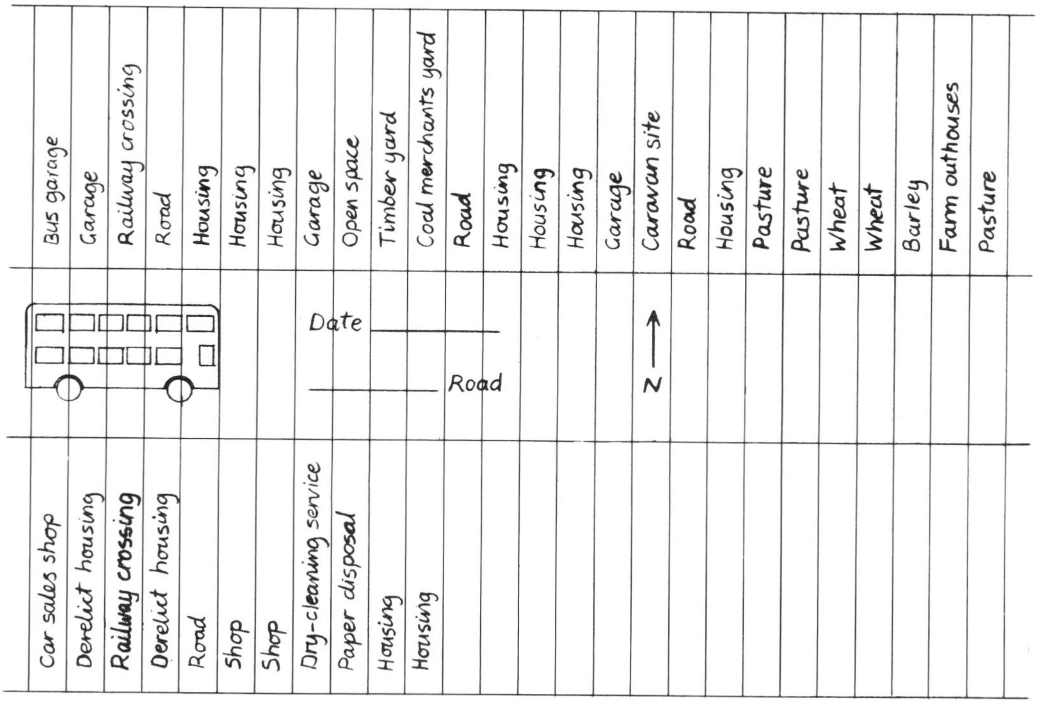

FIG. 24.8 FIELDWORK IN THE URBAN-RURAL FRINGE

Conclusions

The following question may help you draw some conclusions about this fieldwork.

1. Did any particular pattern emerge? Compare your results with the fieldwork carried out on the other roads by the other students.
2. Which land uses seemed to dominate the urban-rural fringe? Were there more or less services than perhaps you would find nearer the centre?
3. Explain three ways, made more obvious from your fieldwork, in which farmers' livelihoods are made more difficult in the urban-rural fringe.
4. Ask your teacher about the ways in which you might graph your information, e.g. as histograms or pie charts.

63

25. New Towns

GREEN BELTS

The idea of the **green belt** has prevented some of the problems which were caused by urban sprawl in the rural-urban fringe. These are areas of 'green' countryside which are being rigidly preserved around the edge of the present city limits. Any change of land use or building is either refused or very carefully controlled. The idea of a green belt is designed to
- preserve the amenities offered by the country side.
- prevent the merging of adjacent towns.
- restrict the sprawl of large built up areas.

London's green belt was designated in the 1947 Town and Country Planning Act. It still is very similar to the original set out by Abercrombie in the Greater London Plan of 1944. It is 8–16 km wide with an area until recently of 3120 sq. km. (See Fig. 25.1.) Some green belt has been lost to the new development of the M25, and more may be released for development in certain areas. The one main problem with the green belt is that if the population of the city grows the people have to be housed. As building is not permitted in the green belt it has to be developed beyond it, or, a **new town** might be built at some distance away to take the population overspill.

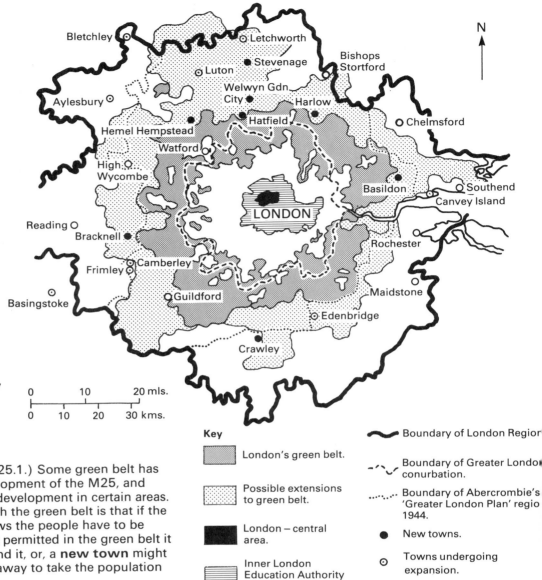

Key

▦	London's green belt.
⣿	Possible extensions to green belt.
⬛	London – central area.
▤	Inner London Education Authority Area.

〜	Boundary of London Region
-ᴧ-	Boundary of Greater London conurbation.
·····ᴧ·	Boundary of Abercrombie's 'Greater London Plan' region 1944.
●	New towns.
⊙	Towns undergoing expansion.
○	Other major centres.

FIG. 25.1 LONDON'S GREEN BELT

THE HISTORY OF NEW TOWNS

In **1844** the **Chadwick Report** drew attention to the insanitary conditions in which urban workers lived. Some rich industrialists tried to improve conditions in their areas. The Cadbury family built Bournville. Lord Leverhulme built Port Sunlight. These towns were still attached to urban areas.

In **1898 Ebenezer Howard** wrote about **'Garden Cities of Tomorrow'**. His idea was to build a city which was removed from the existing urban centres. He thought the population of such a city should be controlled at about 30 000 people and that it should be surrounded by a 'green belt' for farming and recreation. There should be spaces for gardens, trees and parks for everyone. The land should be owned by one authority who would develop the whole city. In **1899 The Garden City Association** was founded which later became the Town and Country Planning Association. (see p. 59).

In **1940** the **Barlow Report** recommended the dispersal of industry and population from congested areas.

In **1944 Sir Patrick Abercrombie** proposed in his Greater London Plan that 1 million people should be dispersed from London to new towns at least 40 to 48 km away.

In **1945** Lord Reith led the **New Towns Committee** and in **1946** came the **New Towns Act**, followed by others in 1965 and 1968. Power was given to the Secretary of State to designate any land for the development of a new town. Between 1946 and 1949 eight new towns were designated for the Greater London area. They were Stevenage, Crawley, Hemel Hempstead, Harlow, Hatfield, Welwyn Garden City, Basildon and Bracknell. (See Fig. 25.1 and 25.2.)

THE AIM OF NEW TOWNS

The idea of a new town is to:
. Relieve overcrowding in the cities.
. Provide a thriving industrial sector with room for expansion.
. Be as self contained as possible. New jobs to be supplied along with new houses.
. Provide a better environment for a more satisfying life.
. Become a centre for it's surrounding area rather than being a **dormitory** town, e.g. for London. (See glossary p. 121.)

ADMINISTRATION AND FINANCE

A parliamentary fund was set up to finance the new towns, repayable over 60 years. £50 million was allocated in 1946 and by 1975 this had risen to £1500 m. New towns are seen as a national investment. The older new towns are now making returns. A Development Corporation is set up for each new town, composed of architects, engineers, planners, economists etc. It has the power to buy land compulsory, at the price it would get if a town had **not** been designated. The Corporation prepares a master plan to develop the new town as a whole. Every stage of the development has to be in consultation with the local authority and the Secretary of State. Even the residents air their views in public enquiries. Only when the new town is complete does the Development Corporation dissolve, authority being taken over by the local borough council and the New Towns Commission.

FIG. 25.2 NEW TOWNS IN THE UNITED KINGDOM

MILTON KEYNES

For the first time in the United Kingdom a major **city** was designated in 1965. This was to be Milton Keynes and a Development Corporation was established in March 1967. Its plan was published and started in 1970, the first aim being to relieve the pressures of population in the Greater London area. The site of 9000 ha. (22 000 acres) included the settlements of Bletchley, Stony Stratford, Wolverton and 13 villages. Many new towns have been criticised for their lack of character. It is hoped that the character of these settlements will be preserved yet integrated by the planners into the one new settlement of Milton Keynes.

Fig. 25.3 shows the excellent location of Milton Keynes. It is 80 km north-west of London on the main rail and road route-way from London to Birmingham. It is also well placed for airports. For firms who specialise in the distribution of goods the accessibility is an attraction. Growth has been rapid. The idea was to build a little of everything at the same place, so not only would a house be available with a job but clinics, schools, churches and facilities for recreation and entertainment would also be available. The projected population by the year 2000 is 250 000.

The following page attempts to show some of the characteristics of Milton Keynes.

FIG. 25.3 THE LOCATION OF MILTON KEYNES

which new towns relieve the following major urban areas and underline as indicated: Merseyside (4 new towns in green); Greater London (11 new towns in red – but not Corby); Glasgow and Edinburgh (6 new towns in orange); Belfast (2 new towns in brown).

3. A number of new towns are not underlined. These were developed to cater for the special needs of their areas. Try to find out more about one of them.

4. Mark with a star those new towns which already have existing large populations and are now undergoing planned expansion, i.e. Northampton, Peterborough, Warrington, Londonderry, Newtown and Preston (Central Lancashire).

5. Make a visit to your nearest new town or read other material on new towns. Also study the information and diagrams on these pages.
Describe in detail:
(a) the main advantages of living, working or locating an industry or office in a new town.
(b) the main disadvantages and problems of new towns. (Would you want to live in a new town? Explain your answer.)
(c) the designs you would put forward as a town planner, architect or landscape architect, which would persuade people that your new town was a superb place to live.

Questions

1. Make your own **enlarged** copy of Fig. 25.2.

2. Telford and Redditch were designed to relieve population pressure and housing problems in Birmingham. Underline these in blue. Work out

MILTON KEYNES

HOUSING

Cheaper than anywhere else in south-east England
Good variety of styles
Much landscaping, open spaces and play areas
Rental houses immediately available for a new company and its work force
Careful balance maintained between provision of housing, jobs and labour

CENTRAL MILTON KEYNES
More than 140 shops under one roof, including.
Department and specialist stores
Indoor and outdoor markets
Exhibition areas
93 000 m² retail floor space
Important office location
Civic buildings (central library, law courts etc)
Inter-City railway station
Bus station and ample ground level parking

RECREATION AND LEISURE
185 leisure and recreation projects have been completed including the Bowl, a large open air amphitheatre (50 000 capacity), 3 leisure centres, each with a swimming pool and theatre, lakes, canals, rivers, open spaces, golf courses, sports grounds etc.

TRANSPORT
The new road system has been completed on a grid plan. No traffic congestion as employment areas are dispersed. On average, it takes people 15 minutes to get to work. Public transport serves every part of the city. There are four railway stations including the new Central Milton Keynes and 110 km of 'Redways' for pedestrians and cyclists.

INDUSTRY
Names include Volkswagen, Coca-Cola, Bendix and Minolta
Ideal location, choice of sites and premises
Room for expansion
Cheaper rates and rents
Careful designs, attractively landscaped
Factories and offices ready for immediate occupation
Information Technology Training Centre
Central Business Exchange (CBX)
Researches into the fields of electronics, engineering, computing and statistics

26. City Models

FIG. 26.1
A MODEL FOR A
TYPICAL MEDIUM-
SIZED BRITISH CITY.
(MANN'S MODEL.)

A Middle class sector
B Lower middle class
   sector
C Working class sector
   and council estates
D Industry and lowest
   working class sector
1 Central Business
   District
2 Zone in transition:
   deterioration, constant
   change and
   redevelopment
3 Zone of small terrace
   houses in sectors C, D;
   larger by-law housing
   in B; large old houses
   in A
4 Post 1918 residential
   areas with post 1945
   development mainly on
   the periphery
5 Commuting distance 'dormitory towns'

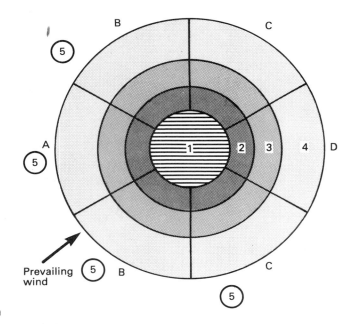

In an attempt to explain the organisation of urban land-use or functional zones a number of theories or models have been developed. The 3 most common of these are the **concentric**, **sector** and **multiple nuclei** models shown at the bottom of the page.

Fig. 26.1 shows a model for a typical medium sized British city. It has one city centre and a number of villages around it from which people can commute to the city for work. **A prevailing westerly wind** has had some influence on the quality and cost of housing. The model combines both concentric rings and sectors.

Questions

1. What is the relationship between the prevailing wind and the location of the middle and working class houses? Why do you think this is so? (See Fig. 30.5, p. 82.)

2. Do you think that the models actually reflect the real pattern found in cities? Try applying Mann's model or any of the others to a city in which you have carried out practical studies.

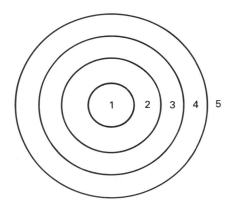

CONCENTRIC MODEL (BURGESS)

1. CBD
2. Zone in transition
3. Zone of workingmen's homes
4. Residential zone
5. Commuter zone

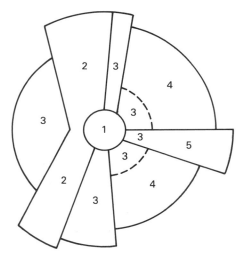

SECTOR MODEL (HOYT)

1. CBD
2. Wholesale, light manufacturing
3. Low-class residential
4. Medium-class residential
5. High-class residential

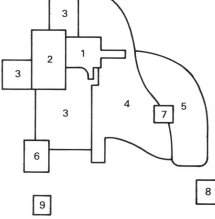

MULTIPLE NUCLEI MODEL
(HARRIS AND ULLMAN)

1. Central Business District
2. Wholesale, light manufacturing
3. Low-class residential
4. Medium-class residential
5. High-class residential
6. Heavy manufacturing
7. Outlying business district
8. Residential suburb
9. Industrial suburb

FIG. 26.2 BURGESS'S MODEL   FIG. 26.3 HOYT'S MODEL

FIG. 26.4
HARRIS AND ULLMAN'S MODEL

27. Industry

Preparation

Prepare an outline map of a local industrial estate, science or business park which you can visit easily. Name any important roads, rivers etc. and mark north.

Make a further rough copy of this map to take with you on your survey.

In advance of your visit, make contact with two firms who could help you with more detailed questions.

Make a list of at least 10 industries you might find represented, for example, food and drink, engineering, furnishing, chemicals and plastics etc.

Method

Divide the work load between the group.

Visit each of the firms in the area.

Name each firm and number them all in order of appearance. See Table 27.1.

Record what is produced by the firm.

Record how many people are **employed** there.

Return to the classroom. Adjust your list of categories of industry to cover the range you found. Decide on a colour or type of shading for each category.

Results

Make up a table from the information you have collected similar to the one shown below. This will act as the key to your map.

Transfer the number you gave to each firm onto your outline map. Shade in each premises in the correct colour or shading. (See Fig. 27.1.) Your map and key should match!

Use the employment figures to construct a pie chart. (See instructions on p. 3.)

Conclusions

Study the map, table and graph.

Describe the relief of the whole site. Was it flat, undulating, hilly?

What main types of industry were represented? (Use the glossary of terms below.) Which categories from your list seemed to be particularly dominant?

Here are some factors which may decide where an industry is located:

Site (including water), **Raw materials** (local and/or imported), **Transport** (road, rail, canal etc.), **Markets** (who will buy the products) **Labour**, (skilled, unskilled etc.), **Capital** (money invested in the industry, shares), a source of **Power** (electricity, gas etc.), **Waste disposal**.

Choose one or two firms to find out how these factors have affected them. Write a detailed account of your findings.

4. Were there any obvious signs of pollution from any of the industries, particularly air, water or noise pollution?

5. Does the presence of any of these industries give rise to any other environmental problem for example, unsightly appearance, danger of explosions, releasing noxious gases etc.

Primary industries involve the extraction and production of raw materials, e.g. mining, farming.

Secondary industries are concerned with making or manufacturing goods which may be finished e.g. a car, or component parts for assembly, e.g. a horn.

Tertiary industries are those which provide a service.

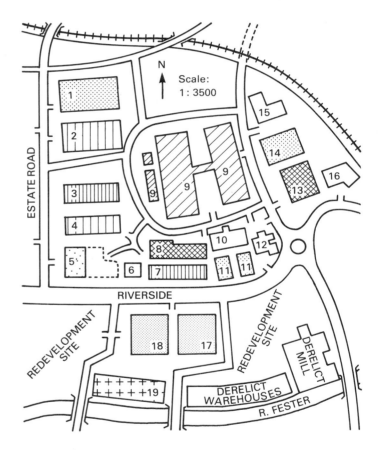

FIG. 27.1 DIAGRAM OF AN IMAGINARY INDUSTRIAL AREA.

TABLE 27.1 (UNFINISHED EXAMPLE)

CATEGORY OF INDUSTRY	COLOUR OR SHADING	NAMES OF FIRM(S) ENGAGED IN THIS TYPE OF INDUSTRY	NUMBER ON OUTLINE MAP	TOTAL NUMBER OF EMPLOYEES
FURNISHING		SWISH (CURTAIN RAILS) LTD. MINTY	3 7	75
FOOD AND DRINK		R. WHITE LTD. GOLDEN WONDER	8 13	88
ENGINEERING		ROSE BRO'S LTD. WILLS CIGARETTE MACHINES	2 4	55
CHEMICALS		MACBRIDE'S LTD.	17	

28. Planning

FIG. 28.1 LONDON'S COVENT GARDEN BEFORE AND AFTER REDEVELOPMENT

In Britain up until the early twentieth century, houses and factories were built almost anywhere they were wanted. This lead to congestion in the centre of towns and a haphazard sprawl of buildings around the edges known as **suburban sprawl**. This often covered good agricultural land and rich mineral deposits. Industries, homes, transport and leisure activities all competed for space. Some sort of control was needed over making decisions about how the land was to be used. The housing boom after the 1st World War only made matters worse. Only one third of the present homes in England and Wales were built before 1939. Britain is also densely populated with some 230 persons per km². The United States by comparison only has 25 persons per km².

THE DEVELOPMENT OF PLANNING CONTROL IN ENGLAND AND WALES

1909 The Housing, Town and Country Planning Act. This was chiefly concerned with public health and housing. It gave local authorities **permissive** power to take on and administer planning schemes.

1932 The Town and Country Planning Act. Local authorities began to have control over most of the land in their areas. They could plan urban or rural schemes. Provisions were made for preserving buildings and protecting trees and woodlands.

1947 The Town and Country Planning Act. This gave local authorities **compulsory** powers and duties. Most forms of development were now subject to the authorities' consent, working on the principle that all development rights belonged to the state. A **compulsory purchase** could be made for land to be used for public purposes. The owner was only paid its existing use value as compensation. They had control over:
- the location, size and character of towns and villages,
- the siting of industry,
- the development by gas, electricity and water boards,
- in some cases by the development transport authorities,
- the working of minerals,
- the protection of agriculture and forestry,
- the conservation of the countryside and coast

1959 The Town and Country Planning Act.

1961
1973 } The Land Compensation Acts.

Now land which had been compulsorily purchased should receive the market value for compensation. Compensation was also improved where only part of a property was taken. (Imagine how your house might be devalued – worth less – if a new by-pass chopped off part of your garden.)

1971 The Town and Country Planning Act. This updated the laws of the 1947 act.

Now all 'development' (including forms of construction, engineering, mining and material change in the use of land or existing buildings) requires prior consent or planning permission from the local planning authority.

PLANNING AT GOVERNMENT LEVEL

The **Department of the Environment** (D.O.E.) has responsibility for town and country planning in England and is headed by the **Secretary of State for the Environment**, assisted by three ministers:

The **Minister for Transport**, who is responsible for general transport policy, roads, road safety, railways, ports etc.

The **Minister for Planning and Local Government** who is responsible for land use and regional planning, new towns, minerals, the countryside, water and sewerage.

The **Minister for Housing and Construction** who is responsible for the housing programme, the construction industries etc.

PLANNING AT A LOCAL LEVEL

Local authorities are given the power by central government to carry out all the ground work on planning brought in by the various planning acts.

County Councils: e.g. Oxford County Council. There are 45 county councils in England. They deal with large and expensive planning and administrative matters over wide areas, for example the building of a motorway extension. Until recently 6 of these were very large and known as the Metropolitan Counties. They were abolished on 1 April 1986 and their functions transferred to the borough or district councils in an attempt to stop unnecessary costs and duplication of roles.

District Councils: e.g. Cherwell District Council. There are 332 district councils within the county councils. They deal with planning on a very local scale, for example planning permission for a house or an extension.

Borough Councils: London is administered by 32 borough councils and the City of London. The Greater London Council (GLC) was responsible for unifying plans over the whole area but after its abolition on 1 April 1986, along with its 6 Metropolitan counterparts, its services and responsibilities were devolved to the boroughs and the City Corporation.

FIG. 28.2
TO SHOW THE ROLE
OF LOCAL PLANNING
AUTHORITIES

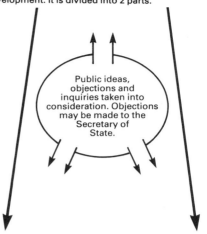

DEVELOPMENT PLAN

A written statement and maps to show the local authority's main objectives for land use in its area over a period of years. It is designed to create a pleasant environment rather than just stopping undesirable development. It is divided into 2 parts.

Public ideas, objections and inquiries taken into consideration. Objections may be made to the Secretary of State.

STRUCTURE PLAN
prepared by County Council

A written statement and maps setting out and justifying proposals for the development of land in that area. It suggests any areas where action should be taken in next 10 yrs. ('Action Areas'). It requires approval of the minister.

LOCAL PLAN
(one or more)
prepared by District Council

A written statement and map showing the nature and location of the development and other land use in the area. It doesn't need approval from the minister to be adopted.

FINALISED PLANS

Henley Buildings, Boundary Street Estate

FIG. 28.3 COUNCIL HOUSING IN A LONDON BOROUGH

FIG. 28.4 EARLSTREES INDUSTRIAL ESTATE – ENTERPRISE ZONE 1986, CORBY

Corby Industrial Development Centre

REGIONAL PLANNING

Regional economic planning councils and boards were set up in 1964 because some parts of Britain were notably less prosperous than others. They hope to achieve a better balance between the decline of industries, such as coal mining and heavy engineering, and the level of unemployment and the rate of economic growth throughout the country. Within these regions have been designated 'development areas' to encourage industrial growth. They receive special grants. Corby is one example. When the steel works closed in 1980 it had a disastrous unemployment crisis. One particular area with 112 ha of land ripe for development was made the first 'enterprise zone' in 1981. This means that for 10 years the zone is:
● exempt from Development Land Tax.
● exempt from local authority rates on industrial and commercial property.
● under a simplified planning regime, making permission to build easier.

By 1984 few sites remained, 5000 new jobs were created by 250 new firms and new investments worth £500 millions were made.

LONDON STREET, NORWICH

Many factors had to be taken into consideration when the draft plan was drawn up for London Street, especially those which affected **traders, pedestrians, motorists** and the historical and architectural **character** of Norwich. This scheme was to be one small part of an overall 30 year plan for Norwich to make two large pedestrian areas around the castle, shops and the cathedral. Only buses and service vehicles would be allowed to cross these areas on carefully designed routes. The need for careful planning can be seen in the following points.

Two way traffic had always been difficult due to the narrow street. Pedestrians often spilled off the pavement into the road itself. There were real accident risk areas, for example at the junction of Swan Lane, which was already pedestrianised and London Street.

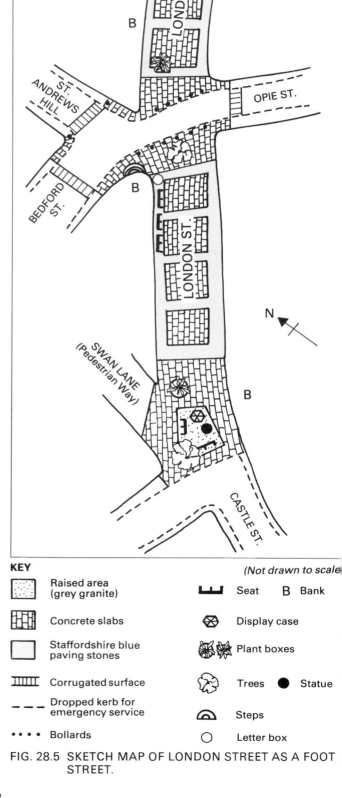

KEY   *(Not drawn to scale)*

▦ Raised area (grey granite)	⊔⊔ Seat	B Bank
▦ Concrete slabs	⬡ Display case	
▢ Staffordshire blue paving stones	❀❀ Plant boxes	
▥ Corrugated surface	☘ Trees ● Statue	
– – – Dropped kerb for emergency service	⌒ Steps	
• • • • Bollards	○ Letter box	

FIG. 28.5 SKETCH MAP OF LONDON STREET AS A FOOT STREET.

the shopping streets were based on a medieval street pattern which could not provide rear access to the shops. Therefore, 'service only' streets would have to be formed adjoining the foot street. Goods would have to be delivered by trolley at a maximum distance of 40 metres to the shops. Emergency vehicles would still need access to the street so paving slabs would have to be reinforced to withstand weights up to 12 tonnes and bollards etc. would have to be a minimum of 4 m apart. For security reasons five major banks in the street were concerned about access for servicing. They were encouraged to revise their business methods and persuade their branch banks, elsewhere in the city, to handle the main flow of cash. Also the shopkeepers needed to be convinced that trade would not suffer if vehicles were banned. After a trial closure, 28 out of 42 shops did better trade and pedestrian traffic increased by 45%. Traders, pedestrians and even motorists were found to be in favour of the foot street. Planning permission for London Street was finalised in 1969.

A **precinct** is a traffic free area for pedestrians, often in the main shopping zone.

A **foot street** is a pedestrian shopping street which cannot provide rear access for service deliveries.

Questions

Study Figs. 28.5 and 28.6.
1. Choose three major problems for the planners. Describe what they were and how they were overcome successfully.
2. In what way have the planners made the street more **aesthetically** pleasing to the pedestrians and traders?
3. What advantages are there for shoppers in a pedestrian only area?

Practical Study

1. Either use Fig. 28.7 or an area in a nearby town or city chosen by your teacher. Gather information to form a draft plan for a shopping precinct. The following work will help. (Omit Question 4 if you are using Fig. 28.7 and only answer relevant sections in the other questions.)
2. Carry out a survey of the traffic flow on Market Day or Saturday and one other mid-week day. Record the number of vehicles per hour travelling east and west on these days. Also record the weather conditions.

FIG. 28.6 VIEWS OF LONDON STREET, NORWICH, BEFORE AND AFTER PEDESTRIANISATION

Norwich City Planning Department

73

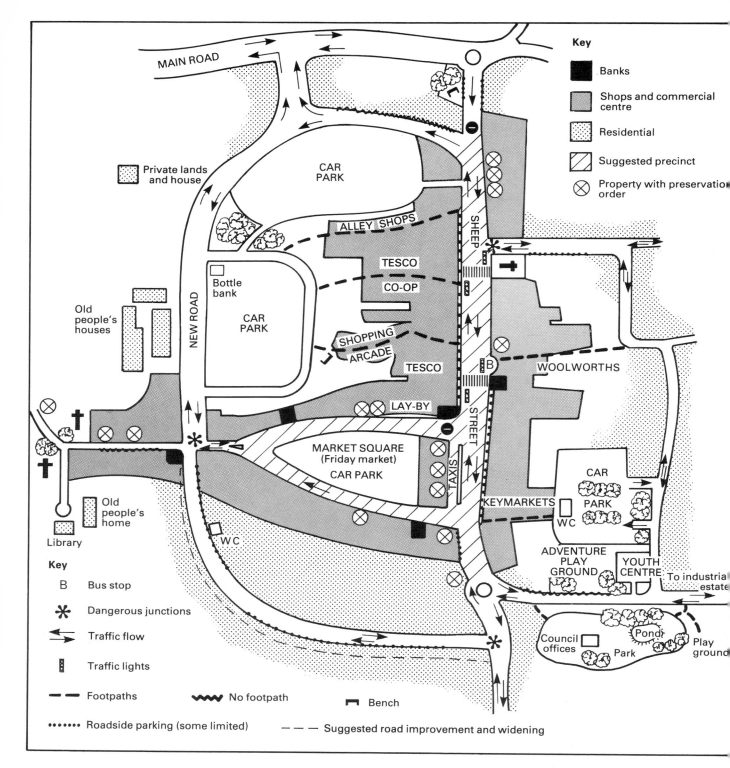

FIG. 28.7 IMAGINARY MAP FOR SHOPPING PRECINCT EXERCISE

Key (map legend):
- Banks
- Shops and commercial centre
- Residential
- Suggested precinct
- ⊗ Property with preservation order
- B Bus stop
- ✳ Dangerous junctions
- ← Traffic flow
- Traffic lights
- – – Footpaths
- ∿∿∿ No footpath
- ⌐ Bench
- •••• Roadside parking (some limited)
- — — Suggested road improvement and widening

Map labels: MAIN ROAD, CAR PARK, Private lands and house, NEW ROAD, Bottle bank, CAR PARK, Old people's houses, ALLEY SHOPS, TESCO, CO-OP, SHOPPING ARCADE, TESCO, LAY-BY, SHEEP STREET, WOOLWORTHS, Old people's home, Library, WC, MARKET SQUARE (Friday market) CAR PARK, TAXIS, KEYMARKETS, WC, CAR PARK, ADVENTURE PLAY GROUND, YOUTH CENTRE, To industrial estate, Council offices, Park, Pond, Play ground, B

3. Study the area concerned and make notes on the following:
   - Amenities such as shelter, lavatories, lighting, seats, car parks and landscaping.
   - Accident risk area for pedestrians/traffic.
   - Footpaths, zebra crossings, pavement obstacles, allies etc.
4. Carry out a questionnaire on pedestrians and traders to see what they would like.
5. Consider the following factors where appropriate. Make notes and then outline any **major problems** which arise.
   - Safety. ● Ease of shopping. ● Parking.
   - The young, disabled and elderly.
   - Service roads. ● Rear access.
   - Competition between shops.
   - Value of land abutting the precinct.
   - The load of displaced traffic on other roads.
   - Buses and taxis. ● Emergency vehicles.
   - Pollution, noise, exhaust fumes.
   - Building foundations and preservation.
   - Aesthetic appeal.
6. Draft out a plan with a written statement and map(s).
   If you are carrying out your own fieldwork show it to the people on the street, i.e. shopkeepers, police, traders etc. Get their views before you finalise your plans.
7. After a meeting of your planning committee finalise the plans.

29. Dereliction/Reclamation

Scottish Development Agency

FIG. 29.1
REDEVELOPMENT ON THE
CLYDEBANK, GLASGOW

The British government definition of derelict land is **'land so damaged by industrial or other development that it is incapable of beneficial use without treatment'**
There are estimated to be 100 000 hectares of derelict land in Britain. This is not a great amount – only about 0.5% of the total land area – however, it often occurs:

● in densely populated areas.
● in areas important or once important for industry. (Most of these arose before planning controls so the owner or operator had no legal obligation to restore the land.)
● in certain counties more than others, for example, Lancashire, Durham and Cornwall are heavily affected whereas Lincolnshire and Gloucestershire have very little.
● in first class farming areas.

Most dereliction today is in fact due to present or past extractive industries, for example, coal, sand, gravel, clay, tin etc. Some of these are also processed where they are extracted, leaving huge piles of waste, e.g. slag heaps from coal.

The responsibility for the reclamation of already formed derelict land lies with the local authorities who can claim government grants of up to 50% in most places. Economically depressed areas such as Durham can claim up to 85% but it is still difficult to find the extra 15% because funds are dependant on the rates. Planning controls are now much stricter. When permission is granted for the working of a new site various conditions are laid down, for example,

● the minimal amount of disturbance,
● restricted heights for tipping,
● the stabilization of heaps,
● storing topsoil and re-spreading it after work has ceased, e.g. open-cast mining,
● filling in pits,
● leaving quarry floors tidy,
● generally restoring the land to its former use, e.g. farmland, or landscaping it for a future use, e.g. recreation, housing or new industries.

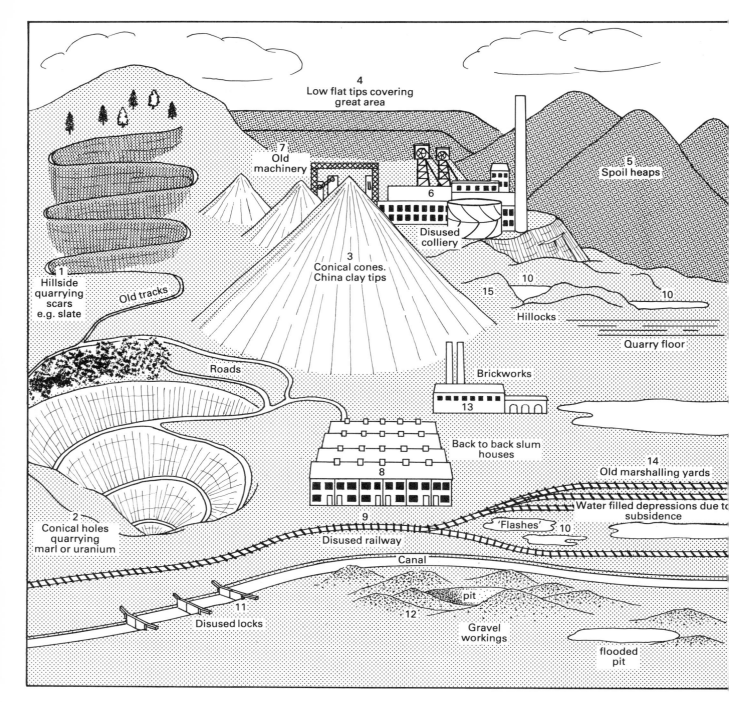

4 Low flat tips covering great area

7 Old machinery

5 Spoil heaps

Disused colliery

6

3 Conical cones. China clay tips

15   **10**

10

Hillocks

1 Hillside quarrying scars e.g. slate

Old tracks

Quarry floor

Roads

Brickworks

13

Back to back slum houses

8

14 Old marshalling yards

Water filled depressions due to subsidence

2 Conical holes quarrying marl or uranium

9 Disused railway

'Flashes'   **10**

Canal

pit

12 Gravel workings

11 Disused locks

flooded pit

FIG. 29.2 DERELICT LAND

These problems are still evident in many reclamation programmes.

1. The cost of reclamation, including landscaping, is very high, perhaps some £1500 per acre. As most of this becomes the responsibility of the company working the land this puts additional costs on their product and dereliction still outpaces reclamation.
2. The public see a heap and a hole. Why can't one be used to fill the other? Often the distance (even small distances) and the volume of material makes it just too expensive to be transported.
3. The removal of a mineral layer can cause problems with the soil structure and the water table when restored to farmland. Waterlogging and poor yields are common complaints.

Questions

1. Study the 'before' and 'after' photographs on p. 75.

Describe the scene before the reclamation programme. What might have been the main problems in reclaiming this land? What might have caused the greatest costs?
2. What is the symbol for derelict land used in the Second Land Utilisation Survey of Britain? On an extract provided by your teacher identify derelict land and suggest new uses for it, bearing in mind the local environment.
3. Lincolnshire has very little derelict land compared with its size. What there is comes in unusual shapes and sizes, e.g. disused aerodromes and disused railways. The later are unique because they are very long and very narrow, occasionally broadening at a station and stationyard.
Make a table of possible linear (l) and non-linear (n-l) uses for a disused railway. For example, a station might become a private house (n-l), a cutting a refuse tip (n-l) and the old trackbed a walkway (l).

Trash. Garbage. Refuse. Waste It's All Rubbish!

TRUE OR FALSE?

Domestic refuse has doubled in the last 20 years?

Landfill sites for dumping are more difficult and expensive to find?

Industrial waste is greater than ever. Electricity power stations in Great Britain produce 10 million tonnes of pulverised ash per annum?

The litter problem on our streets is worse than ever and costs more to collect?

There is more hazardous waste, i.e. toxic, reactive, corrosive, infections and ignitable?

There are more disposable goods?

Manufacturers are using more packaging on their products to keep it fresher or give it more appeal?

Paper and plastic are now the most common refuse items?

The consumer pays three times for each item, once to buy, once to have it collected and once to pay for its disposal?

The present trend is for non-returnable bottles?

It takes 40–80 years for a fir tree to grow and less than one minute to cut it down?

We will soon need refuse collecting satellites in space!

Answer. All true!

FIG. 29.3 EXTRACTING WASTE FOR RECYCLING

FIG. 29.4 A BOTTLE BANK

FIG. 29.5 (below left) GULLS AT A RUBBISH TIP

FIG. 29.6 AN UNOFFICIAL DUMP BEHIND RAILINGS: CANS LITTER A CITY STREET

RUBBISH JARGON

Landfill. A tipping or dumping site where *ideally* each day's addition is covered by a layer of earth to prevent odours and vermin.

Incineration. Burning waste to reduce its volume and weight and leave a harmless residue.

Pulverisation. To reduce to dust, fine powder or granules, for example, ash.

Composting. Moisture and air are added to screened refuse in controlled amounts. After 5 days in a revolving drum a humus-like material is made by the action of micro-organisms.

Reuse. To use the item again for the same or a different purpose, e.g. milk bottle, a paper bag.

Reclamation. To reclaim or take back, making a product or resource which is thought to be waste or derelict, available for future use.

Recycle. To reprocess a waste product, for example newspaper → pulp → toilet paper.

Degrade. To wear down or decompose naturally.

Biodegradable. A substance which can be broken down by living organisms. Recent research is being carried out to find a biodegradable plastic.

Inert. Chemically inactive. Harmless.

Noxious. Hurtful. Poisonous.

Toxic. Poisonous.

Pyrolysis. This is an incineration process which takes place in the absence of oxygen. It produces less air pollution than other methods of incineration and produces fuels which can be sold or used, for example, to heat a nearby housing estate.

Windrowing. This is one form of composting. Crude refuse is tipped in long linear heaps, called windrows, across a field. The heaps may be treated with special cultures, wetted and turned periodically, until they have fermented. The compost is then separated from the non-compost.

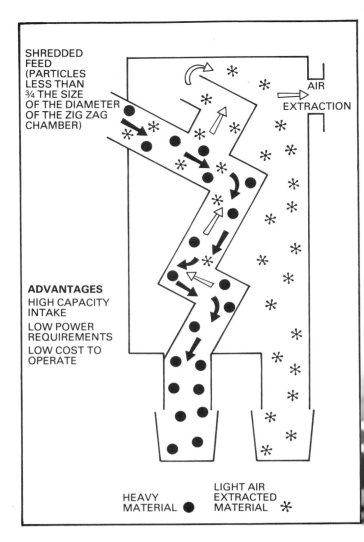

FIG. 29.7 ZIG ZAG AIR SEPARATOR

(image labels) SHREDDED FEED (PARTICLES LESS THAN ¾ THE SIZE OF THE DIAMETER OF THE ZIG ZAG CHAMBER) · AIR EXTRACTION · ADVANTAGES HIGH CAPACITY INTAKE LOW POWER REQUIREMENTS LOW COST TO OPERATE · HEAVY MATERIAL ● · LIGHT AIR EXTRACTED MATERIAL ✳

Questions

1. Forty percent of American household refuse is packaging. Examine your last shopping load. Which goods do you think were '**over-packaged**'? Was it necessary? Who pays for the packaging? What changes would you like to see made in shops to reduce future rubbish loads or create easily degradable rubbish?
2. **Rubber gloves and gas masks ready**! Lay out the contents of one full school waste paper bin.
   Sort it into vegetable matter (rotting food) and all the different groups of packaging materials found in the table opposite. Further examine the plastics. How many obviously different kinds were there?
3. Find out about the Zabbaline people in Cairo, Egypt and what they do with their rubbish.
4. Find out how 'bottle banks' operate?
5. Write an essay on 'Rubbish, an unnecessary waste.'

Did you know?
In Tokyo, door to door 'salesmen' collect newspapers, magazines and cartons in exchange for fresh rolls of toilet paper. They call themselves the toilet-paper exchangers!

TABLE 29.2 METHODS OF DOMESTIC REFUSE
DISPOSAL IN GREAT BRITAIN

METHOD	%	
Landfill untreated	74.5	Less expensive ↑
Other landfill	12.4	
Landfill after shredding	3.0	
Direct incineration	8.3	
Separation and incineration	1.5	↓ More expensive
Other – including composting	0.3	

Construct a pie chart of this information

TABLE. 29.2 THE WASTE OF PACKAGING?

PACKAGING	PAPER	PLASTICS POLYTHENE	POLYSTYRENE	GLASS	CLOTH/WOOD	METALS ALUMINIUM	CANS
RESOURCES ENERGY	Timber	Oil (Petro-chemicals).	Oil (Petro-chemicals).	High grade Sand. Limestone.	Petro-chemicals. Timber. Cotton. Jute etc.	Aluminium (All imported to U.K.).	Tin. Steel. Aluminium.
USE	Wrappers. Bags Outer packing. Waxed. Plastic coated. Cellophane.	Bottles. Bags Film	Coating paper. Pack delicate items, e.g. radios, fruit.	Bottles, some returnable, e.g. milk.	Clothing. String. Sacks. Boxes. Cases.	Cans for drinks. Kitchen foil. Freezer tubs.	Aerosols. Cans mostly used for food.
LITTER PROBLEM	Most decompose in time except wax and plastic.	Does not degrade. Animals may choke on it, children suffocate.	Does not degrade. Light, easily blown	Danger of broken glass.	Do not add much to overall littler problem.	Does not degrade.	Do not degrade quickly. Noisy when blown.
CONTROLLED DUMPING	Easily compacted. Blows about. Decomposes, but not as fast as vegetable matter.	Blows about. Resistant to chemical and biological degradation. They remain the same when buried.	Blows about.	No problems.	Easily compacted. Eventually degrade.	Does not degrade. Not usually a problem.	No problems.
INCINERATION	Volume reduced by burning.	Melts. May clog incinerator grates. No toxic fumes.	Noxious fumes when burnt.	Melts. Forms clinker with ash.	Burns well.	Unaffected by fire.	No. Aerosols explode.
PULVERISATION	Easy to pulverise.	OK	OK	Easy.	Easy.	OK	Baled or fist-sized lumps only.
COMPOSTING	Good. Bio-degradable.	Remains inert.	Remains inert.	No good. Have to be removed.	Biodegradable. Takes longer.	No good. Have to be removed.	No good. Have to be removed.
DEGRADABILITY	Complete in time (not wax or plastic coating).	Present plastics not degradable but they are inert.		Not degradable but inert.	Complete in time.	Not degradable.	Will rust eventually.
REFUSE	Often reused before throwing away.	Some containers can be reused, e.g. ice cream cartons, egg cartons.		Milk bottles may do 30 drips.	Can be reused if not damaged.	Foil can be reused if handled carefully. Not cans.	Not reusable.
RECYCLING	Yes. Loss of strength + ink contamination but good for loo paper, tissue, insulation etc.	Too may types. Difficulty of sorting into groups. Need to be colour coded.		YES. Sort colours. Smashed to produce more glass or abrasives.	Wood as fuel. Not usually recycled. Not enough.	Would have to separate before the dustbin to recycle. Needs too much energy.	YES. Extracted with magnets. De-tinning to reclaim tin.

30. Pollution

This occurs when chemical or physical agents (pollutants) which may have a bad effect on living and non-living things are released into the environment – air, land or water. This may include gases, liquids, solids and noise.

RSPB/M W Richards

FIG. 30.1 OILED SEABIRD

FIG. 30.2 ACID RAIN 'HATS'

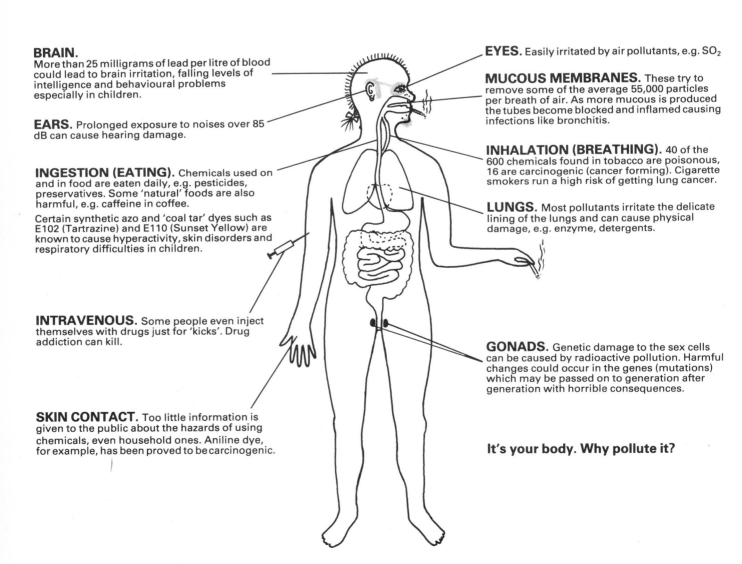

BRAIN.
More than 25 milligrams of lead per litre of blood could lead to brain irritation, falling levels of intelligence and behavioural problems especially in children.

EARS. Prolonged exposure to noises over 85 dB can cause hearing damage.

INGESTION (EATING). Chemicals used on and in food are eaten daily, e.g. pesticides, preservatives. Some 'natural' foods are also harmful, e.g. caffeine in coffee.

Certain synthetic azo and 'coal tar' dyes such as E102 (Tartrazine) and E110 (Sunset Yellow) are known to cause hyperactivity, skin disorders and respiratory difficulties in children.

INTRAVENOUS. Some people even inject themselves with drugs just for 'kicks'. Drug addiction can kill.

SKIN CONTACT. Too little information is given to the public about the hazards of using chemicals, even household ones. Aniline dye, for example, has been proved to be carcinogenic.

EYES. Easily irritated by air pollutants, e.g. SO_2

MUCOUS MEMBRANES. These try to remove some of the average 55,000 particles per breath of air. As more mucous is produced the tubes become blocked and inflamed causing infections like bronchitis.

INHALATION (BREATHING). 40 of the 600 chemicals found in tobacco are poisonous, 16 are carcinogenic (cancer forming). Cigarette smokers run a high risk of getting lung cancer.

LUNGS. Most pollutants irritate the delicate lining of the lungs and can cause physical damage, e.g. enzyme, detergents.

GONADS. Genetic damage to the sex cells can be caused by radioactive pollution. Harmful changes could occur in the genes (mutations) which may be passed on to generation after generation with horrible consequences.

It's your body. Why pollute it?

FIG. 30.3 HOW DIFFERENT PARTS OF OUR BODY ARE AFFECTED BY POLLUTANTS

Air Pollution

Pollutant	Source	Effects. Notes.
Sulphur S **Sulphur dioxide** SO_2 Sulphur trioxide SO_3 Sulphuric acid H_2SO_4 Various sulphates	Burning sulphur-bearing **fossil fuels**, e.g. coal, oil, during which process sulphur is oxidised and released into the air, e.g. power stations, domestic fires.	Thought to be the most dangerous pollutant to health. Causes lung irritation leading to bronchitis, emphysema etc. especially in the very young and aged. Lowers crop yields due to yellowing and dying back of plants. Blackens buildings, corrodes metal, crumbles stonework. Acid lakes (see Fig. 30.7) devoid of living organisms. Indirect effect on the timber, fishing and tourist industries.
Nitrogen oxides Nitrogen monoxide NO Nitrogen dioxide NO_2	Formed during the burning of fuel. High temperatures cause the chemical combining of oxygen and nitrogen in the air, e.g. factories, motor vehicle exhausts, power stations.	Encourages the formation of acid rain, (See Fig. 30.7), i.e. dilute nitric acid. Chemical reactions involving sunlight, nitrogen oxides and hydrocarbons can cause the build up of ozone in the atmosphere.
Ozone O_3	Formed at ground level as sunlight reacts with exhaust fumes.	Causes lung irritation and has harmful effects on vegetation.
CFCs (chloro-fluorocarbons e.g. freons	Aerosol sprays, expanded polystyrene containers, e.g. egg boxes, fast food boxes, refrigerators.	The ozone layer forms a barrier to harmful ultra-violet radiation from the sun which could cause reduced crop yields, skin cancer and a warming of the atmosphere. A vast 'hole' has appeared in the ozone layer over the Antarctic and now the Arctic Circle. It is causing international alarm. Look for the 'ozone friendly' signs on packaging.
Carbon C **Carbon monoxide** CO	Burning fuel. Incomplete burning of carbon in fossil fuels. If there is plenty of oxygen present this is usually turned into CO_2, but the internal combustion engine operates without extra air and so CO is released from motor vehicle exhausts.	Particles settle on leaves, reducing photosynthesis and therefore crop yields. CO is poisonous to man and animals. It combines with haemoglobin in the blood, taking the place of oxygen, so that oxygen cannot reach the body cells.
Carbon dioxide CO_2	Burning fuels.	CO_2 is released in increasing amounts. Scientists are concerned about the greenhouse effect. (See p. 4.) A build-up of CO_2 might prevent heat which is reflected from the earth from escaping. This may in turn raise the atmospheric temperatures and so alter the weather.
Hydrocarbons	Gaseous chemicals composed of carbon and hydrogen. Mostly from vehicle exhaust fumes or petrol refining.	Play a major part in the formation of ozone from exhaust fumes.
Particulate matter Dust, carbon, soil, pollen, soot, ash, asbestos etc. (Metals see below.)	Agricultural burning, e.g. stubble, Industrial processes. Burning of fuel. Natural sources.	The heavy particles settle out close to the source causing soiled washing and paintwork, also grime on leaves which reduces photosynthesis and lower crop yields. Fine particles ($10-1\mu$) remain suspended and are carried further before being deposited. Very fine particles ($0.1-0.3\mu$) produce a visible haze in the atmosphere.
Lead Pb	Exhaust fumes from vehicles using leaded petrol. Certain factories.	Lead accumulates in the body if breathed in or eaten on food. It is very poisonous and interferes with the body's enzyme activities. Many countries now offer unleaded petrol. (See also pp. 83–84.)
Flourine F	Brickworks. Aluminium smelting.	Causes mottled teeth and bones. Livestock are unable to eat and may die.
Noise	Machines. Traffic. Aircraft.	Fear of noise can reduce milk yields, fertility and causes stillbirths in livestock. The British Government hope to eventually reduce the levels for lorries to 80 dBA and cars to 75 dBA. Sonic booms are not allowed over the land.

FIG 30.4 SMOG IN LOS ANGELES, USA

IDEAS FOR CONTROLLING AIR POLLUTION

● Change to fuels with a low sulphur content, for example, natural gas.
● Use alternative sources of energy, not fossil fuels, for example HEP, solar energy etc.
● Change the nature of the industrial process so that there are less emissions anyway.
● Disperse the pollutants more widely, for example use taller smoke stacks.
● Add more equipment to remove the pollutants before they are released into the atmosphere, for example, the catalytic convertor converts exhaust fumes into the less harmful nitrogen, carbon dioxide and water before it leaves the exhaust pipe. (See electrostatic precipitators p. 121.)
● Switch to different modes of transport, such as electric trains rather than motor vehicles.
● Use other means of propulsion, for example, hydrogen, steam turbine or electric battery.
● Introduce more legislation (laws), for example, Clean Air Acts.

Air Pollution and the Weather

1. The direction and speed of the wind can decide
   (a) where pollutants are carried to.
   (b) the concentration of the pollutants.
2. If the air is turbulent and allows the air layers to mix the pollutants may be dispersed easily and widely.
3. A **smog** may develop when
   (a) the pollutants combine with fog in calm air conditions.
   (b) there is a **temperature inversion**.
       See Fig. 30.6.

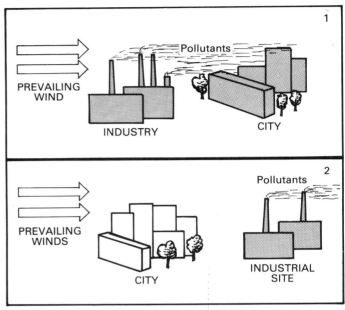

FIG. 30.5 DIAGRAM TO SHOW THE EFFECT OF PREVAILING WIND ON AIR POLLUTION

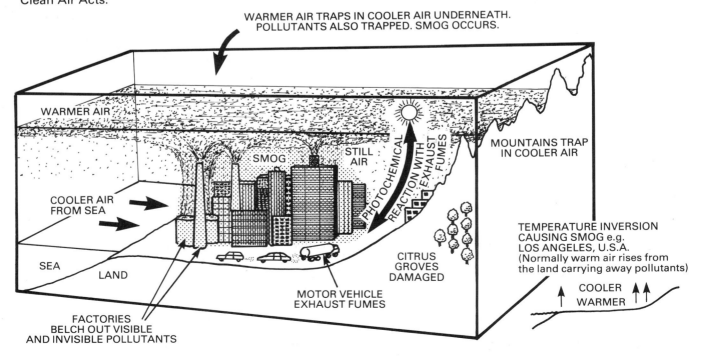

FIG 30.6 TEMPERATURE INVERSION CAUSING SMOG, e.g. LOS ANGELES, USA

THE LEAD ISSUE

Lead is added to petrol to increase car engine efficiency. It is emmitted in exhaust fumes. The white paper presented to the British parliament in May 1970 on 'The Fight Against Pollution' suggested that:

> 'Lead is a well known poison, but the amount that is emitted from motor vehicle exhausts is, in this country, trivial.'

But, in April 1983 it was reported that the goverment had accepted a recommendation by the Royal Commission on Environmental Pollution to introduce **lead free petrol**. All new cars produced from 1990 would have to be designed to run on lead free petrol, which some countries already use.

Questions

1. Find out what effects lead poisoning has on the body. Why are children particularly at risk?
2. What problems will the 1990 law bring for garage owners and car designers? Find out about the system already in use in North America.
3. In what ways would you encourage the control of lead paint and lead plumbing, which are also sources of lead pollution?
4. Mercury is also an extremely poisonous metal. Research, from other sources, the **Minamata Bay** incident in **Japan**. Write up an account either as a sensationalised newspaper report or for use in a school assembly.

AMOCO CADIZ

In 1978 a huge supertanker was wrecked off the coast of Brittany, France. 223 000 tonnes of crude oil were spilled causing extensive pollution. Tourists beaches were ruined and hundreds of sea birds and other marine life were destroyed. Detergents used to disperse oil in earlier disasters have since proved to be damaging to wildlife.

Losses from the production and movement of oil have been estimated at over 2 million tonnes per year. Sixty per cent of this total occurs in marine environments due to:

1. Deliberate and accidental discharges at sea, including the flushing of oil tanks. (The penalties for offenders are still very low.)

2. Transfer losses at the oil terminals.

3. Major accidents, often due to very busy shipping lanes in narrow channels, e.g. the Torrey Canyon disaster when 30 400 tonnes of crude oil were lost off Land's End at the entrance to the English Channel.

4. Accidents during offshore production – likely to increase in the future.

5. Increased size of supertankers (300 000–400 000 tonnes).

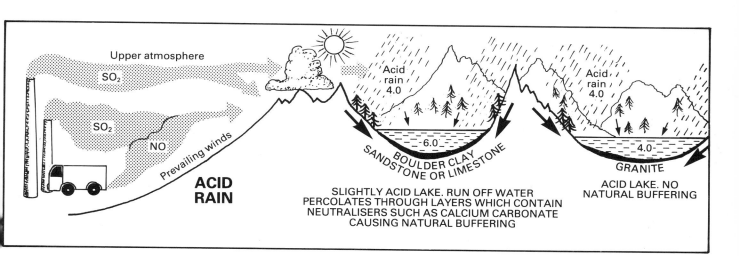

FIG. 30.7 ACID RAIN

ACID RAIN

Sulphur dioxide (SO_2) and **nitrogen monoxide** (NO) are released into the air daily as a result of burning coal, oil and natural gas. Thirty million tonnes of sulphur get trapped in the upper atmosphere annually. With the addition of rain-water, dilute sulphuric and nitric acids are formed, hence the name **acid rain** (usually below pH 4.0).

Areas most at risk from acid rain are mountainous regions with thin soils which are in the line of prevailing winds and so receive much rain. Great Britain 'exports' her sulphur dioxide to Scandinavia! Here are some of the known effects of acid rain on the environment:

● Lakes and rivers become acid, unless they have natural buffering (see Fig.30.7), often with a pH of less than 4.0. Fish, spawn and other forms of freshwater life are destroyed.
● The tops of spruce trees may die. This is economically disasterous for timber producing countries.
● Increased leaching of calcium from the soil leads to poor growth of trees and crops. Additional leaching of aluminium poisons the water.
● Local wells are turning acid, causing copper poisoning of drinking water and corroding central heating systems.
● Marble and limestone used for buildings and statues are weathered more rapidly and metals are corroded.

Water Pollution

Pollutant	Source	Effects. Notes.
Sewage	Raw effluent pumped into oceans and estuaries. 'Treated' effluent in rivers.	Spreads waterborne diseases, e.g. cholera, typhoid. Causes eutrophication (see p. 45), unpleasant odour and sight. Intensively farmed livestock can cause more disposal problems than humans do. The cost of bringing treatment up to a satisfactory level everywhere is too expensive.
Industrial waste e.g. detergent e.g. Mercury	Effluent from factories. Used as a catalyst in the production of plastics, as a fungicide in pulp mills and on seeds (now banned in some countries). Mercury compounds may be accidentally released in industrial effluent.	Often interferes with 'natural' self purification processes in the water. A cumulative poison which affects the nervous system. Causes brain irritation, paralysis, abnormalities in babies and eventually death. 45 died in the Minamata Bay incident in Japan. 10 000 were still at risk in the mid 1970's, mainly as a result of eating mercury poisoned fish and shellfish.
e.g. Lead	Washed from roadsides (exhaust fumes) into water courses.	Causes headaches, depression, impaired mental health, increased chance of stillbirths and miscarriage. Symptoms appear in people with lead levels of 100 milligrams per litre of blood. Over 25 mg/litre is considered dangerous.
e.g. Dioxin	Bleached paper products	Toxic to water life, humans using bleached disposable nappies, coffee filters, tampons, paper hankies, toilet paper etc.
Agricultural waste	Run off from land. Accidental spills.	Chemicals such as DDT build up in food chains, killing carnivorous fish, birds and mammals. Fertilisers cause eutrophication. See p. 45.
Heat	From industries which use water for cooling, e.g. power stations.	Thermal pollution kills some animals and plants outright. It may increase bacterial growth in the water. Water is returned to rivers, lakes and oceans with a 5–10°C temperature increase. Industries argue that to cool water down further costs too much money.
Acid rain	Rainwater combines with SO_2 and NO which are released from the burning of fossil fuels.	It can increase the acidity of rivers and lakes, especially if they have little calcium carbonate present to neutralise the acid. Few living organisms can tolerate the increased acidity, e.g. pH 4. See Fig. 30.7 on p. 83.
Solid waste	Dumped in the oceans. 9 m tonnes are dumped annually into the ocean from New York. 5 m tonnes from London into the Outer Thames Estuary, annually. 75% of dumping in oceans is from ships.	Unsightly. Many parts float and are resistant to being worn down. Animals become entangled in wire, net, rope and plastic sheets. Some items provide new habitats for barnacles and algae.
Radioactive waste	From nuclear devices, for example, nuclear powered vessels, bomb detonations and nuclear power stations.	These are mostly low level emissions due to national legislation (laws). The corrosive powers of the sea have to be considered if containers of radioactive waste are dumped.
Oil	Shipping operations are responsible for 60% of the total losses.	Causes soiled beaches, surface films of oil, slicks and tarballs, death of marine organisms, including seabirds. See p. 80.

PRACTICAL WORK

A lichen is a simple plant formed from a **symbiotic relationship** between a **fungus** and an **alga**. The alga is green and can make food by photosynthesis. Some of this food is released to the fungus in return absorbs mineral salts from the rock or bark on which the lichen grows and forms an anchor. Most of the 'body' of the lichen is from the fungus. (See Fig. 30.8.) Lichens (and mosses) are very sensitive to pollution. A few crusty species or none at all suggests a high level of pollution. (See Fig. 30.9.)

CARRY OUT THE FOLLOWING PRACTICAL WORK:

1. Prepare a table, as below, to take out on your fieldwork. Use large sheets of line paper.

Street/Area	Zone	Observations
North St.	0	No lichens
St. John's St.	1	V. poor specimens. Discoloured. No apothecia.

2. Divide the class into working groups. Each group should cover a different section of town starting in the centre working outwards.
3. Use Fig. 30.9 to help you complete your table. Record injury symptoms such as discoloration, bleaching (reduced rate of photosynthesis), stunted growth, few fruiting bodies (apothecia).
4. Back in the classroom transfer all the zone numbers, in pencil, onto an outline map of the town.
5. Give each zone a colour. Grade the colours from high to low levels of pollution, e.g. mauve → green → yellow. Use the colours to shade in the different zones as started in Fig. 30.10.
6. Write up how and when you carried out the practical work. State the obvious!
7. Discuss the results as a class.

Write up your conclusions. Include comments on the following:
● Any patterns of zoning which emerged, e.g. concentric rings. ● Injury symptoms observed.
● Evidence from the lichens that fits in with the figures in Table 30.1. Do they make good indicators?

TABLE 30.1

Distance from City centre (km)	Mean annual SO₂ (μg/m³)
0–2·5	>240
2·5–4·0	200–240
4·0–5·5	170–200
5·5–9·0	120–170
Over 9·0	>125

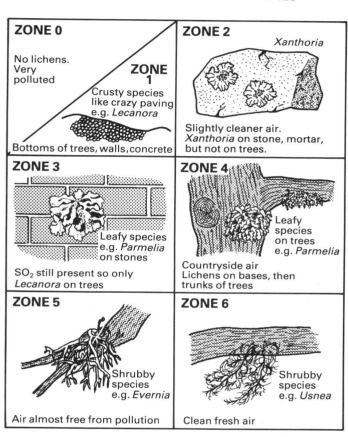

FIG. 30.9 ZONES FOR LICHENS AS POLLUTION INDICATORS

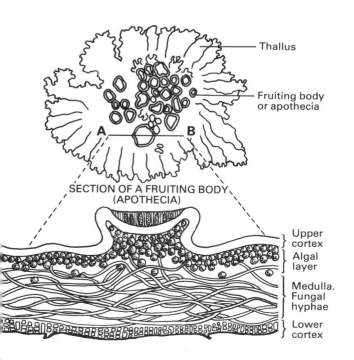

FIG. 30.8 *XANTHORIA PARIETINA* – A LEAFY LICHEN

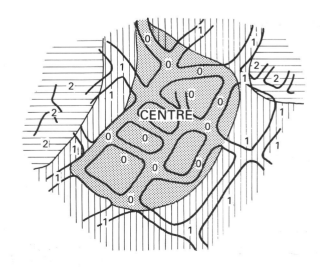

FIG. 30.10 ZONING MAP

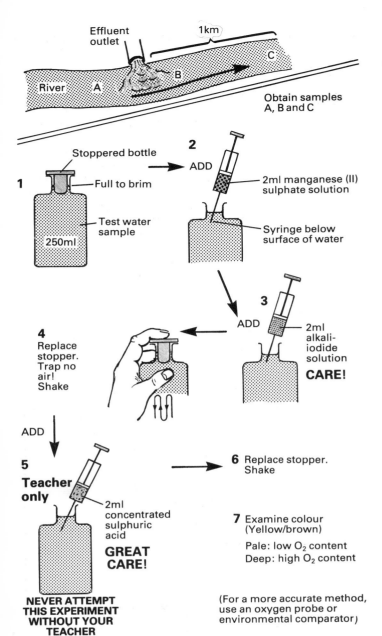

FIG. 30.11 O₂ TEST

Labels within figure:
- Effluent outlet
- 1km
- River
- A, B, C
- Obtain samples A, B and C
- Stoppered bottle
- **1** Full to brim — Test water sample — 250ml
- **2** ADD — 2ml manganese (II) sulphate solution — Syringe below surface of water
- **3** ADD — 2ml alkali-iodide solution — CARE!
- **4** Replace stopper. Trap no air! Shake
- ADD
- **5** Teacher only — 2ml concentrated sulphuric acid — GREAT CARE! — NEVER ATTEMPT THIS EXPERIMENT WITHOUT YOUR TEACHER
- **6** Replace stopper. Shake
- **7** Examine colour (Yellow/brown) — Pale: low O₂ content — Deep: high O₂ content
- (For a more accurate method, use an oxygen probe or environmental comparator)

POLLUTED RIVER STUDY

Find a river with a factory or sewage works effluent outlet. (WASH YOUR HANDS AFTER FIELDWORK!) Record the temperature of the water at points A, B and C. Take water samples at A, B and C. Freshwater animals can be good indicators of polluted water. Sample and record animals found at the three sites using the sampling techniques on p. 112.

Carry out **all** the following experiments on **each** sample back in the laboratory.

1. **Smell**. Half fill a 500 ml flask with sample water. Leave it corked for 24 hrs. Release the cork and smell carefully.
2. **Setting solids**. Allow the solids in 100 ml (1 litre) of well shaken sample water to settle in a measuring cylinder and record the height to which the solids settle. Clean water may have less than 0.5 cm³ per litre of water. Sewage may have 15 cm³ per litre of water.
3. **Frothing test**. This suggests the presence of detergents which may contain phosphates and cause eutrophication. Shake 500 ml of sample water for one minute in a closed jam jar. Time and record how long it takes for the froth to break down. Compare each sample with 500 ml of tap water and 500 ml of tap water containing ¼ teaspoonful of detergent.
4. **Oxygen content**. See Fig. 30.11.
5. **Nitrogen**. Add 4 ml of Nessler's reagent to 100 ml of a water sample. If nitrogen, in the form of ammonia, is present a yellow reaction will take place. A deeper colour indicates the presence of more nitrogen.

Tabulate the results as follows:

Sample	Above Effluent (A)	Below Effluent (B)	1 km Downstream from Effluent (C)
SMELL			
SETTLING SOLIDS			

Compare the results for the 3 sites.
Write up your results and conclusions.

LABORATORY EXPERIMENT

1. Use pretreated seeds bought from a biological supplier. (5000r means they have been exposed to 5000 röntgen of radiation etc.)
2. Sow the seeds as in Fig. 30.12.
3. Label the rows. Place in a greenhouse. Water as necessary. Observe and record at 2 day intervals.
4. Pot on seedlings which grow over 50 mm into larger pots. Continue growing until they flower.
5. Tabulate and compare the results. Write up your results and conclusions.

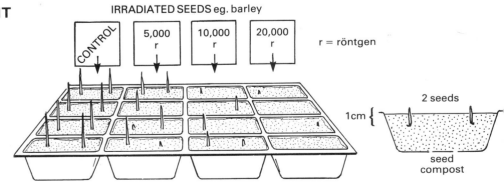

IRRADIATED SEEDS eg. barley

- CONTROL
- 5,000 r
- 10,000 r
- 20,000 r
- r = röntgen
- 2 seeds
- 1cm
- seed compost

FIG. 30.12 IRRADIATING BARLEY SEEDS

Level of Radiation	% Germination	Number to reach 100 mm	Number to Flower	Other Observations
Control	100	8	8	Sturdy
5000r	70	3		

Radioactive Pollution

Radioactive substances occur naturally in the environment. They gradually 'decay' to release energy in the form of heat and the radiation of particles from their atoms. Cosmic rays from outer space and gamma rays from the earth's crust ensure that we live with a background dose.

The activities of people and their discovery of nuclear fuels has added to the amount of **background radiation** in the environment. For example, the testing of atomic bombs in the 1950's and 1960's released radioactive 'fallout' into the upper atmosphere. Radioactive Strontium 90 was recorded thousands of miles from the test areas, in grass, milk and babies' bones. There was some evidence to suggest that it greatly increased the risk of children developing leukaemia. The Test Ban Treaty of 1963 was signed by many countries to say that they would agree not to test nuclear explosive devices in the atmosphere.

The combustion of nuclear fuels such as **uranium** in nuclear power stations is used to generate electricity. However, radioactive waste is formed from the reaction. Some is of low level radioactivity, which is released into the air, rivers and seas. Some is of high level radioactivity such as **plutonium 239**, which is very dangerous and difficult to store.

THE PROBLEMS

1. The risk of an **accident** or **major leak** of nuclear substances from the reactor core of a nuclear power station, especially as they are being built closer to urban areas.
2. The serious **damage** that could be caused **to living tissues**. The LD_{50} for man (the dose which might kill 50% of the population) has been estimated at 400 rads but is probably nearer 700 rads in healthy young adults. Nausia and vomiting might be followed in the third week after exposure by loss of hair and appetite, fever, wasting away and in some cases death.
3. Wherever radioactive substances are used, **waste** is produced which is still radioactive! No safe and permanent method has been found to dispose of this waste.
4. The long time taken for some radioactive substances to 'decay'. Plutonium 239 has a half life (i.e. it is reduced to half its quantity) of 24 000 years. Strontium 90 takes 30 years.

THE BENEFITS

Radioactive substances have had many uses since their discovery.

1. Taking **X-rays**.
2. **Radiotherapy**. Large doses of radiation are used on specific areas to kill cancerous growths in the body.
3. **Diagnosis**. Radioisotopes are given to a patient by mouth or injection. Their distribution in the body is measured with a gamma camera and the results are used to diagnose heart disease, thrombosis, liver and lung function.
Alternatively, no radioactive substance is given to the patient but samples of body fluids are taken and examined using radioactive techniques. This is very useful for monitoring hormone levels during pregnancy and checking for abnormalities.

4. **Labelled compounds**. A normal atom is replaced with a radioactive one. By **tracing** where it is this can be used, for example, to,
   - detect a leak in a pipeline.
   - learn more about genetics.
   - find out how living things move substances around their bodies. Such information could be used to develop new pesticides.
5. **Industry**. Radioisotopes are used in industrial gauges to **measure** things continuously and without physical contact, for example, the thickness of coatings and plating of foil, plastic film, paper and steel. They can also be used to check the contents of packets and cans on an assembly line.
6. **Sterilising** food and medical equipment by killing bacteria.
7. Working out the **age** of archeological specimens (Carbon14 dating)

Questions

1. Record T.V. or radio reports and keep newspaper cuttings about pollution incidents.

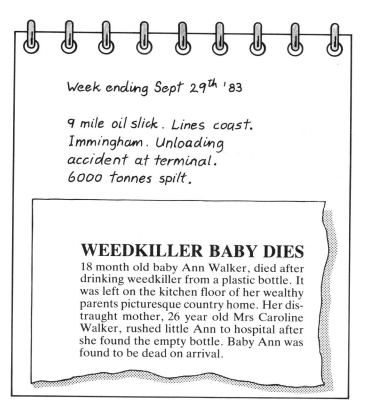

Week ending Sept 29th '83

9 mile oil slick. Lines coast. Immingham. Unloading accident at terminal. 6000 tonnes spilt.

WEEDKILLER BABY DIES
18 month old baby Ann Walker, died after drinking weedkiller from a plastic bottle. It was left on the kitchen floor of her wealthy parents picturesque country home. Her distraught mother, 26 year old Mrs Caroline Walker, rushed little Ann to hospital after she found the empty bottle. Baby Ann was found to be dead on arrival.

2. Here possible alternatives for the **disposal** of low level (a) and high level (b & c) radioactive waste:
   (a) Dilute and disperse low level waste by water or air.
   (b) Store waste in cases of concrete, steel or glass until it has decayed to less harmful levels.
   (c) Bury it at sea or underground.
   Write a criticism of each method of disposal. Here are some key words to help you. **Corrosion, earthquake, transportation, decay rates, sites**.

3. Examine the list of 'Ideas for Controlling Air Pollution' on page 82. Use your common sense and research to suggest **two** problems of each solution. For example, using taller stacks does not get rid of pollutants, it just spreads the burden further in the upper atmosphere.

31. Conservation

To preserve: to keep in its original state.
To protect: to keep from harm.
To restore: to return to its original condition.
To control: to regulate, restrain, check or test.
To conserve: to keep entire, to keep from harm, loss or decay, to retain or preserve.

Obviously the term '**conservation**' involves a great deal of protection, preservation, restoration and control within its meaning. It is easier to restore and preserve a steam locomotive or stately home than a wetland or wood as these are habitats which need to be conserved in a special way. This will involve careful monitoring and management.

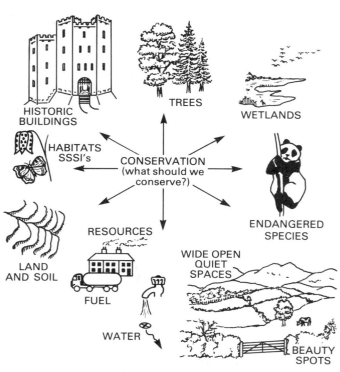

FIG. 31.1 CONSERVATION

Why Conserve?

1. Because the **world's population increases daily**. The more people there are, the greater the pressure on the same amount of land. It has been estimated that every individual needs approximately 5 hectares to support them.
2. Because of **improved methods of farming**. More intensive methods are now being used to provide food for a growing population using machinery and chemicals. The effect of this is to reduce wildlife habitats.
3. Because of the **consumption of natural resources**. People are rapidly using up raw materials such as timber, oil, gas, coal and minerals. Water is often heavily polluted and land spoiled.
4. In order to **plan ahead**. So that we don't leave an ugly, polluted and wasted countryside, lacking all natural resources to our children and children's children.

Questions

1. **The Country Code**
   (a) What might be the consequences if people don't follow these codes?
   Fasten all gates. Take your litter home. Keep dogs under close control. Keep to public paths across farmland.
   (b) How would you
   Guard against fire?
   Make no unneccessary noise?
   Help to keep water clean and free from dangers such as glass or fishing line?
   (c) Why is it sensible to
   Use gates and stiles to cross fences, hedges and walls?
   Leave livestock, crops and machinery alone?
   Take special care when driving on country roads?
   Explain all your answers.

2. **North Sea Oil**. Organise a short discussion in your class using three teams of pupils to represent the following groups:
   (a) Side 1. Represent the views of a government who want to save their economy from disaster by boosting it with the income from the oil revenue.
   (b) Side 2. Represent the view of the oil company who wants quick profits.
   (c) Side 3. Represent the views of the conservationists who would like to see production spread over a greater number of years.
   After hearing all the 'evidence' write up your own opinion about how North Sea Oil should be produced and consumed up to and beyond the year 2000.

FIG. 31.2 ASTON ROWANT NATIONAL NATURE RESERVE OXON

THE NATURE CONSERVANCY COUNCIL

The NCC is a government organisation. Its main functions are:

1. To promote nature conservation in Great Britain.
2. To advise the government on nature conservation.
3. To select, establish and manage more than 200 **National Nature Reserves** covering over 150 000 ha. These are either owned by the NCC, leased or an agreement is made with the owner. They include some of the best examples of different types of habitat.
4. To carry out ecological research, looking into, for example, the effect of sheep grazing on chalk grassland to find out the best ways of maintaining it with its typical plants and animals.
5. To identify the most important places for wildlife as **Sites of Special Scientific Interest** (SSSI). There are over 4500 **SSSI** on another 1.5 million hectares. The **Wildlife and Countryside Act 1981** now requires the owners or occupiers to tell the NCC if they intend to carry out any operation, e.g. draining or spraying, which may damage the SSSI. The NCC can then advise on a less harmful approach or offer some financial help to avoid such action.
6. To promote public awareness, using information books, reports and leaflets. *Wildlife, the Law and You*, sponsored by Shell is a must for your studies. It stresses the main points about the law of protecting species in the 1981 Act.

- Killing, injuring, taking or selling animals, such as the otter, badger and red squirrel is against the law.

- Disturbing them in their places of shelter is also against the law.

- All wild birds, their nests and eggs are protected (with exceptions for pest and sporting species) and there are special penalties for harming certain rarities.

- Specially protected plants must not be uprooted, picked or sold and uprooting any wild plant is illegal.

THE COUNTRYSIDE COMMISSION replaced the National Parks Commission under the Countryside Act, 1968.

1. It has the power to designate National Parks in England and Wales.
2. It advises the government on National Park policies, administration and finance.
3. It keeps under review all matters relating to conservation and enhancing the natural beauty of the countryside in general.
4. It is required to provide and improve facilities for the public to enjoy the countryside.
5. It produces many reports and publicity material.
6. It can grant aid to certain projects, for example, providing and maintaining recreational footpaths and long distance paths.

THE ROYAL SOCIETY FOR NATURE CONSERVATION (RSNC) This is a voluntary organisation. It is the national association for 40

Nature Conservation Trusts which covered Great Britain by 1965. For example, **BBONT** is the Naturalist Trust for Bucks, Berks and Oxon. The RSNC advises and gives assistance to the trusts. It represents them at national level. In 1915 it was the body who proposed that conservation in the future should be the responsibility of the government and worked towards the creation of the Nature Conservancy Council. Its other main priorities are to raise money, to select, acquire, fund and manage over 1000 **local nature reserves** and to educate the public with its pamphlets, conferences and visitor centres at the reserves. It also advises local authorities, water authorities and farmers about the management of wildlife habitats.

Caswell Bay, S Gower

FIG. 31.3 VIEWS FROM TWO SSSI

Annet, Isles of Scilly

© Nature Conservancy Council

FRIENDS OF THE EARTH (FoE) This is an environmental pressure group. They are part of a world wide organisation and get their funds from voluntary contributions. They campaign for example, for the better use of national resources, the protection of endangered species, the better use of land etc. In the 1970's they led 'The Resource Campaign' to try and persuade the public, manufacturers and governments that they were wasting raw materials such as timber and metal, by not recycling it. (See p. 79.) Below is an eye catching poster from their publicity material, 'If you go down to the woods today . . .'.

'If you go down to the woods today . . .'

Friends of the Earth

THE WORLD WILDLIFE FUND (WWF) The WWF is an international organisation working in Britain and 24 other countries. It raises money for conservation projects all over the world especially for the protection of threatened wild animals, plants and their habitats.

THE INTERNATIONAL UNION FOR THE CONSERVATION OF NATURE AND NATURAL RESOURCES (IUCN) This is another international body representing over 100 countries. It has a staff of expert scientists concerned with conservation. It advises nations and helps them to see the need for national parks and nature reserves. It advises the WWF and suggests which projects are the most urgent for each year.

Founded in 1904 **THE ROYAL SOCIETY FOR THE PROTECTION OF BIRDS (RSPB)** aims to:
- encourage the conservation of wild birds by arousing public interest in their beauty and place in nature
- carry out scientific research
- enforce protection laws
- manage over 100 reserves
- educate the public with films, 'BIRDS' magazine etc.

The society has a membership for over 412 000 and also a Young Ornithologists Club (up to age 14) of 80 000.

THE NATIONAL TRUST

This was founded in 1895. It works for the preservation of places of historic interest and natural beauty in the United Kingdom. As a charity it depends on voluntary support from the public. It is the largest private landowner and conservation society in Britain. Its properties include unspoilt coastline, fells, dales, lakes, forests, 22 whole villages, 109 gardens and 274 historic buildings open to visitors. The latter are often given to the Trust by their former owners with an endowment for their future upkeep.

One of their properties in Kinder Scout in the Peak District National Park, for which they had to raise £200 000 in an emergency appeal. (See Fig. 32.1 on p. 91.)

Find out more about the work of the following organisations:
The Society for the Protection of Rural England. The Ramblers Association. Greenpeace. The British Trust for Conservation Volunteers.

Bodiam Castle

Waddesdon Manor

FIG. 31.4 HISTORIC BUILDINGS

West Wycombe Park

Mike Shorthouse

32. National Parks

The first national park was founded in Yellowstone, U.S.A. in 1872. It took until 1945 for the National Parks Committee to be set up in England and Wales, followed by the National Parks and Access to the Countryside Act in 1949. This act was set up for 'the purpose of preserving and enhancing the natural beauty of the areas specified . . . and for the purpose of promoting their enjoyment by the public.'

Ten parks were designated under the supervision of the National Parks Commission. (See Table 32.1.) They cover 9% of the total land area in England and Wales. The Countryside Act of 1968 transformed the National Parks Commission into the Countryside Commission with much more responsibility for recreation in the countryside as a whole. After the re-organisation of local government in 1974 each park now has its own committee or planning board, whose first job was to produce a national park plan.

Questions

1. Fig. 32.1 points out some of the conflicts in National Parks. (See boxes.) Discuss each one and write down why they might arise and what could be done to remedy them.
2. Use an atlas to check the locations of the National Parks. What have the majority got in common? How are they located in relation to the main centres of population?
3. Who owns the land in the National Parks? Do you think the name National Park totally suitable?

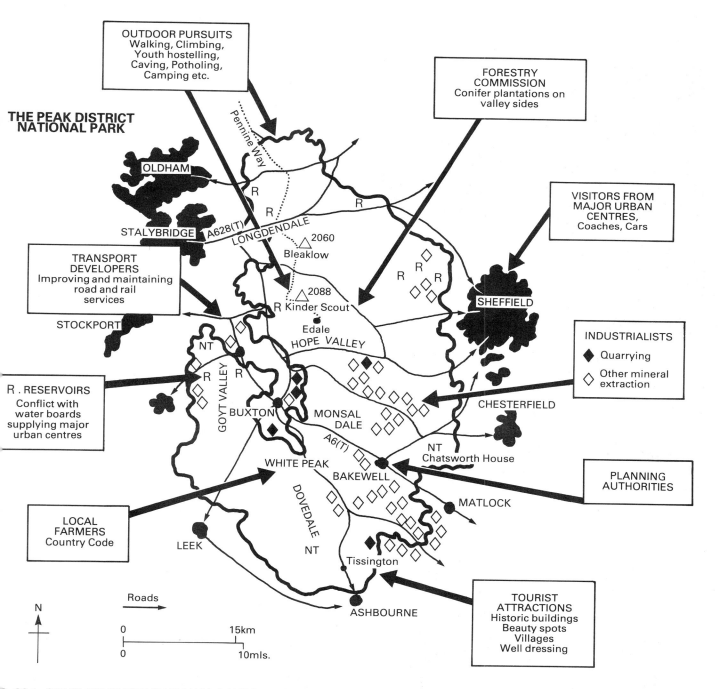

Fig. 32.1 CONFLICT IN THE NATIONAL PARKS

Countryside Commission

FIG. 32.2 LOOKING DOWN THE HARTHORPE VALLEY,
NORTHUMBERLAND: A NATIONAL PARK

National Park	Date of Confirmation	Area Designated (km²)	Population 1971
Peak District	1951	1404	36 708
Lake District	1951	2243	44 050
Snowdonia	1951	2171	26 272
Dartmoor	1951	945	28 064
Pembrokeshire coast	1952	583	20 553
North York Moors	1952	1432	21 800
Yorkshire Dales	1954	1761	18 189
Exmoor	1954	686	10 458
Northumberland	1956	1031	3 297
Brecon Beacons	1957	1344	29 372
Totals		13 600	238 763

TABLE 32.1 NATIONAL PARKS IN ENGLAND AND WALES

As from 1 April 1989, the Norfolk and Suffolk Broads
will have the status and responsibilities of a National
Park. (Area 280 km². Population 5500.)

COUNTRY PARKS

After the Countryside Act 1968, local authorities were
encouraged to provide, equip and manage country
parks. These are small areas of countryside (but not less
than 10 ha/25 acres) near to urban areas which would
help to reduce the pressure on national parks. There are
over 120 approved country parks in Great Britain to
which the public are allowed access for **informal
outdoor recreation**. They have basic facilities such as
car parks, lavatories and wardens.
Recreational amenities may include walks, nature study
routes and display centres, fishing, sailing, riding,
gardens, picnic areas etc. The park may receive extra
financial help from the Countryside Commission to help
buy land, provide facilities, clear litter etc.

AONB

There are 33 **Areas of Outstanding Natural Beauty**
covering about 10% of England and Wales (14500
sq. km). They are all scenically attractive but the
landscapes are very varied. Some examples are the
rolling hills of the Lincolnshire Wolds, the wooded
valley of the River Wye, beautiful coastlines such as the
Gower Peninsula or areas important for tourism such as
Cornwall or the Isle of Wight (see Fig. 32.5). Up to the
present day local authorities have controlled their
development. There have been problems, such as:

● the area may cover land administered by several local
authorities,

● most of the farming and forestry activities have been
outside their planning control,

● they don't have to provide recreation facilities,
although these areas attract visitors, especially in
cars.

The Countryside Commission is now suggesting that
each AONB has its own committee (like the National
Parks) to plan and manage the area. It is hoped that this
would improve the beauty and character of the areas by
bringing about more harmony between planning
authorities, inappropriate development, public
enjoyment, improvement of farming and forestry, and
conservation.

LONG DISTANCE FOOTPATHS

These are continuous routes over 100 km long, open to
walkers and in some cases cyclists and horse-riders.
They cross some of the finest countryside in England
and Wales, usually through National Parks and AONB
avoiding motorist routes. By 1983 12 were open, the
first being the Pennine Way in 1965. (See Fig. 32.5.) All
are marked with the **acorn** symbol. Good maps and a
compass may also be needed. They can be used for
short walks lasting an hour or a day or for walks lasting
two or three weeks including camping or the use of
local accommodation. Setting up a path recommended
by the Countryside Commission means that public
rights of way have to be negotiated with the
landowners by the local authorities. Grants of 100% are
paid to the local authorities by the Exchequer for the
upkeep of the paths and compensation to landowners.

Recreational paths are named paths longer than
10 km but much shorter than long distance paths,
attractive for a family stroll or a more serious walk, also
in scenic or interesting countryside. Examples are the
Tissington Trail (Peak District), the Derwent Walk (Co.
Durham) and the Staffordshire Way.

FIG. 32.3 DERWENT WALK, COUNTRY PARK AND
RECREATIONAL PATH

Questions

1. What is the difference between a country park and a
national park? Which authorities are responsible for
each? Why are country parks an important addition
to recreational facilities near major centres of
population?

2. What is the difference between a long distance path
and a recreational path?

3. Write your own account, complete with a sketch
map, of **one** long distance path. Describe what it
offers the walker and how it can be used as a
recreational facility. (See Fig. 32.5)
*Ref. Long Distance Path by the Countryside
Commission.*

4. Study the newspaper cutting. It hints at one problem
recently reported in a national park.
What is a 'honeypot'?
What has been done to remedy the problem by the
park's committee? Was this the ideal solution?

Trampling feet put a blight on honeypots

BELOW the shining limestone cliff at Malham Cove in the Yorkshire Dales, a surprise awaits walkers who return this spring to this dramatic beauty spot – a stone staircase cut into the 240ft sheer precipice.

They were completed just before Easter, convenient for those who wish to reach the superb viewpoint above, but as officials of the Yorkshire Dales national park readily admit, are "rather drastic in an unspoilt area".

Such artificial features are becoming more common at the most popular beauty spots, known as "honeypots" because they attract the greatest swarm of visitors. The question worrying national park and other countryside planners is: how can the honeypots' natural beauty be preserved while providing facilities for the holiday hordes?

The Sunday Times, 10 April 1983

FIG. 32.4 HERITAGE COAST, GOWER PENINSULA (Park Mill looking towards Three Cliffs Bay)

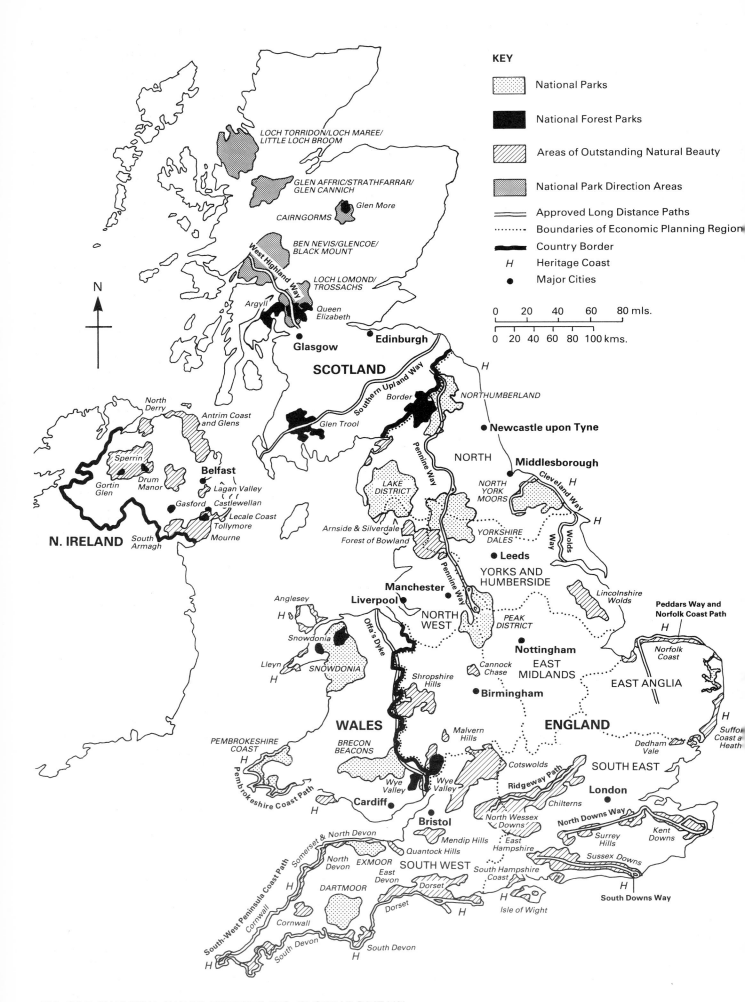

KEY

National Parks

National Forest Parks

Areas of Outstanding Natural Beauty

National Park Direction Areas

Approved Long Distance Paths

Boundaries of Economic Planning Region

Country Border

H Heritage Coast

● Major Cities

0   20   40   60   80 mls.

0   20   40   60   80   100 kms.

N

SCOTLAND

LOCH TORRIDON/LOCH MAREE/ LITTLE LOCH BROOM

GLEN AFFRIC/STRATHFARRAR/ GLEN CANNICH

Glen More

CAIRNGORMS

BEN NEVIS/GLENCOE/ BLACK MOUNT

West Highland Way

LOCH LOMOND/ TROSSACHS

Argyll

Queen Elizabeth

Glasgow

Edinburgh

Southern Upland Way

Border

NORTHUMBERLAND

H

Newcastle upon Tyne

Glen Trool

NORTH

Middlesborough

Cleveland Way

H

Pennine Way

NORTH YORK MOORS

LAKE DISTRICT

H

Wolds Way

YORKSHIRE DALES

North Derry

Antrim Coast and Glens

Sperrin

Belfast

Gortin Glen

Drum Manor

Lagan Valley

Gasford

Castlewellan

Lecale Coast

Tollymore

N. IRELAND

South Armagh

Mourne

Arnside & Silverdale

Forest of Bowland

Leeds

YORKS AND HUMBERSIDE

Lincolnshire Wolds

Anglesey

Manchester

Liverpool

NORTH WEST

PEAK DISTRICT

H

H

Snowdonia

Offa's Dyke

Peddars Way and Norfolk Coast Path

Lleyn

SNOWDONIA

H

Nottingham

Cannock Chase

EAST MIDLANDS

Norfolk Coast

H

EAST ANGLIA

Shropshire Hills

Birmingham

WALES

Malvern Hills

ENGLAND

Suffolk Coast and Heath

H

PEMBROKESHIRE COAST

BRECON BEACONS

Cotswolds

SOUTH EAST

Dedham Vale

H

Wye Valley

Wye Valley

Ridgeway Path

London

Pembrokeshire Coast Path

Cardiff

H

Chilterns

Bristol

North Wessex Downs

North Downs Way

Somerset & North Devon

Mendip Hills

East Hampshire

Surrey Hills

Kent Downs

North Devon

EXMOOR

SOUTH WEST

Quantock Hills

Sussex Downs

East Devon

South Hampshire Coast

DARTMOOR

Dorset

H

South-West Peninsula Coast Path

Cornwall

Cornwall

Dorset

Isle of Wight

H

H

South Downs Way

South Devon

South Devon

H

FIG. 32.5 NATIONAL PARKS, FORESTS ETC. IN GREAT BRITAIN

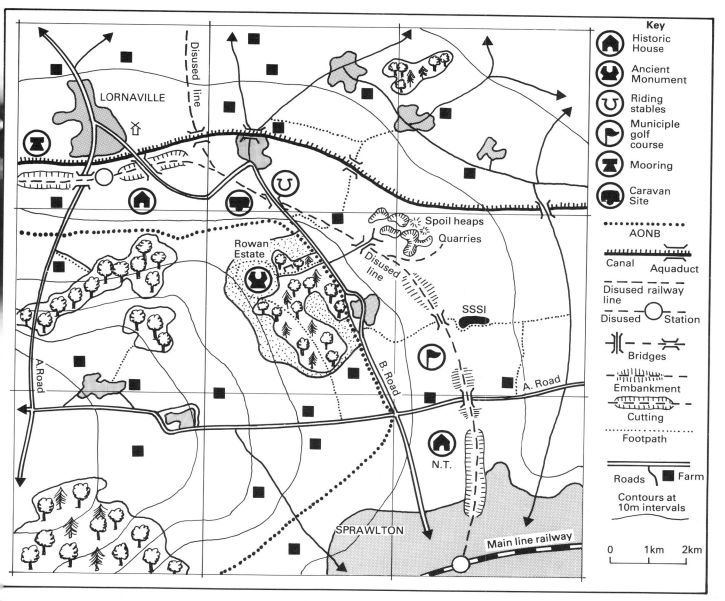

Key

(house)	Historic House
(monument)	Ancient Monument
(U)	Riding stables
(flag)	Municiple golf course
(mooring)	Mooring
(caravan)	Caravan Site

- - - - - AONB

Canal   Aquaduct

Disused railway line

Disused ◯ Station

Bridges

Embankment

Cutting

······· Footpath

═══ Roads   ■ Farm

Contours at 10m intervals

0   1km   2km

LORNAVILLE

Rowan Estate

Spoil heaps

Quarries

Disused line

SSSI

B. Road

A. Road

N.T.

SPRAWLTON

Main line railway

FIG. 32.6

COUNTRY PARK SIMULATION EXERCISE

The planning department of the local authority hope to develop a **country park** in this area encorporating some of the existing recreational facilities and offering as many informal outdoor recreational pursuits as possible. They aim to provide for the large population to the south and east of the mapped area and to relieve the pressure in the AONB. The disused railway has already been bought by the local authority with a view to making it the axis or corridor in which the facilities will be focussed. Rowan estate is huge but privately owned. Access to the ancient monument has been restricted to a limited number of days in the year.

1. What do you understand by the term country park?
2. What is an SSSI?
3. Suggest two ways in which a disused railway line could be used as a recreational facility. Suggest two such uses for a disused station. Suggest two uses for a disused railway yard.
4. If you were a planning officer what arguments would you put in favour of the disused line being the axis or corridor of the park?
5. Assuming you have little difficulty acquiring necessary land and access, within reason, explain:
   (a) where you would develop water sports facilities and what form they would take,
   (b) where you would develop facilities including at least one circular walk,
   (c) at least **three** places where you might develop car parking and lavatories, picnic sites and at least **one** wardens' centre,
   (d) **three** places where you would expect to carry out some landscaping with trees and shrubs.
   (e) where you would develop other amenities which have not so far been mentioned (at least **two**).
6. Where might be the potential problem areas for the warden? Are there any areas or facilities which may be vulnerable to overuse?
7. Using a **tracing overlay** outline the area you would define as the country park. Mark all the facilities you would include (those pre-existing and those you have mentioned above) inventing symbols where necessary.

33. Chokeham

Chokeham is a typical small town congested with local and through traffic. Imagine the scene: **parked cars, narrow roads, moving vehicles, heavy lorries, rush hour, traffic jams, accidents, pedestrians, noise, fumes, vibrations, traffic lights, crossing and headaches!**

What are the alternatives?
1. **Improve traffic flow using:**
   ● One-way systems.
   ● Bus lanes.
   ● Better car parking.

2. **Discourage vehicles from using the centre or CBD.**
   ● Parking restrictions.
   ● Pedestrian precincts.
   ● Park and ride. (Good povision of car parks, including multistorey, on the perimeters of the most congested area.)

3. **Widen roads.** Apart from the removal of parked car this is often impossible in an old town centre where buildings would have to be demolished.

4. **Construct a ring road.**

5. **Build a bypass.**

6. Have a **public transport option**, for example, an underground or rapid transit system.

Questions

1. Make your own copy of Fig. 33.1. Prepare a transparent overlay of the same size.
2. Discuss the alternatives 1–5 for relieving Chokeham of its traffic problem in the town centre, where the roads are narrower.
3. Firstly, work out what short term improvements you could make using alternatives 1–2. Mark them on your plan (in pencil first) and explain the reasons for your suggestions in writing.
4. Secondly, assume that some financial help from the government will be granted to build a ring road or bypass.
   Mark in red on the overlay your idea of improving the road system using these alternatives assuming there was an unlimited budget.
5. Now consider these points:
   ● **The cost.** Every 2 km of ring road or bypass on your plan will cost £1 million. A roundabout or bridge will cost £200 000.
   ● **The industrial estates.** Should a new road system offer easier access to the estates or will the short term improvements be sufficient?
   ● **Physical problems**, e.g. marsh.
   ● **Major objections.** e.g. by landowners, villagers.
   If you were given a **budget of £3½ million** work out two possible improved systems. Mark them in blue and green on your overlay.
6. Make a final decision and mark the budget route in red on your actual plan.
7. Complete your written report for the town council explaining why you think your system is the best.

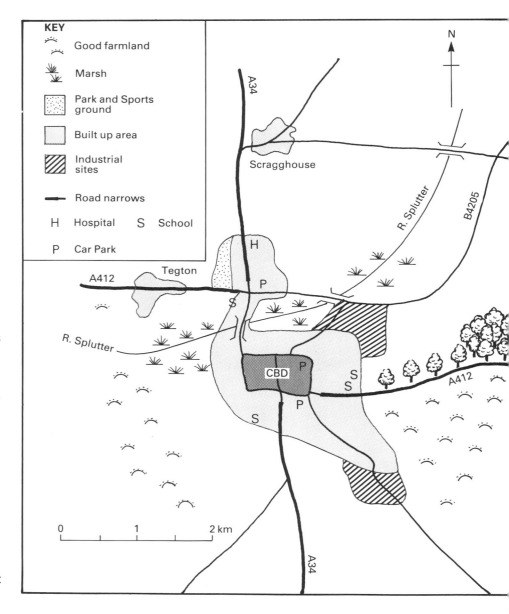

KEY

~ Good farmland

Marsh

Park and Sports ground

Built up area

Industrial sites

Road narrows

H Hospital   S School
P Car Park

N

A34
Scragghouse
R. Splutter
B4205
H
P
A412   Tegton
S
R. Splutter
CBD   P
S
S
P
S
A412
A34

0   1   2 km

FIG. 33.1 CHOKEHAM. AN IMAGINARY CASE OF TRAFFIC CONGESTION

34. Southam Airport

Noise is unwanted sound. An enjoyable sound for some might be unacceptable to others. Certain daytime noises might be irritating at night. High levels of noise may lead to permanent deafness if they are endured for long periods of time. The milk production of dairy herds kept in the vicinity of airports has been known to fall.
Noise levels are measured in decibels. (See p. 81.)

TYPE OF NOISE	DECIBELS
Normal breathing	10
Quiet office	40
Conversation	60
Average car/ Vacuum cleaner at 3 m	70
Heavy traffic	90
Damage to hearing on prolonged exposure	80—90
Jet overhead/ Lorries	100
Unsilenced motorcycle	110
Jet taking off/ landing	120
Loud disco music	120
Threshold of pain	120–130
Thunderclap	140

With heavier traffic moving on urban roads not designed to carry it the noise levels have increased greatly in recent years. Air traffic noise, however, is even louder and affects more people over a wider area.

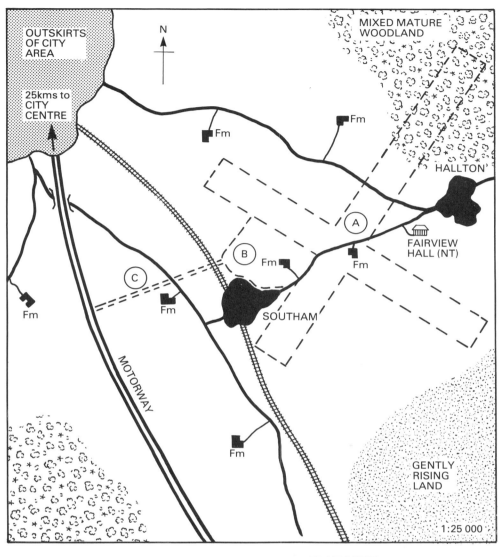

FIG. 34.1 THE SITING OF A NEW AIRPORT. A SIMULATION EXERCISE

The map in Fig. 34.1 shows an area just beyond the built-up suburbs of a large city and some 25 km from the city centre. It is a rural area with two villages and a number of farms. The land is fertile and fairly flat. Market gardening and other arable agriculture is practiced.

A motorway and main-line railway run from the city across the south-west corner of the area. A number of local roads serve the villages and farms. The mature woodland provides a suitable habitat for a number of rare species of butterflies and wild flowers. Fairview Hall is an important example of a tudor manor-house and is a much visited National Trust property.

The government are searching for a suitable site for the construction of a second airport to serve the city. They require a large, flat area with good access to the city. Fig. 34.1 shows how the proposed airport would fit into the area. (A–Runways, B–terminal buildings, C–link motorway.)

Questions

1. Write a report for the government outlining the **advantages** of this site for a new airport. Include as much detail as possible such as:
   - the suitability of existing communications and the ease or difficulty of improving them,
   - safety problems,
   - disturbance, noise, loss of homes and livelihoods
2. These local interest groups are **against** the siting and construction of the airport:
   (a) the villagers,
   (b) the farmers (the two most northerly farms are dairy farms),
   (c) the National Trust,
   (d) another **named** organisation of your choice.
   Prepare a case for each, explaining carefully their objections.
3. What would be **your** final decision on whether or not to build the airport? Remember to consider both local and national interests.

97

35. Roads

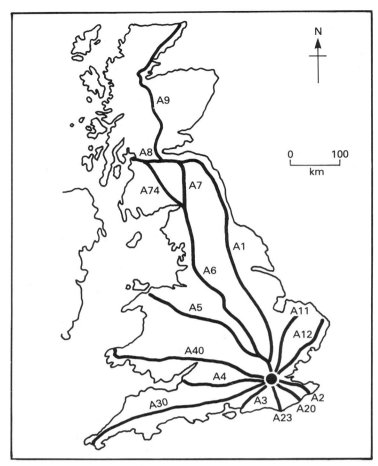

FIG. 35.1 'A' CLASS TRUNK ROADS IN GREAT BRITAIN

Much of the road network in Great Britain is based on an ancient system more suited to the drovers, packhorses and coaches which were the main means of transport before the industrial revolution. The old roads followed valleys and boundaries formed by enclosures. They avoided hills, gradients and water as far as possible. As industrial towns developed, new roads (**turnpikes**) and bridges were built. Money was raised by **tolls** to meet the expense. Telford and MacAdam brought about huge improvements before there was a decline in the use of roads brought about by the railway boom.

Roads have come under increasing pressure since the increase in the number of licensed vehicles after the First and Second World Wars. General improvements and by-passes were not sufficient in themselves to cope with the increase. After 1956 a system of motorways was developed. (See Fig. 35.2) The 'H' arrangement or 'figure of 8' serves the major centres of population well but leaves the other areas devoid of motorways. Fig. 35.1 shows the main trunk roads which supplement the system. In 1985 there were 21.2 million licensed vehicles on over 346 900 km of road.

Questions

1. Work out how many licensed vehicles there are to every kilometre of road in Great Britain.
2. Unfortunately, the number of vehicles, their wear and tear on the roads, is not spread out evenly. How would you measure traffic **flow** (how many vehicles there are on the road daily) and traffic **trends** (which kinds of traffic are increasingly using the roads) in order to investigate whether a road needs to be improved?

Year	Private Cars	Heavy Goods Vehicles*
1974	13 399	677
1975	13 517	668
1976	13 792	647
1978	13 801	606
1979	14 307	624
1980	14 772	574
1981	14 943	558
1982	15 303	549
1983	15 543	565
1984	16 055	576
1985	16 453	582

*Heavy goods vehicles = greater than $3\frac{1}{2}$ tonnes unladen but not less than $1\frac{1}{2}$ tonnes unladen.

3. Graph the figures in the table above. Use suitable symbols to show the difference between private cars and goods vehicles.
   Comment on your findings.
4. Find out if there is a limit to the size of lorries on British roads.
   (a) What is it?
   (b) Has it increased in recent years?
   (c) Why might environmentalists be against further increases?
   (d) What alternatives are there to carrying goods (freight) around the countryside?
       How might such alternatives be encouraged?
   (e) What do you think about the idea of banning lorries over a certain size from 'B' class and minor roads?
5. According to most Americans vehicles and roads in the USA are 'bigger and better'. Carry out your own research into the American system. Write an essay on this subject, bearing in mind the size, population and lifestyle of the USA.

What are the advantages a motorway offers over an ordinary road?
- A direct route between major settlements.
- A quick journey
- The capacity to carry more vehicles.
- Less accidents. A safer journey due to:
  The separation of opposing streams of traffic,
  Six lanes (usually) and a hard shoulder for emergency stops,
  Infrequent exits, less junctions, an absence of right turns and slip-roads for ease of joining and leaving,
  No sharp bends, or gradients, embankments in valleys and cuttings through hills.
- A reduction in unnecessary town traffic.
- A reduction in congestion on other routes.
- A possible increase in firms and employment close to the route of the motorway.
- A reduction in the cost of delivered goods due to:
  Larger loads being carried,
  Less time taken over delivery,
  Firms reducing the number of vehicles they need to own.

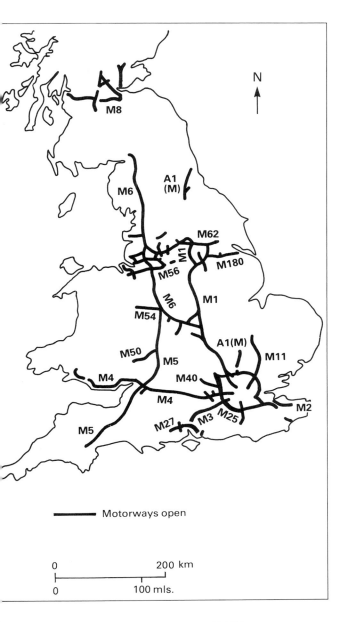

Motorways open

0 ——————— 200 km

0 ——————— 100 mls.

FIG. 35.2 MOTORWAYS IN GREAT BRITAIN

CONSIDERATIONS

Monotony for drivers. Some curves and gradients have to be introduced to break the monotony.

Scale. Cuttings, embankments. bridges and viaducts are very expensive and require skilled engineering and building on a huge scale. Few companies have the capital, equipment or expertise for such a contract.

Route. The route must be carefully planned so that gentle curves and gradients can be used. Underlying rock must be checked for firm foundations,

Effect on the landscape. The completed motorway should blend in with its surroundings. Special consideration should be given to avoid damaging areas of outstanding beauty or scientific interest.

Planning. More time is often taken planning than it is building to try and safeguard everyone's interests. Public enquiries are held to allow everyone to voice their opinions.

Effect on people. New industrial development may be attracted along the line of the motorway, especially at interchanges. This creates new jobs. House prices may be affected, going up in desirable commuter areas and down in urban areas where demolition close to a motorway hasn't taken place, or where it passes uncomfortably close. Houses may be demolished. Land may be compulsorily purchased. Farmers may lose their farms or have them split in two.

Inconvenience. During construction, increased works traffic results in pollution, traffic jams and other incoveniences for local communities.

Cost. All gains and losses, both commercial and social, liable to be made along a proposed route are given a **monetary value.** This is known to the engineers and planners as a **cost-benefit analysis.** The whole project must prove to be worth the cost. It has been roughly estimated that in 1984 an urban dual three way motorway cost £7.5 million per km. The M25 involved many compulsory purchases, public enquiries and subsiduary work. An average estimated cost per kilometre for 1986 might be £4.7 million.

Loss of land. Motorways use a lot of land. It is estimated that interchanges alone take between 4 hectares (diamond shape) and 30 hectares (4 level interchange).

Footnote. Motorway construction costs per km vary significantly depending on the standard and location of the road concerned. The figure represents very broad average costs. In addition to work expenditure other costs may add between 20% and 30% onto the costs of building motorways.

FIG. 35.3 THE WESTWAY, A40(M)

36. M40 Inquiry

Wed 25/8/82

SAVE OTMOOR MOVE DEFEATED

The Oxfordshire County Council's environmental committee has backed by one vote, the Government proposal that the M40 should run across Otmoor.

Wed 18/9/81

Bicester's long awaited bypass should open the same time as the M40 extension through the area, junior transport Minister Kenneth Clarke announced this week.

Mr Hollis has always campaigned that unless the bypass were built at the same time as the M40 the town would become a huge funnel for traffic trying to reach the motorway.

Wed 29/9/82

... the proposed M40 extension would be delayed by three or more years if the route across Otmoor were not used.

Wed 6/10/82

... could bring new jobs to towns along the route, claimed the Secretary of the M40 Support Group.

Wed 8/12/82

... 'attempt to solve too many traffic problems at one go'.

Wed 15/12/82

FLOODS COULD SPOIL FARMLAND

Farmland at one of Oxfordshire's most unspoiled and beautiful spots

could be flooded if the M40 extension is built on the proposed rou ... the Department of Transport h not allowed for the poor drainage the area ... it is estimated that t noise levels for the farm will rise 62 decibels.

Wed 19/1/

He added that the Friends of t Earth were very concerned at t impact of the motorway on Otmo and Bernwood Forest. The ent Otmoor area has been designated being of special scientific intere with Bernwood Forest as a natio ally famous butterfly sanctuary. I the home for 29 types of butter including the rare marsh fritillary ... It would be a disaster to put t M40 across Otmoor because of t dangers of sudden fog, it w claimed at the inquiry ... ... Unexploded bombs, undetect for over 20 years, could seriou endanger the lives of men buildi the M40 extension ...

Wed 26/1/

... the possibilities of the effects accidents, traffic pile-ups and so become horrific and qu unacceptable.

Wed 2/2/

A motorway across Otmoor cou never be hidden ... the damp cl foundations, drainage problems a fog would mean the motorw would have to be raised on an er bankment ... ... Fencott and Murcott have bee regarded as one community f hundreds of years, and the moto way running between the two wou be an immense physical barrier di iding them. ... The three mile Green Belt str between the city and the motorw would be seen as 'dead' land in which industry and housing cou naturally expand, the former Mast of St. Catherine's warned.

Wed 23/3/

The proposed M40 extension is a extravagant luxury, according to t Council for the Protection of Rur England ... the council's secreta said the £235 million of publ money it would cost to extend t M40 would reduce travelling tim between Oxford and Birmingham b only 17 minutes.

Wed 27/4/

... the Friends of the Earth a planning a scheme which coul throw thousands of legal snags in t way.

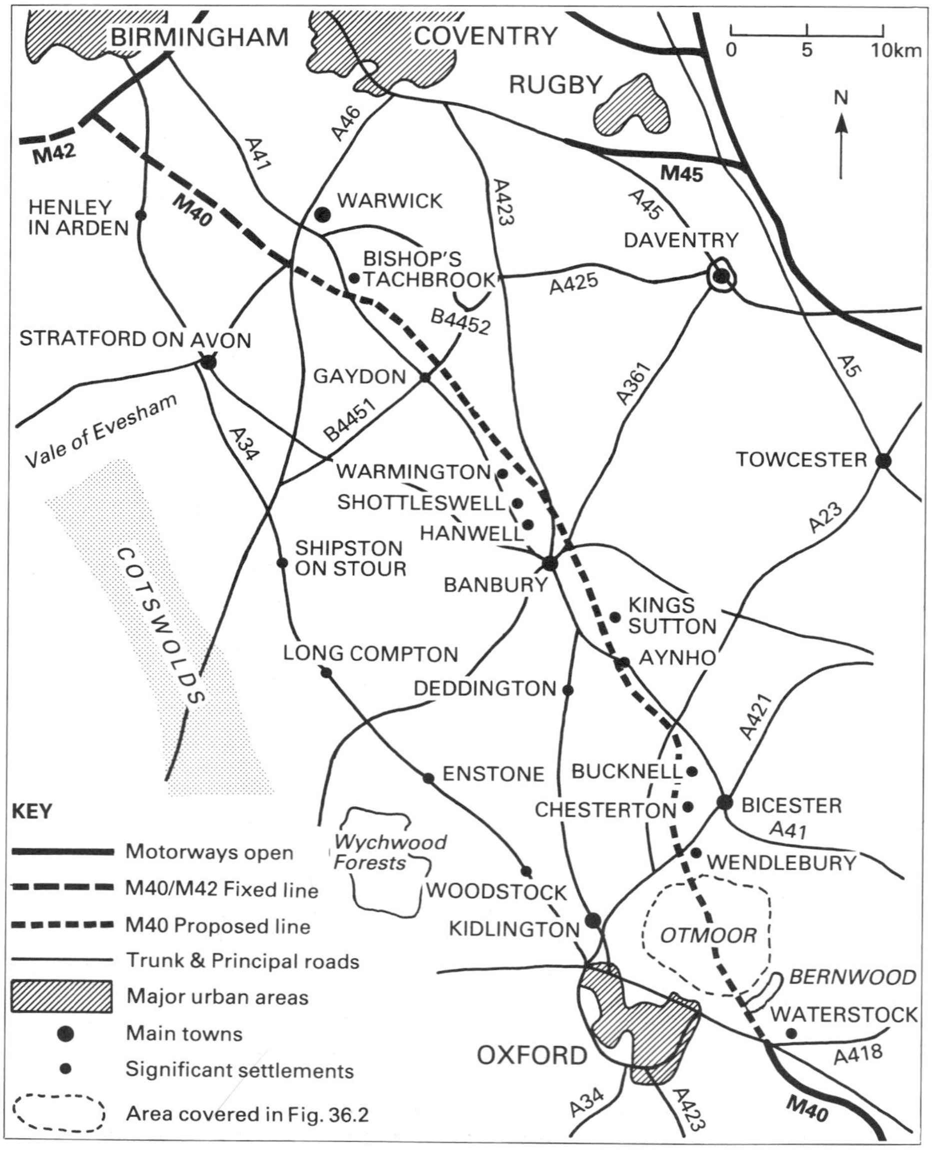

FIG. 36.1 PROPOSED ROUTE OF THE M40

KEY
- Motorways open
- M40/M42 Fixed line
- M40 Proposed line
- Trunk & Principal roads
- Major urban areas
- Main towns
- Significant settlements
- Area covered in Fig. 36.2

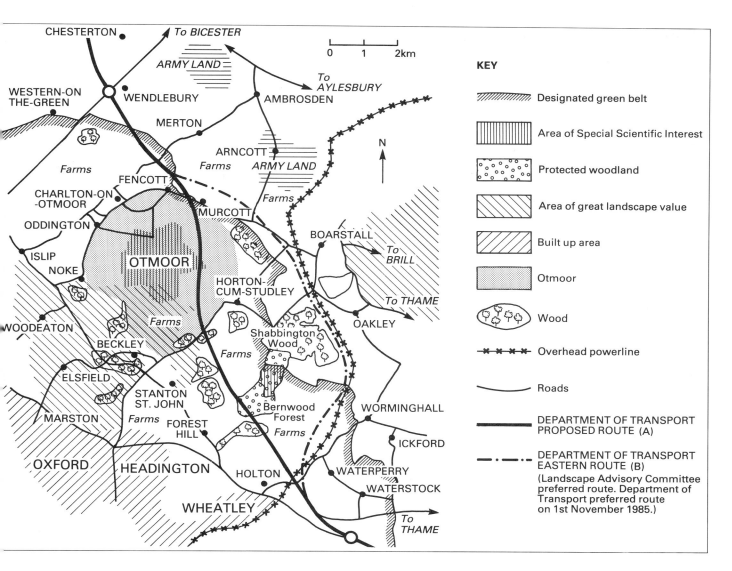

FIG. 36.2 TWO ALTERNATIVE ROUTES

KEY

/////////	Designated green belt
‖‖‖‖‖‖	Area of Special Scientific Interest
∷∷∷∷∷	Protected woodland
⧄⧄⧄⧄	Area of great landscape value
⧄⧄⧄⧄	Built up area
░░░░░	Otmoor
🌳🌳🌳	Wood
✕✕✕✕	Overhead powerline
⎯⎯⎯	Roads
▬▬▬▬	DEPARTMENT OF TRANSPORT PROPOSED ROUTE (A)
─·─·─	DEPARTMENT OF TRANSPORT EASTERN ROUTE (B) (Landscape Advisory Committee preferred route. Department of Transport preferred route on 1st November 1985.)

Questions

1. Study Fig. 36.1 and Fig. 36.2
   Read all the newspaper cuttings.

2. Draw a table similar to the one below and list all the organisations which were represented at the public enquiry according to the newspaper cuttings. Complete the table by saying which ones were for and which ones were against the M40 extension. Briefly outline their argument.

Organisation	For	Against	Brief account of their argument
CPRE		√	Money would be better spent improving the present road system.

3. Did any individual landowners raise any important issues at the inquiry which were particularly in the public's interest?
   Explain your answers.

4. What made Otmoor such an important issue? Explain this by preparing a statement summarising the case against the original proposal for the M40 extension (route A) across Otmoor.

5. Using Fig. 36.2 consider the routes A and B. Note down any issues which might arise both for and against these routes. (Remember to include some of the previous ones already raised in the previous pages.)

6. **T** Divide the class into 7 groups, hopefully with a minimum of 3 students in each group.
   1. Groups to speak **for** and **against** route **A**.
   2. Groups to speak **for** and **against** route **B**.
   3. Groups to speak **for** and **against** route **C**.
   4. A public inquiry **inspectors** group.
   Give each group time to thoroughly discuss their ideas and information.

Select **one** spokesman **for** and **one** spokesman **against each route**, from the groups. Select 3 people from the public inquiry inspectors group to conduct the inquiry with **one** of them to act as **chairman**. This person will be responsible for making a final decision with the help of his/her colleagues.

Conduct your own public inquiry to decide which of these three proposed sections of the M40 should be selected as the missing link in the M40 motorway extension.

37. Ecology

These terms will be useful to you. Learn them thoroughly before going on to the following pages.

Ecology. This is the study of living organisms (plants and animals) in relationship to their environments.
Ecosystem. An ecosystem involves the interaction between **living** (biotic) and **non-living** (abiotic) parts of the environment. The Amazon rain forest is a large ecosystem. A pond is a good example of a small ecosystem. (See Fig. 37.3.) The three main biotic components of an ecosystem are producers, consumers and decomposers.
Producers. These are the green plants which are capable of producing their own food by a process known as photosynthesis. They are also known as **autotrophs** (*auto* – self, *troph* – feeding).
Consumers. These are animals who obtain their food by eating plants or other animals. They are also known as **heterotrophs** (*hetero* – other, *troph* – feeding), (see Fig. 37.1).
Decomposers. These are usually micro-organisms such as bacteria and fungi which speed up the process of decay and release simple inorganic elements back into the soil, water or air, so that they can be reused by plants.

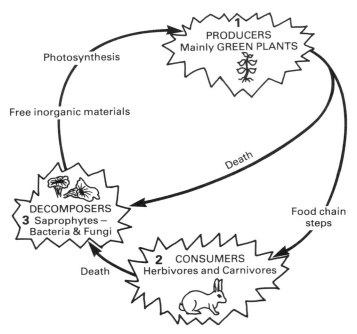

FIG. 37.1

Habitat. The habitat is where a species of plant or animal lives. Within that habitat the species finds all its requirements for food and shelter. A pond (Fig. 37.3) is a habitat of the Great Pond Snail (*Limnaea stagnalis*). A wood is a habitat of the Bluebell (*Endymion non-scriptus*).
Ecological Niche. The niche of a species is its function and role in the ecosystem, i.e. how that species exploits the food and shelter, its feeding habits, behaviour etc. A niche may include more than one habitat, for example, a newt may live in a damp compost heap and a pond at different times in its life cycle.

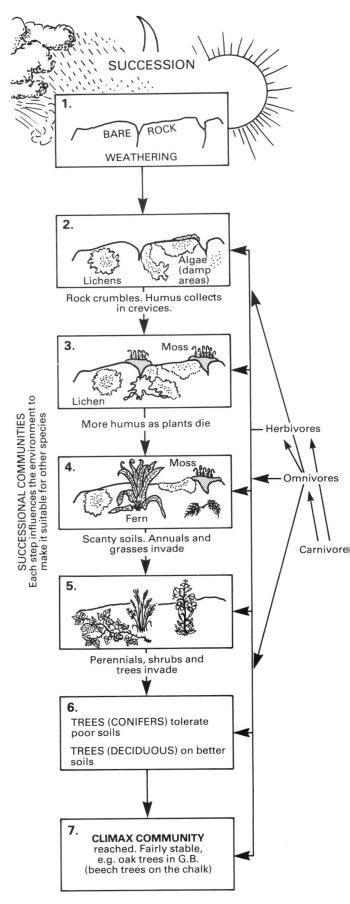

FIG. 37.2 SUCCESSION

Competition. Species compete for food, water and space in which to grow and multiply their numbers. This is known as competition. It can take place between individuals of the same species or between individuals of different species.

102

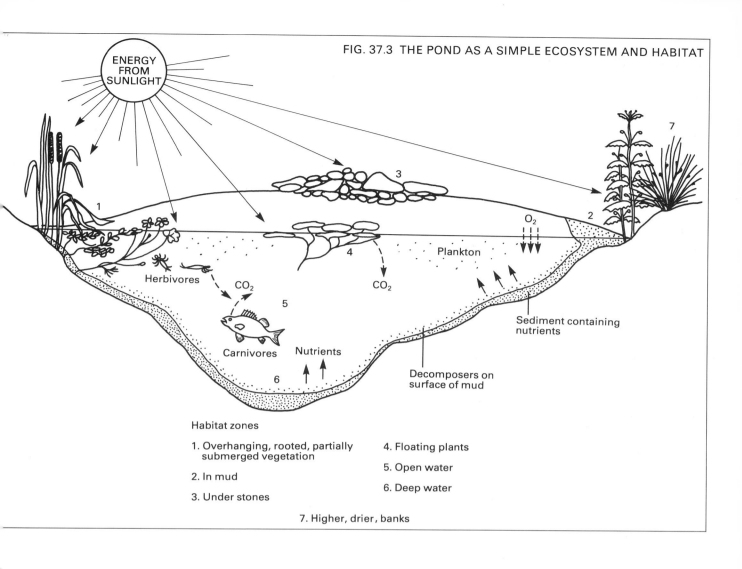

FIG. 37.3 THE POND AS A SIMPLE ECOSYSTEM AND HABITAT

ENERGY FROM SUNLIGHT

O₂

3

1

2

7

Plankton

4

Herbivores

CO_2

CO_2

5

Carnivores

Nutrients

6

Sediment containing nutrients

Decomposers on surface of mud

Habitat zones

1. Overhanging, rooted, partially submerged vegetation

2. In mud

3. Under stones

4. Floating plants

5. Open water

6. Deep water

7. Higher, drier, banks

PRODUCER	→	PRIMARY CONSUMER	→	SECONDARY CONSUMER	→	TERTIARY CONSUMER
Green plants		Herbivore		Carnivore 1		Carnivore 2
Rose leaves	→	Aphid	→	Bluetit	→	Hawk

FOOD CHAINS

Here are a series of living organisms, eating and being eaten. At every stage in this **food chain** energy is being transferred. A food chain is an **energy pathway**. Light energy (radiant energy) from the sun is trapped by the green plants (producers) as they make their food by photosynthesis. The plant becomes a source of food and therefore energy (chemical energy) for the snail. At each stage in the chain most of the energy is 'lost' in the form of heat as the consumers move around, hunt, keep warm, reproduce etc., but a small percentage is stored in the body to be eaten as food by the next consumer in the chain. Each energy level is known as a **trophic (feeding) level**. In the chain below the aphids are feeding at the same trophic level as the snail in the first chain.

FIG. 37.4 A FOOD CHAIN REPRESENTED AS A PYRAMID OF NUMBERS

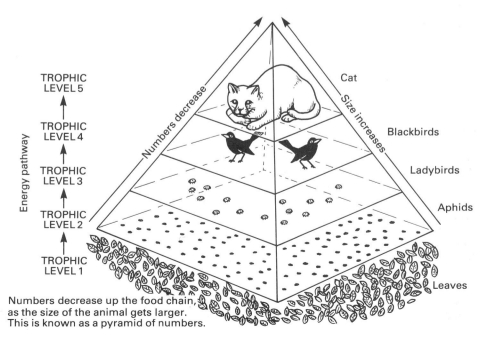

TROPHIC LEVEL 5

TROPHIC LEVEL 4

TROPHIC LEVEL 3

TROPHIC LEVEL 2

TROPHIC LEVEL 1

Energy pathway

Numbers decrease

Size increases

Cat

Blackbirds

Ladybirds

Aphids

Leaves

Numbers decrease up the food chain, as the size of the animal gets larger. This is known as a pyramid of numbers.

FOOD WEBS

It would be unusual for an animal to make only one food choice. A blackbird might eat ladybirds but it may prefer earthworms, grubs, other insects, seeds etc. Species also change their feeding habits from one season to another. So, we do not end up with a simple food chain but a complicated web composed of many inter-relating chains. See Fig. 37.5.

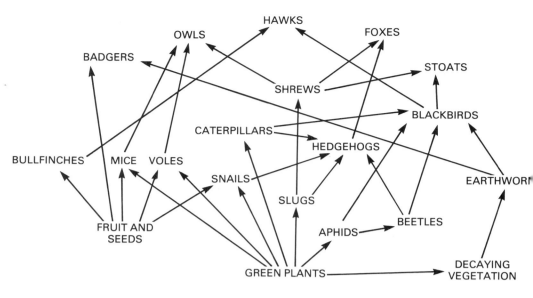

FIG. 37.5 A FOOD WEB

Questions

1. Why do lichens make good first colonisers? Use the lichen to describe what a symbiotic relationship is (see glossary p. 121).
2. Described ways in which people cause changes in the balance of animal and plant communities in an ecosystem. For example, here are some clue words: fire, trampling, grazing, chemicals.
3. Suggest suitable habitats for the following species: badgers, hermit crabs, brooklime, clover.
4. Devise food chains for the following animals: a fox, a whale, a heron and a hawk.
5. Draw a food web typical of a freshwater pond using the following: tadpoles, algae, protozoa, water crowfoot, water boatman, herbivorous fish, duckweed, water fleas (*Daphnia*) water snails, carnivorous fish.
   (a) Name 2 primary consumers.
   (b) Name 2 secondary consumers.
   (c) Write out 3 food chains.
   (d) Describe in what habitat this web might have developed.

Ground cover. The cover is usually taken to be the area covered by the aerial parts of the plant. It shows the relative importance of the species present.

The **Domin scale** for estimating cover:

Cover	Scale
Cover 100%	10
Cover 75–100%	9
Cover 50–75%	8
Cover 33–50%	7
Cover 25–33%	6
Cover about 20%	5
Cover about 5%	4
Scattered cover	3
Very scattered cover	2
Scarce	1
Isolated	X

Sampling Techniques

PLANTS

It is impossible, usually, to describe and analyse all the plants and animals in a community so a sample is taken.

Random Sampling. Throwing, for example, a quadrat at random in an area under investigation means that the quadrat should have an **equal chance of landing anywhere in that area**.

Systematic sampling. A sample is taken according to a definite pattern, for example, quadrats may be laid down end to end or in parallel line.

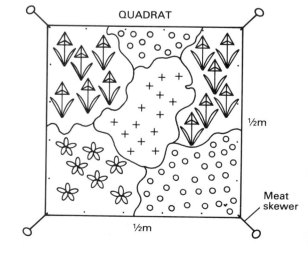

FIG. 37.6 A QUADRAT

VALENCE ANALYSIS

LOCATION: DATE

PLANT SPECIES	1	2	3	4	5		98	99	100	TOTAL OUT OF 100
MEADOW GRASS	✓	✓	✓		✓		✓	✓	✓	96
BUTTERCUP	✓	✓	✓	✓					✓	72
LADIES SMOCK	✓	✓					✓			55

FIG. 37.7 RECORD SHEET

Aim
- To find out which species live in a particular community, or habitat.
- To find out which species are characteristic of the area.

It is useful on a large area, such as saltmarsh, grassland, moorland and heathland.

Method
1. Throw the quadrat (see Fig. 37.6) **at random**. This means it should have an equal chance of landing anywhere, e.g. walk ten paces in any direction and drop over left shoulder. DON'T HOOPLA WITH IT!
2. Take 100 quadrat samples for more accurate recordings. (Divide the work load amongst the class and copy up the results.)
3. List all the species of plant as they arise in each quadrat and tick their presence as in Fig. 37.7.
4. Mark in how many times, out of the total of 100, you found each species, in the last column.
5. Discuss your results and write up the results and conclusions.

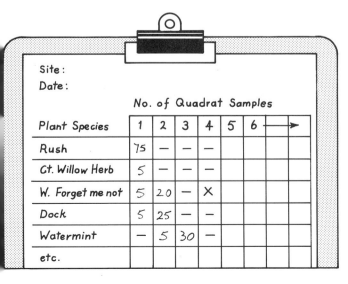

Site : Date :						
	No. of Quadrat Samples					→
Plant Species	1	2	3	4	5	6
Rush	75	—	—	—		
Gt. Willow Herb	5	—	—	—		
W. Forget me not	5	20	—	X		
Dock	5	25	—	—		
Watermint	—	5	30	—		
etc.						

FIG. 37.8 RECORDING A BELT TRANSECT

BELT TRANSECT

- It is a useful way of measuring quantities of vegetation.
- It is a useful way to measure changes in vegetation along a gradient (not necessarily a slope), e.g. from shade to full light, from the top to the bottom of a wall etc.

It is very important to measure environmental factors which may have considerable influence on the vegetation, e.g. light intensity, pH, angle of slope.

Method (See Figs. 37.8, and 37.9)

1. Lay down a tape or rope along the line of the transect.
2. Use a quadrat, e.g. 0.5 × 0.5 m, to sample the whole transect or even intervals along the transect.
3. Record the area covered by each species in each quadrat sample, on graph paper. estimate the ground covered by each plant species within the quadrat using the Domin scale. A single isolated plant should be recorded with an X. Complete a table as in Fig. 37.9.
4. Record the density of each species, i.e. the number of individual plants per quadrat sample. (This may be very difficult, for example, where one grass plant ends and another begins.) Individual record sheets for each quadrat would be best if **cover and density** are to be measured.
5. Discuss the results. Write up your conclusions.

Site : Date :		
Quadrat number : 1. Size : 1 m²		
Species	Cover (Domin)	Density (No. of plants)
Rush	9	2
Gt. Willow Herb	4	4
W. Forget me not	4	6
Dock	4	1

FIG. 37.9 INDIVIDUAL RECORD SHEET

ESTIMATING ABUNDANCE

When quick observations are required this might be a useful method.
1. Make a list of all the plants growing in the area.
2. Give each a coded letter as follows:
   A Abundant   O Occasional
   C Common   R Rare
   F Frequent
3. If the species only grows in one particular place within the area add the letter L which stands for locally, e.g. LR: Locally rare.

Sampling Animals

THE POOTER

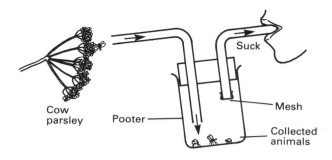

FIG. 37.10 THE POOTER

Aim
- To sample small insects, including those that fly, in meadows and grassy places.
- To investigate all the species of animal visiting one grass or flower type.

Method
1. Sweep over the long grass with a fine mesh sweep net. Turn the net so that the frame is vertical with the net hanging against in and the animals cannot escape.
2. Line up each animal with the tube which draws air into the bottle.
3. Suck sharply through the other tube.
4. The animal should enter the bottle but should not enter your mouth because wire mesh or muslin covers the entrance to this tube!
5. Get your teacher to show you how to 'knock out' the animals, using ethyl acetate. **BE CAREFUL YOU DO NOT BREATHE IN ANY FUMES**.
6. Sort the animals into groups, e.g. 1 pr. wings, 6 legs; 2 pr. wings, 6 legs; no wings, 6 legs, etc. Count and put them in stoppered specimen jars in case they come round. Release them only when you have finished sorting, identifying and sampling your chosen area.
7. Graph your results as a bar graph.

Capture/Recapture Method

This method can be used in a well defined area especially where there are loose bricks or stones.

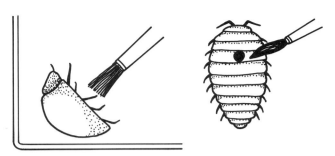

FIG. 37.11 CAPTURE, RECAPTURE METHOD

1. Using paintbrushes, specimen jars and a white enamel dish, collect all the animals you can find in your chosen area.
2. Collect, identify and count the species.
3. Separate them into groups of the same species so that the predators don't eat their prey.
4. Mark each animal on its back with a **small** painted spot, clearly visible to a trained eye. **Do not use a toxic paint or one which will be permanent**. A water-based powder paint in green is best. A bright colour may attract predators.
5. Release the marked animals in the same area.
6. After one day, catch and recount as many animals, spotted and unspotted, as you can find.
7. Work out the population of the area using the following formula:

$$\frac{\text{CATCH 1} \times \text{CATCH 2}}{\text{SPOTTED ANIMALS IN CATCH 2}}$$

Example

$$\frac{68 \times 50}{40} = 85 \text{ (TOTAL POPULATION)}$$

THE LONGWORTH MAMMAL TRAP
Only use this with the guidance of your teacher, as it is an **offence to take or kill shrews** under The Wildlife and Countryside Act (1981).
1. Set up the trap in line with small runways or tunnels in the vegetation.
2. Put suitable bedding and bait into the 'living quarters' of the trap.
3. Small mammals lose heat rapidly, need to feed very regularly and easily die of shock. **NEVER LEAVE A TRAP UNATTENDED FOR MORE THAN 4 HOURS** (2–3 hours if shrews might be accidently trapped).
4. Identify the mammal; record its colour, sex etc. by releasing it into a large polythene bag or wide necked sweet jar. They can jump high!
5. Record weight **last** by transferring the mammal by the scruff of the neck into a loosely woven draw string bag of known weight. Weigh this on a spring balance. Return the mammal to its habitat as soon as possible.

FIG. 37.12 LONGWORTH MAMMAL TRAP

38. In the Lab

The **choice chamber** offers the small invertebrate a choice of environmental conditions. The animal will tend to stay in the area it prefers.

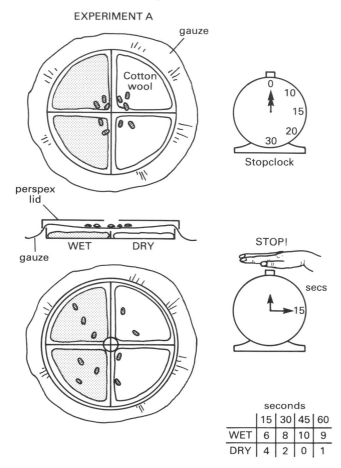

FIG. 38.1 EXPERIMENTS WITH A CHOICE CHAMBER

seconds	15	30	45	60
WET	6	8	10	9
DRY	4	2	0	1

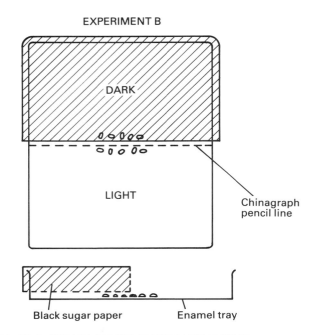

FIG. 38.2 'HOME-MADE' CHOICE CHAMBER

Use a manufactured choice chamber (Fig. 38.1) or make your own from a white enamel tray or ice cream carton. (Fig. 38.2.)

Experiment A

Method
1. On one side of the chamber set up **damp** conditions. Put in a mat or mats of cotton wool dampened with 10 ml of water. Set up **dry** conditions on the other side by using dry cotton wool.
2. Reset the gauze.
3. Line up a stop clock and a beaker containing 10 woodlice of the same species.
4. Carefully, using a small paintbrush, put the woodlice into the centre of the gauze or tray.
5. Reset the lid. There is an air hole in the top. Leave the homemade tray open. Set the stopclock immediately. Stop it at 15 seconds and count how many woodlice are in the damp and dry sections through the transparent lid.
6. Start the clock again. After 15 seconds record the numbers again. Repeat this at least 15–20 times.

Experiment B. Light versus dark.

Experiment C. Warm versus cold.

Experiment D. Wet and dark versus dry and light

Experiment E. Different light intensities.

Experiment F. Different litter choices.

Experiment G. Different food choices.

Experiment H. Different species.

Use your imagination and try out some of the variations above. The experiment works very well with woodlice but you could also use slugs, snails, centipedes, pill millipedes etc. Larger animals may need deeper trays or tanks. Black sugar paper or black felt can be used to achieve darkness. Bench lamps can be used to vary the light intensity and temperature. (Remember to measure the intensity or temperature!)

DON'T BE CRUEL. For example, there is no need to lower a bench lamp so low that the woodlice shrivel up and die before they even get a chance to move off! Let the animals go as soon as possible into a suitable environment.

Results and conclusions
1. The woodlouse is a **terrestrial crustacean**. It respires with the use of **gills** on the underside of its body. These must be kept moist to aid the exchange of oxygen and carbon dioxide for respiration. Woodlice feed on detritus: dead plant and animal remains.
   Examine a dead woodlouse under a hand lens. In what sort of environment are most other well known crustaceans found, e.g. shrimps and prawns?
2. Given the choice of damp, dry, dark or light conditions what might a woodlouse prefer? Suggest reasons why. How did these conditions affect their behaviour? Suggest reasons why.
3. Use your answers to write up your results and conclusions.

39. Keys

There are millions of different kinds of animals and plants, many of which look alike. To identify one species from another, lists of clues called **keys** are used.

Here is an extremely simple example of a key.

Name the small mammal **A** in Fig. 39.1 below using this pair of clues:

Small mammal with a black tipped tail – Stoat.
Small mammal without a black tipped tail – Weasel.

FIG. 39.1 THE WEASEL AND STOAT

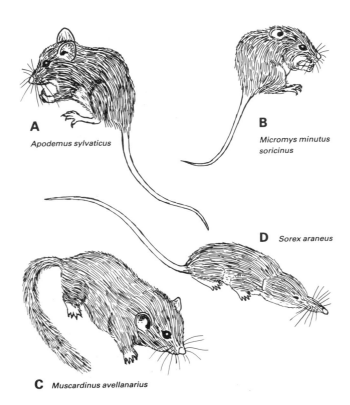

FIG. 39.2 SMALL MAMMALS

To name several different small mammals a longer list of clues would be needed.

Name all the small mammals in Fig. 39.2 by using the list of clues found below:

1 Animals without bushy tails (go to clue 2)
  Animal with a bushy tail – DORMOUSE
2 Animals with small ears (go to 3)
  Animal with large rounded ears – WOODMOUSE
3 Animal with pointed snout and small eyes – COMMON SHREW
  Animal without pointed snout and large eyes – HARVEST MOUSE

ANSWERS
A. WOODMOUSE   C. DORMOUSE
B. HARVEST MOUSE   D. COMMON SHREW

Some of the latest keys are not solely of this *dichotomous* type. Below is a tabular form of key produced by the Field Studies Council as part of the AIDGAP project. They are trying to produce simple, well written and well tested keys or *Aids for the Identification of Difficult Groups of Animals and Plants*. This is part of one by R. A. D. Cameron, N. Jackson and B. Eversham which can be used to identify the families of slugs in the British Isles (for terminology see p. 118 and p. 121):

A If the slug has a small external shell (at the hind end of the body) it is a member of the **TESTACELLIDAE**.

B If the slug has no external shell, use the table below.

KEEL and TAIL	MANTLE	PNEUMO-STOME	FAMILY
No true keel. Blunt tail with mucus gland.	Granular, no concentric rings.	in front half of mantle.	**ARIONIDAE**
Keel extends from tail up to ⅔ distance to mantle. Tail pointed.	Pattern of fingerprint like concentric ridges. **(Use hand lens)**	In rear half of mantle.	**LIMACIDAE**
Keel extends from tail to mantle. Tail pointed.	Mantle texture varies, but with pronounced grooves.	In rear half of mantle.	**MILACIDAE**

40. Environmental Factors

An ecological study should attempt to measure, observe and record environmental factors which may affect the plants and animals living in the community.

EDAPHIC FACTORS (SOIL)

1. **Acidity or alkalinity**. Use the experiment on p. 22 or the pH probe on an environmental comparator. Use universal indicator paper in freshwater streams and ponds.
2. The **nutrient supply**. See p. 45.
3. **Water, air and humus** content. Use the standard experiments to find the percentage in a sample, found in most biology text books.
4. **Particle size**. The particles are grouped according to size. These groups are called **fractions**. Clay is an important fraction because it holds water and nutrients in the soil.

Soil fraction	Diameter
Coarse sand	2.0–0.2 mm
Fine sand	0.2–0.02 mm
Silt	0.02–0.002 mm
Clay	less than 0.002 mm

Use the experiment shown in Fig. 40.1 to analyse a sample of soil taken with a soil auger. The humus content tends to float.

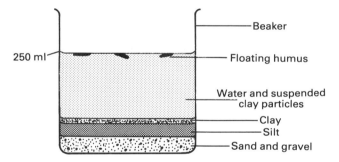

Add a heaped tablespoonful of the soil sample taken with a soil auger to 250 ml of water. Stir well with a glass rod and allow particles to settle. Observe and record the proportions of fractions present.

FIG. 40.1 EXPERIMENT TO ANALYSE SOIL SAMPLE

5. **Texture**. Different proportions of sand, silt and clay determine the texture. This in turn affects:
   - the size of pores between the particles,
   - drainage,
   - air in the soil for root respiration,
   - root penetration and anchorage.

Climatic Factors

1. Light
Light varies in three important ways.
- Its quality or **wavelength**. (See Fig. 1.6 on p. 4 and Fig. 12.1 on p. 33). Ultraviolet and infrared light are not used in photosynthesis. Green chlorophyll absorbs mostly red and blue light from the visible wavelength.

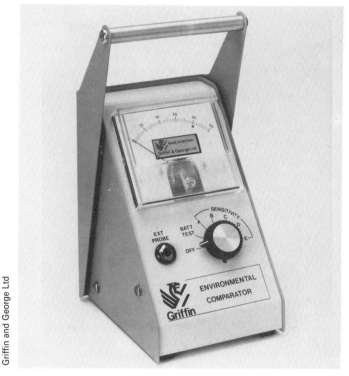

Griffin and George Ltd

FIG. 40.2 ENVIRONMENTAL COMPARATOR

- Its **intensity**. This can be measured with a **light probe** on an environmental comparator or a **light meter**. (See Fig. 40.2.)
- Its **duration**, i.e. the number of light hours recieved each day. The response of an organism to the length of day is known as **photoperiodism**. In plants it can affect flowering, leaf fall and dormancy (time at rest). In animals it can affect migration, nesting and change of colour. (This factor is closely linked with temperature.)

2. Temperature
Most living things in the biosphere function between a temperature of 0°C and 50°C. Each species has a **minimum, maximum** and **optimum** temperature requirement for carrying out activities. Temperature controls the rate of body activities in cold blooded animals and plants. It influences the availability of water by affecting the rate of evaporation from the soil or an organism's body. Use **maximum and minimum thermometers** to record the shade temperatures during a study. If these are not available use an ordinary centigrade thermometer or the temperature probe on an environmental comparator to take readings at regular intervals, for example, every half hour. Taking depth readings in water is illustrated here.

Measuring temperature in deep water

3. Water

- The percentage of water in the cells of living organisms can vary between 40% and 90%. Chemical activities in the cells need water for their reactions.
- Water is used in organisms to transport substances, and also to cool the organism by evaporation.
- Plants require water for support. When the cells have sufficient water they are rigid; wilting occurs when they do not have enough.

Measure the amount of rainfall using a **rain gauge** over a period of at least one week.

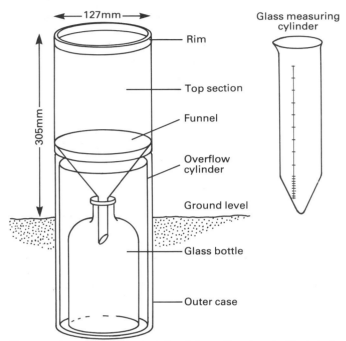

Measure the rain daily by pouring it from the glass bottle into the measuring cylinder. Reset the gauge.

FIG. 40.3 RAIN GAUGE

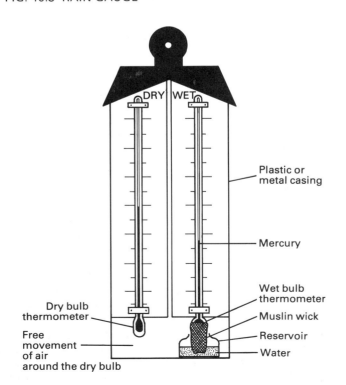

FIG. 40.4 WET AND DRY BULB THERMOMETER

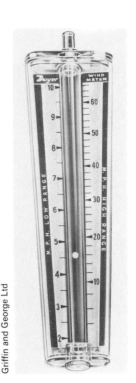

FIG. 40.5 A CLINOMETER FOR MEASURING ANGLE OF SLOPE

FIG. 40.6 HAND HELD WIND METER

4. Relative Humidity

This is the amount of water vapour in the air. It can be measured by using a **potometer** or a **wet and dry bulb thermometer**.

The 'dry' bulb thermometer records the actual air temperature. The 'wet' bulb thermometer records the temperature as if the air was saturated with water. If the wet bulb reading is taken away from the dry bulb reading and the difference looked up on the table which comes with the apparatus, the percentage of relative humidity can be found.

5. Wind

- Affects the rate of evaporation, the relative humidity and temperature.
- Causes actual physical damage to plants and affects their growth.

Use a **Davy instrument** or any other hand held **anemometer** to record the wind speed in different locations and at different heights.

Topographic Factors

1. **Altitude**. Use an altimeter.
2. **Aspect**. Use a compass to find out in which direction a slope is facing.
3. **Angle of slope**. Use a clinometer.

BIOTIC FACTORS

This particularly includes factors caused by the interference of people. For example:
1. Trampling.
2. The use of pesticides.
3. The removal of hedgerows and cutting down of trees.
4. The planting and harvesting of crops.

41. The Pond

DO'S

1. **Do** use a **pencil** rather than a pen to record fieldwork.
2. **Do** remember the **Country Code**. See p. 88.
3. **Do** structure your work so that you haven't disturbed all the animals or trampled on the plants before you start to sample them.
4. **Do** put water plants in with animal specimens to **oxygenate** the water.
5. **Do** leave all collected specimens in the **shade**.
6. **Do record as you work**. (All of you!) Write up at the earliest opportunity.
7. **Do** return all species to the water as soon as possible after recording and identifying.
8. **Do** use simple apparatus, a strong fine mesh large net, a household sieve, artists' paintbrushes, pipettes, penknife, white enamel trays and a variety of specimen jars, screw top jars and large old orange squash containers.

DON'TS

1. **Don't** assume you will not be going if it rains!
2. **Don't** fill specimen jars to the very top. Allow oxygen to diffuse in at the surface.
3. **Don't** leave carnivores in with other valuable specimens!
4. **Don't drink pond** or stream **water**. Wash your hands carefully after the study.
5. **Don't** forget your wellingtons!

LEARN, MARK AND INWARDLY DIGEST!

1. A pond needs an adequate supply of **water**! Many species have adaptations which help them to deal with drought and the colder winter months when they go through a 'resting' stage in the bottom mud.
2. A pond needs **sunlight**.
   - For plants to carry out photosynthesis.
   - For warmth. Variation in water temperature is less than it is on the land. Warmer water means it has less dissolved oxygen in it.

Microscopic plants (phytoplankton) and animals (zooplankton) live in the lighter, warmer surface waters. Little light can penetrate into the depths so the water is cooler and darker.

3. **Oxygen**. The oxygen content in water is lower than it is in air. Oxygen diffuses into the water from the surface. A pond or lake which is shallow but has a large surface area will have a higher dissolved oxygen content than one which is deep and has a small surface area.

   Green plants in and around the water add to the oxygen content during the day by the process of photosynthesis. Carbon dioxide is used and oxygen is given off in this process.

   Respiration by plants and animals takes place by day and by night. Oxygen is taken in and carbon dioxide is given out. At night time, therefore, oxygen levels can be at their lowest.

   Aquatic animals vary in their oxygen requirements. Microscopic animals absorb oxygen by **diffusion**, over the whole body. Larger animals may have special adaptations to obtain oxygen, e.g. **tracheal gills** in insect nymphs and crustaceans, **red pigment (haemoglobin)** in mud dwellers such as *Chironomous* larvae.

4. **B.O.D. Biological Oxygen Demand**. This is the amount of oxygen (mg/l) consumed within a given sample of pond water over 5 days at 20°C in a closed dark container. It suggests how rapidly the water might become deoxygenated if, for example, it was polluted with sewage or needed large amounts of oxygen to decompose a high organic content. (See No. 6.)

5. **Buoyancy**. Water supports the bodies of animals and plants. Many make use of the surface film of water, for example, pond skaters.

6. **Decomposition**. Micro-organisms (decomposers) rot down organic matter (dead plants and animals). To do so they need oxygen. A pond choked with algae and weeds may use so much oxygen for decomposition that there is little left for other forms of life.

7. **Nutrients**. The decomposers in the bottom of the pond help to release important nutrients, for example, **nitrates, phosphates** and **potash** which are then recycled by plants and then animals in the water. Run-off water from the surrounding land often contains dissolved chemicals which may lead to a build up of too many salts, with the following results:

   - **A change in the pH level** of the water which in turn will affect which species choose to live there. (See Acid Rain. p. 83.)
   - **Eutrophication**. This occurs when the water is excessively enriched with nutrients. Algae begin to grow rapidly, shading out other plants. The activity of aerobic bacteria is increased during the decomposition of these algae which in turn reduces oxygen levels in the water to such low levels that may freshwater animals die.
   - A high concentration of salts can cause water to be drawn out of the bodies of organisms by **osmosis** and lead to rapid death, e.g. fish.

8. **Temperature**. The surface waters of the pond may warm up and lay over cooler water at the bottom. Nutrients become exhausted in the surface layer as the organisms increase their activities. Until the water cools again, little mixing occurs with the bottom layers to replenish the nutrients. In winter ice may form on the surface at temperatures below 4°C and this helps to prevent further cooling of the lower layers.

Questions

1. Record the date and location of the pond.
2. Sketch a large labelled drawing of the pond and its immediate surroundings.
3. Distinguish and mark these zones:
   Aquatic zone. The area which always has water in it, except in very dry summers.
   Swamp zone. The area where the water level fluctuates.
   Marsh zone. The area which remains damp (perhaps under a drier crust) in summer and waterlogged in winter.
4. Mark on the appropriate dimensions of the pond.
5. Mark on other noticeable features, e.g. luxuriant or poor plant growth, trampling by grazing animals, shelter from bushes and trees, overhanging canopy, nesting birds etc.
6. Record the weather on the day of the survey. Has there been a recent dry period? In the last 3 days, has there been heavy, light or no rain?

SAMPLING ANIMALS

1. Choose 4 or more of the habitat zones shown in Fig. 37.3.
2. Carry out 10–15 samples in each zone. For example, 15 sweeps with a net in open water.
3. Using keys and books, quickly identify the species. Some common ones are shown below.
4. Record the number found of **each** species in your own version of the table below. This is known as **direct counting**.
5. Don't release specimens back into the same area until you have finished all your samples!
6. Investigate the following environmental factors in each zone: light intensity, pH of mud or water, dissolved oxygen and temperature (air and water). See pages 22, 109, 110.
   ● For each zone work out food chains and webs, by studying mouthparts, behaviour and researching feeding habits.
   ● Choose two invertebrate animals and write an account of how they are adapted to their zone.

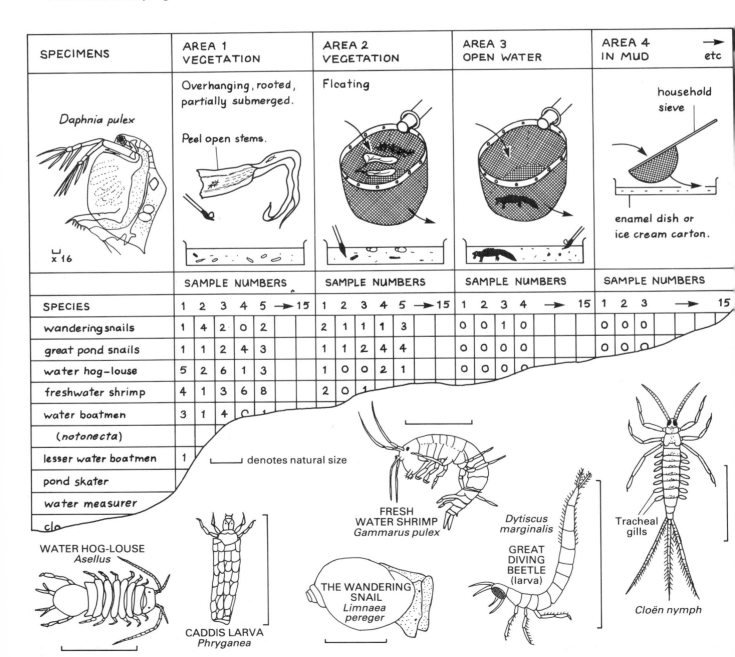

FIG. 41.1 RECORDING ANIMALS FOUND BY THE DIRECT COUNTING METHOD

SAMPLING PLANTS

✺ limited time   ◉ unlimited time

1. Make a quick list of plants growing in and around
✺ the pond. **Estimate the abundance.** (P. 105.)
2. Carry out a **line transect** down the bank into the
◉ water to find out how the species vary down the
   slope. (See Fig. 41.2.)
   ● Stake out two canes at the top and bottom of the
     slope. Tie across a horizontal line, marked in
     10 cm intervals. Check with a spirit level. Cover at
     least three metres.
   ● Measure at each 10 cm interval:
     (a) the distance to the ground,
     (b) the plant species growing there, and
     (c) the height of the plants.
   ● Note the water line.
   ● Graph the results. (See Fig. 41.2.)

3. Carry out a **belt transect** right next to this line
◉ transect, using a metre or a suitable sized quadrat.
   Use the instructions found on p. 105. Use Fig. 37.8
   to show you how to present your results.

Questions

1. Which zone, acquatic, swamp or marsh, had the
   greatest variety of plants growing in it?
   Which method of sampling, the line or the belt, gave
   you the best information to answer this question?
   Explain your answer.
2. Was there much evidence of plants dying in the
   swamp zone? What effect might this have on the
   pond?
3. In what way were the plants in the aquatic zone
   adapted to living in a watery environment? Study
   their stems, leaves and flowers.
Within your conclusions try to include comments on the
following:
● The variety of plants found, including their
  distribution and abundance as well as their
  adaptations to their environment.
● At least two plants (one aquatic) which have been
  studied closely as concerns:
  (a) pollination mechanisms,
  (b) root formations,
  (c) seed dispersal,
  (d) leaf variety and shape, and
  (e) environmental factors influencing habitat.

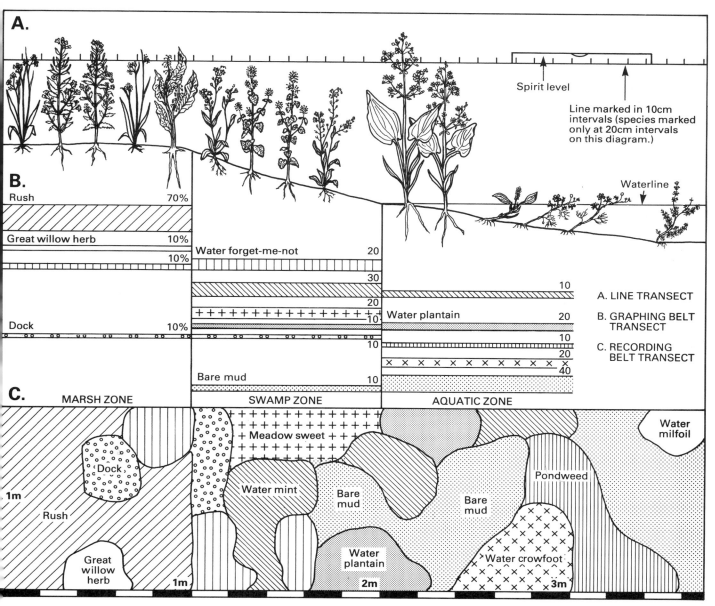

FIG. 41.2 RECORDING PLANT SPECIES ALONG A LINE TRANSECT AND BELT TRANSECT

113

42. The Cemetery

Any investigation in a cemetery must have the permission of the vicar or local council.

TAKE ONE GRAVESTONE!

What could you study? Here are some suggestions:

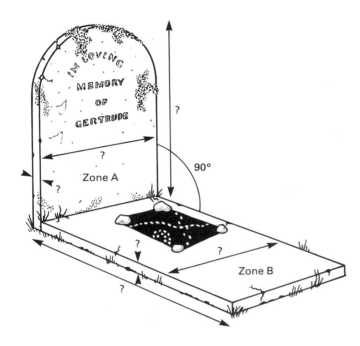

FIG. 42.1 GRAVESTONE

Vertical versus Horizontal?

1. Sketch the gravestone and label important features.
2. Record the rock type of vertical Zone A and horizontal Zone B. Record their dimensions.
3. Record how long the stone has been standing there. Record the points of the compass.
4. Record the date, location and weather conditions.
5. Record at suitable intervals, down Zone A and across Zone B, pH and the build up of organic matter (humus) or scanty soils.
6. Record at even intervals, e.g. $\frac{1}{2}$–1 hr, throughout a working day the light intensity, temperature and humidity, at the same places in each zone.
7. Set up sticky paper traps (the type used to catch flies) and smoked paper sheets, preferably a day in advance of the study. (You need clear dry weather for a day and a night for good results.) See Fig. 42.3.
8. Persuade some well known invertebrates to crawl across one piece of smoked paper prior to the study. Fix the tracks with artists' fixative and use them to identify tracks from your study.

T. Select the gravestones in advance. Identify common species of moss and lichen and be prepared to help pupils **immediately** with their identification. Call difficult ones. Specimen A, B, etc. until they can be identified.

Major investigations

Choose suitable techniques from pp. 104–6 to investigate the following in Zones A and B.

1. Identify the species of lichen and moss, also any ephemerals, annuals and perennials.
2. Investigate their distribution. A smaller quadrat, e.g. 10×10 cm, might be useful here. Tabulate your results.
3. Identify and record all the animals inhabiting and visiting the zones. Tabulate your results.

Answer some of these questions in your conclusions.

● Were there any noticeable differences in the plant and animal communities found in the vertical and horizontal zones?
● Which species had no problems colonising either zone? Had they any special adaptations to do so?
● In your estimation could the environmental factors be responsible for any differences, for example, light and shade? Explain your answers.
● Where was the greatest build up of organic matter (humus) or scanty soils? Might this have had any effect on the distribution of plant and animal communities?

If time permits, compare:
(a) two gravestones of a similar age and stone type,
(b) two gravestones of different age and similar stone type,
(c) two gravestones of different age and different stone type,
(d) raised gravestones with flat ones etc.

FIG. 42.2 LICHEN GROWTH ON A GRAVESTONE

BIRD PELLETS, e.g. Owl

These are regurgitated ('brought up') from the stomach. They contain a mixture of bones of small mammals, carapaces of insects and other indigestible pieces. They are bound together in a well stuck furry pellet about 4–5 cm long. They give a good indication of the diet of an owl.

1. Collect owl pellets from underneath roosting sites, e.g. tall trees, deserted and farm buildings.
2. Keeping the specimens **separate**, unravel the pellet with dissecting tweezers and needles, **carefully**.
3. Use the flow chart in Fig. 42.5 to identify the lower jaws. Examine the other minature bones which you should recognise. They may be bones of a previous meal. Don't expect to get a complete set!
4. If you have time, make a pleasing **labelled** display of the contents of one pellet on black sugar paper. These go down well for club activities or displays for open days!
5. Work out food chains from your result, and finally, a food web.
6. If you can examine enough pellets, record your findings as pie charts or histograms.

FIG. 42.4 REGURGITATED PELLETS OF THE BARN OWL

©Mike Read/Natural Image

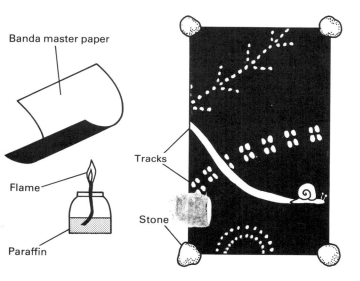

FIG. 42.3 TRACKS ON SMOKED PAPER

Banda master paper

Tracks

Flame

Stone

Paraffin

PREPARING SMOKED PAPER FOR TRACKS

Instructions for use:
- Use paper which has a very shiny surface, Banda paper for example. Smoke it with the spirit lamp.
- Get some common invertebrates, such as a woodlouse, garden spider, earthworm and slug, to move across the smoked paper. Note the difference between the patterns formed by slime trails, many appendages and the tiny bristles, or chitae, on earthworms.
- Record the tracks with artist's fixative.
- Leave new smoked paper out in the areas you wish to study in dry weather for at least three hours. Use blu-tak to anchor them on zone A on gravestones (see p. 114). Stones may be used for anchorage on zone B or on concrete areas of wasteland.
- Compare the tracks with those you have learnt in the laboratory. Identify the visitors to the paper. New animals may be collected in the area and brought to the laboratory to record their tracks as well.

LADYBIRDS

A Specialised Invertebrate Study

Everyone can recognise a *ladybird*, but have you ever bothered to count the number of spots?
The seven spot ladybird (*Coccinella 7-punctata*) is fairly common but you will also find different forms of two spot (*Adalia 2-punctata*) and ten spot ladybirds (*Adalia 10-punctata*). Some forms will look more black than red! An unkept cemetery, derelict land or wasteland, or even your own garden can provide the ideal habitat for an intensive study. Ladybirds will be hunting their prey on plant favourites such as bramble, broad-leaved dock, and thistle. Some very exciting finds can be made on conifers in churchyards. You could be involved in some very original scientific work!

- Equip yourselves with many containers (screw-top jam jars with punctured air holes containing one small dock leaf).
- Also take paintbrushes, magnifying glasses and pooters (see p. 106). Collect all the ladybirds you can find within half an hour from one area. Or, collect all those to be found on one plant species, e.g. dock, or on a specific group of plants, e.g. conifers. Separate the different species and forms. For example, there are four basic forms of *Adalia 2-punctata*:

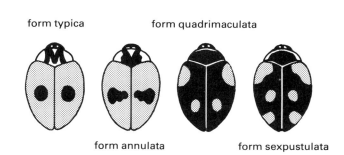

form typica   form quadrimaculata

form annulata   form sexpustulata

There are three basic forms of *Adalia 10-punctata*.

This section is inspired by WATCH, the organisation for young people run by the RSNC, The Green, Nettleham, Lincoln LN2 2NR – a thoroughly recommended study!

115

FIG. 42.5 IDENTIFYING THE CONTENTS OF BIRD PELLETS (Key by Colin Plant, Assistant Curator, Passmore Edwards Museum)

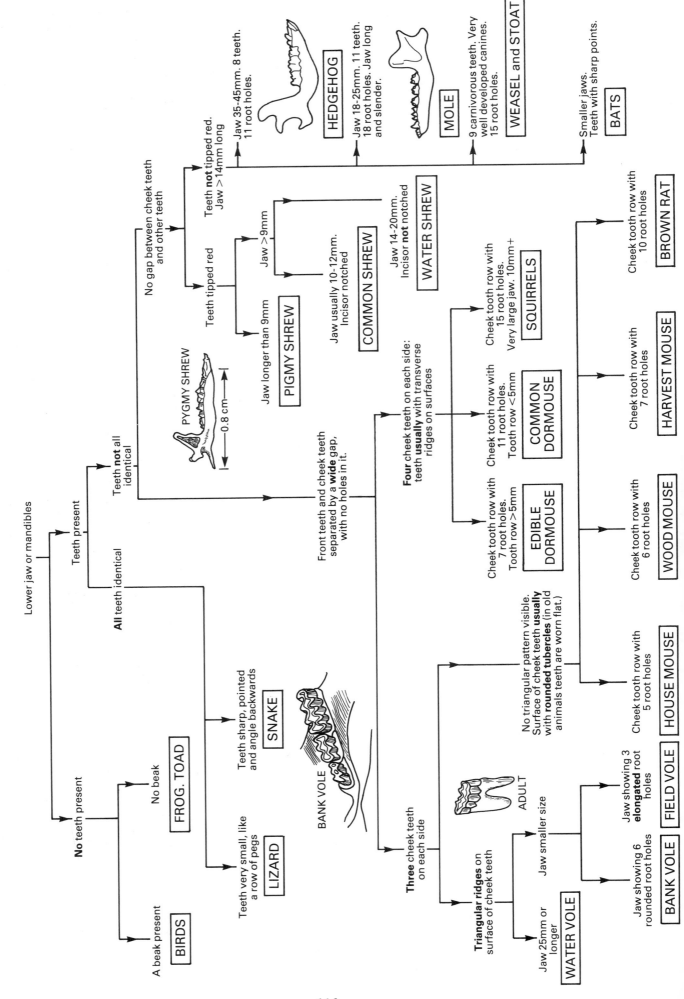

116

43. Wasteland Ecology

Most wasteland shares two main features:
- Neglect.
- Disturbance, for example, tipping, trampling. List the many ways in which people have affected the wasteland shown in Fig. 43.1.

The following stages of development can be recognised in wasteland:

1. The ephemerals and annuals (see glossary) do well as first or **pioneer** plants. They devote most of their life cycle to reproduction, producing and easily dispersing large amounts of seed. Examples are groundsel, ragwort, shepherd's purse and charlock.

2. As the **soil** becomes **enriched** with organic matter (humus) all the ground becomes covered. There is much more shelter, variety and a greater quantity of food. More animal species move in. Perennials such as nettles, dock, couch grass and many other grasses compete successfully with the pioneer plants.

3. **Scrub woodland** develops. It begins with bramble, elder, hawthorn etc. and eventually, after several years, may support some trees, for example sycamore.

These stages are typical of **primary succession**. See p. 102. This is a succession in a place which has not supported an ecosystem before. Where plants become established (recolonise) quickly without the great variety that the annuals give, this may be a case of **secondary succession**. This occurs where an ecosystem previously existed but never reached maturity due to, for example, grazing or fire.

FIG. 43.1 FEATURES OF AN OVERGROWN WASTELAND

Here are some investigations that could be carried out using techniques found on p. 104 and p. 105.

1. Why are (a) members of the **compositae** family or (b) members of the **cruciferae** family effective **pioneer** plants?
   ● Investigate their distribution (valence analysis and percentage cover).
   ● Study how they disperse their seeds (observation and research).
   ● Which animals are regular visitors to these plants? (pooter and observation).

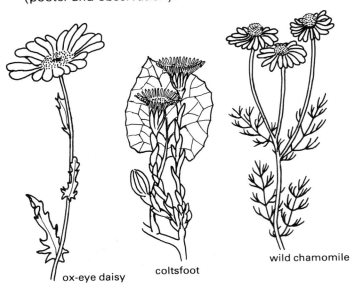

FIG. 43.2 MEMBERS OF THE *COMPOSITAE* FAMILY

ox-eye daisy
coltsfoot
wild chamomile

2. Which species of **mollusc** are well **adapted** to living in a habitat around man-made structures such as walls, foundations and building rubble?
   ● Collect all specimens which fit this description carefully by hand and paintbrush from areas in the wasteland.
   ● Use the key on p. 108 to identify and sort into families, count and record the numbers.
   ● Observe the species and make notes on adaptations, respiration, feeding etc.
   ● Use choice chambers (p. 107) to carry out experiments on choice of food etc.

3. What is the **population of woodlice** in one well defined area? How is their **behaviour** important to their survival?
   ● Use the capture/recapture method on p. 106.
   ● Conduct laboratory experiments using choice chambers, p. 107.

4. How suitable has the wasteland become to support a variety of **small mammals**?
   ● Set up live mammal traps, only during the hours of fieldwork, for at least one week. Identify and record the species and their numbers every 3–4 hours.
   ● Work out some suitable food chains and a food web for the whole habitat. You may need to observe which predators frequent the area. (Use tracks and droppings to help you.) Also you will need to identify and list all the other animals you come across during your studies.

For each study remember to measure the environmental factors such as light, humidity, temperature, pH, angle of slope etc., especially for investigations 2 and 3.

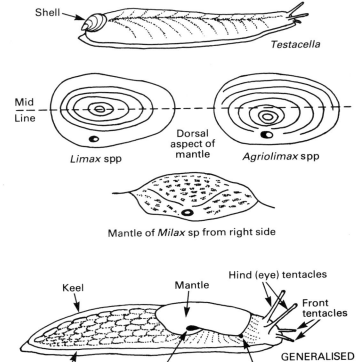

Testacella

Mid Line

Limax spp
Dorsal aspect of mantle
Agriolimax spp

Mantle of *Milax* sp from right side

Keel
Mantle
Hind (eye) tentacles
Front tentacles
GENERALISED SLUG
Foot fringe
Pneumostome (Respiratory orifice)
Genital orifice

FIG. 43.3 DIAGRAMS TO ILLUSTRATE SLUG GENERA

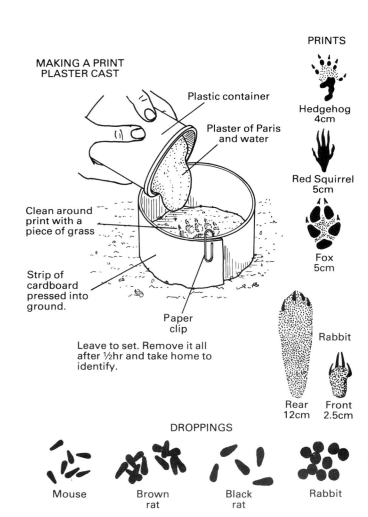

MAKING A PRINT PLASTER CAST

Plastic container
Plaster of Paris and water
Clean around print with a piece of grass
Strip of cardboard pressed into ground.
Paper clip

Leave to set. Remove it all after ½hr and take home to identify.

PRINTS
Hedgehog 4cm
Red Squirrel 5cm
Fox 5cm
Rabbit
Rear 12cm
Front 2.5cm

DROPPINGS
Mouse
Brown rat
Black rat
Rabbit

FIG. 43.4 SIGNS OF UNSEEN GUESTS

44. Newspaper and Magazine Cuttings

Fallout cracks nut sales

FORTY tons of imported hazelnuts contaminated with radiation from the Chernobyl disaster have been intercepted in Britain and sent back to Turkey. Some of the nuts contained nearly twice the level of contamination considered safe by the EEC.

It is the first time that food imports have been rejected in this way in Britain since the disaster, and has served as a sharp reminder that without constant vigilance contaminated food can still get into shops.

It will also damage the traditional Christmas market, with nuts from around the world already scarce due to poor weather conditions. Prices are expected to soar.

The Turkish nuts arrived in two lorryloads at Dover more than a week ago. Port health officials insisted on taking samples which were tested at the Government's research establishment at Harwell.

The incident has worried some Government officials because, although Turkey is recognised as a country whose food shipments should be checked carefully, imports from throughout the EEC are usually allowed into Britain without tests.

These shipments are accompanied by documents which state that the food complies with the EEC radiation limits—but there is a long history of Common Market documentation being abused.

Britain's food manufacturers are now so worried about radiation in imported food used as raw materials that many of them are now having shipments tested privately. Imports from Eastern bloc countries are particularly suspect.

Demand for private tests—costing £45 sample—is now so great that Leatherhead Food RA, a Surrey-based company, is running a 24-hour service to test for caesium isotopes.

Dr Alan Holmes, spokesman for the company, said: "We opened our new radiation testing laboratory at the end of September and we have met with a very steady demand.

"It was obvious in the wake of Chernobyl that people in this country were having difficulty getting samples tested quickly. For various reasons companies often prefer to have their food tested privately rather than in a Government establishment."

Foods tested so far include paprikas, hazelnuts, milk powder, fruit pulp and cereals, a variety of vegetables and in one case a cream liqueur.

None of the samples has so far been above the EEC safety limit.

Daily Telegraph,
November 9, 1986

This is one subject where it would be very helpful to read around and keep up to date. Collecting cuttings about environmental issues is a very useful exercise.

What to look for in a cutting:
1. The source and date of the report and/or incident.
2. The issue being reported.
3. The location (if relevant).
4. The cause.
5. The importance facts or points being made. Highlight these with a marker pen as you read through.

Follow up work
Watch out for follow-up reports on the same issue. They may tell you new or more accurate facts and figures.

Clamp on farmers who spread poison

BRITAIN'S water authorities are demanding tough new controls on farmers as evidence emerges that 1986 will be the worst year on record for rivers and streams poisoned by farm waste.

Farmers are bracing themselves to resist new curbs on silage making and storage of animal effluent in what has become a bigger environmental controversy than straw burning for the agriculture industry.

Millions of fish on fish farms and in the wild have died as a result of discharges from intensive farms. One of the latest victims is the rock star and businessman Roger Daltrey who recently had half a million prime trout wiped out on his fish farm near Blandford, Dorset.

Daltrey, who sprung to fame with the Who pop group, was said yesterday to be "still too upset" to talk about the incident three weeks after first details emerged. It is believed that five years of work at the fishery were wiped out when thousands of gallons of liquid fertiliser spilt from a burst storage tank on a nearby farm.

The incident happened soon after the Water Authorities Association and the Ministry of Agriculture published a detailed report which showed that cases of water pollution from farms rose by 25 per cent in England and Wales last year. Farming had become the worst single water polluter in the country in 1985—but latest information suggests that incidents will rise by half as much again this year.

A spokesman for the Water Authorities Association said: "What happened to Mr Daltrey is only one incident among many. Normally these incidents don't attract the attention of Fleet Street."

The water pollution issue threatens to cause a major split between the Department of the Environment, which is slowly beginning to accept that tighter controls are needed, and the Ministry of Agriculture which is relying heavily on farmers adhering to a voluntary code of practice.

The Sunday Telegraph,
September 7, 1986

Thatcher yields on acid rain

A LIMITED series of measures aimed at placating Scandinavian criticism of British "acid rain" pollution will be announced by Mrs Thatcher in Norway this week.

She is expected to tell the Norwegian government that she is prepared to try to limit the amount of discharges from British coal fired power stations, which the Norwegians and their neighbours claim is killing their forests and poisoning their lakes.

The Sunday Telegraph,
September 7, 1986

Two-horse race for Channel link may end rivalry

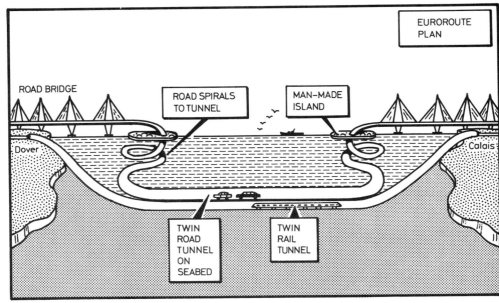

EUROROUTE plan for the Channel Tunnel

THE deadline is near for one of Europe's longest-running pipedreams — the Channel Link. Detailed proposals must be presented by the end of the month. Silly entries excepted, this will be a two-horse race which may end in a compromise.

Friends and foes of the Chunnel acknowledge that the offer of tens of thousands of jobs in time for the next General Election is one this Government will find almost impossible to refuse, especially as it should not cost taxpayers a penny.

So the question is not so much "whether" as "which". The Channel Tunnel Group is proposing two tunnels, to be bored into the chalky layer under the channel, and carrying railway carriages modified to take cars.

At an estimated cost of about £2 billion, this is the type of scheme which has been consistently backed by all past independent investigations into the viability of a Channel link by various Anglo-French banking and other expert groups.

Euroroute, the idea of Ian MacGregor when chairman of British Steel, will allow motorists to drive through from one country to the other on a combined bridge or tunnel link, with the transition taking place on two new artificial islands seven miles offshore. The price is £5 billion.

Both schemes suggest crossing times about 30 to 40 minutes. Neither promises cheap tolls. They are most unlikely to save money as well as time.

What will the two main options mean in practice to the cross channel traveller?

If CTG is chosen, the crossing will begin with a new terminal at Cheriton, Kent. Here passengers will go through British and French customs, health and emigration. No pre-booking will be needed and cars will drive on to what CTG now call their "rolling motorway" extra wide double-decker carriages.

Trains will leave every five minutes. During the journey drivers and passengers may choose to sit in their cars or get out and stretch their legs.

The well-lit carriages will have refreshment vending machines and video monitors displaying weather and traffic information.

On arrival at the other end, they will drive off the rail carriages on to the French motorways.

If Euroroute is built, drivers will motor down to toll, customs and immigration stations at Great Farthinghoe, near Dover. An inshore tunnel will then take them through Shakespeare Cliff on to a seven-mile bridge.

This cable-stay structure could have offered travellers magnificent views and plenty of fresh air. But danger from high winds has meant that 5ft fences would have to be erected all along it.

The Government's decision, however, will be based on more than just travellers' convenience. Employment prospects are vitally important. Both schemes promise a great deal. Euroroute claim 40,000 jobs during a five-year construction period; CTG mention 60,000 over four and a half years. Half the jobs will be in France.

After completion, CTG has the edge with more permanent jobs promised in Kent. CTG also makes much of its scheme being "compatible with the existing sea ferry services."

Ultimately the decision to emerge at the end of January 1986 seems most likely to be a Great Franco-British Compromise. The Transport Ministers Secretary, Mr Nicholas Ridley could express a preference for the CTG scheme and indicate that it would be even better if Euroroute, unable to beat them, joined them instead.

Finally the fate of the link will probably be decided on finance. Euroroute are confident that the Government will not be able to refuse a private investment of £ billion.

CTG are equally sure that cautious civil servants continue to view the link as a riskt venture and would prefer a £2 billion risk. They may well be right.

Turning rivals into allies would give the scheme such high powered international backing that it may, at last, become unsinkable.

Daily Telegraph, October 20, 198?

Using Information

The question of the Channel link is a recent controversial issue in Great Britain and Europe. Read the cutting on this page carefully and use it to answer the following:

1. According to the article, what are the two main proposal plans for the new Channel link?

2. What factors will need to be considered in choosing one or other of these two plans?

3. What are the advantages and disadvantages of each proposal? Divide yourselves into two groups, one in favour of the Euroroute plan and one opposing it and stage a debate.

4. Can you find out whether this issue has been resolved yet or not?

Glossary

Acid rain Polluted rain with an acidity of below pH 4.0, caused by sulphur dioxide and nitrogen oxide mixing with the rain in the atmosphere. It is very damaging to trees, fish and other life forms. Natural rain is weakly acidic with a pH range from 5.6 to 4.5.

Anemometer Instrument for measuring wind speed.

Annual A plant which grows, flowers, seeds and dies within one year.

Arete A steep mountain ridge, often formed where two or more corries have caused erosion.

Background radiation Low level radiation from substances naturally present in the environment.

Barrage A man-made barrier, usually across an estuary, which is used to harness tidal power as an alternative source of energy.

Bedding plane The surface which separates one layer of sedimentary rock from another.

Birth control Limiting the size of the family by using methods of contraception, e.g. pill, sheath and coil.

Capital intensive Involving a high level of money investment.

Carapace A hard covering or exoskeleton found in some arthropods, e.g. insects, crabs.

Carcinogen A cancer forming chemical.

Carrying capacity The natural limit set on the size of a population due to the availability of, for example, food, water and shelter.

Chlorophyll The green colouring found in the green parts of plants designed to trap light energy for use in photosynthesis.

Conduction The transfer of heat from one point to another by the medium or conductor between them. Metal is a good conductor.

Contraception The prevention of pregnancy using 'artificial methods'.

Control experiment An experiment set up under normal conditions and compared with other similar experiments in which certain factors have been either eliminated or varied.

Convection The transfer of heat from one point of a medium to another by movement of the medium itself. Takes place in liquids and gases but not metals.

Corrie or cirque A deep rounded hollow with steep sides formed by the action of snow and ice: a feature of glaciated regions.

Cost-benefit analysis To seek the maximum of benefits from the minimum of costs.

Cross-breeding To produce offspring by mating together, or crossing, two unrelated breeds.

Decibels (dB) The standard unit for the measurement of sound. For traffic the 'A' weighting scale is used relating to the frequency bands to which the human ear is most sensitive. This is called the dBA. The decibels work on a logarithmic scale, i.e. a vehicle producing 80 dBA is ten times noisier than one producing 70 dBA. Because the ear does not register noise in the same way as a meter, it takes an increase of about 9 dBA to make a sound seem twice as loud.

Dichotomous Dividing or branching into two.

Diffusion The molecular movement in liquids or gases which usually results in them being evenly spread, or distributed.

Dormitory town A town from which most of the residents travel away to work.

Electrostatic precipitator Used to attract particles of matter and stop them escaping from factory chimneys.

Enterprise zone Established by the British Government to encourage new investment and create new jobs in previously run-down areas, e.g. London Docklands.

Ephemeral A plant with a short life cycle which may grow and flower several times a year.

Extensive farming A method of farming which uses more land to produce the same amount of crops and livestock as intensive farming would in less space.

Fallout The radioactive particles which are released into the atmosphere from a nuclear explosion.

Fallow Productive land left unploughed, untilled or unsown for a year or more.

Family planning Deciding how many children to have and when to have them.

Food conversion rate The rate at which an animal converts its food into body flesh or meat.

Fossil fuel Fuels formed from dead animals and plants which became buried in the rock layers of the earth's crust, e.g. natural gas, oil and coal.

Gamma radiation Electromagnetic radiation emitted by atomic nuclei, also known as gamma rays.

Genetics The study of the way in which characters are inherited.

Half-life To measure the breakdown of nuclear waste, i.e. the time in which its radioactivity halves. The half-life of strontium 90 is thirty years; of plutonium 239, 24 000 years.

Hardwoods Timber from deciduous trees whose slow growth rate produces compact hard wood.

Heat budget What happens to all of the sun's energy on its way to the earth's surface.

Heavy nucleus Part of a nuclear atom which can be split into smaller fragments by nuclear fission, so producing large amounts of excess energy.

High density housing Many houses built in a relatively small area.

High rise buildings Tall blocks of flats and offices.

Impervious Rocks which do not let rainwater pass through them freely. They may be porous, like clay, or practically non-porous like granite.

Infant mortality rate The average number of children out of every 1000 born that die within one year of birth.

Intensive farming High production farming on a limited, often small, area, i.e. high yield per hectare.

Insolation The radiant energy received from the sun by the earth and other planets of the solar system. It varies considerably over the earth's surface.

Isotope Atoms of the same element which differ in mass because of the different number of neutrons in the nucleus: uranium and uranium 235, for example. Unstable isotopes emit radiation as they decay. They are known as radioisotopes.

Keel (slugs) A raised ridge on the midline of the body ending in the tail where it is most prominent.

Labour intensive A system of farm management involving many workers.

Light nuclei Nuclei of atomic atoms which contain small numbers of protons and neutrons. They can be combined by fusion, so producing large amounts of excess energy.

Long wave radiation Wavelengths above visible light.

Mantle (slugs) A flap of skin and tissues covering part of the body and enclosing the lung, found anterior to the head in most species except *Testacella*, in which it is under the shell.

Marginal land Land only just worth cultivating, for example on the edge of heath or moorland.

Multiplier farms Where pig breeding companies supervise the mating and production of healthy high genetic quality gilts, or young female pigs, which are then sold to pork farmers.

Mutation A sudden change in a gene or chromosome which may noticeably affect the organism.

Nymph A young wingless larval stage of an insect which resembles the adult.
Egg → nymph stages → winged adult.

Open field system Two or three large fields split into small strips and worked by many individuals.

Overpopulation Too many people for the resources available.

Parasitic Living in or on another organism called the host. The host may or may not be harmed.

Parliamentary enclosures When private and general Acts of Parliament were taken to physically enclose a piece of land for individual ownership in the 17th to 19th centuries.

Pasteurisation A process which kills all possible harmful bacteria in milk by raising its temperature to 71°C for 15 seconds and then rapidly cooling it to not more than 10°C.

Perennial Plant which lives and flowers year after year.

Pneumostome (slugs) An external opening of the lung on the right side of the mantle.

Potometer Apparatus used to measure water uptake in a shoot. Often used as an indication of the transpiration rate.

Ppm Parts per million.

Prevailing winds The direction from which the wind generally blows.

Primary energy Energy produced directly from a basic source.

Radiation A natural process by which energy gets from one point to another. The energy is radiated through space as waves. Different sources of radiation produce waves of different lengths. Groups of these wavelengths with similar properties are known as wavebands.

Raw materials Materials in an unprocessed state.

Recycling Reprocessing a waste product for further use.

Röntgen The unit of exposure to radioactivity.

Shortwave radiation Wavelengths below visible light.

Sievert Unit now used instead of the rem to measure the dose of radioactivity received by the body. Below 10 millisieverts there is no detectable effect. The recommended maximum dose for a member of the public is 5 millisieverts per year. For a radiation worker it is 50 millisieverts.

Softwood Timber from a conifer tree.

Soil auger Instrument used to take soil samples from the ground.

Spontaneous combustion To burst into flames without being set alight.

Strawwalkers A series of vibrating 'trays' which pass the separated stems, or straws, out of the combine harvester.

Suburbia Urban development on the fringes of a city.

Symbiosis A relationship between two dissimilar organisms to their mutual benefit, e.g. algae and fungi in lichens, nitrogen fixing bacteria and leguminous plants such as beans and peas.

Terraces Flat sections of land cut into hill slopes for cultivation with walls or embankments to retain irrigation water and soil.

Tides The alternative rise and fall of the sea's surface approximately twice a day, caused by the gravitational pull of the moon and to a lesser extent, the sun.

Tracheal gills Found on the abdomen of aquatic insect larvae for the exchange of gases between the tiny tracheae, or tubes, inside and the water outside their thin walls.

Variation Differences in structure or character among offspring of the same parents or among members of a related group.

Vasectomy An operation in men, involving the cutting and tying of the sperm duct, to prevent the release of sperm during sexual intercourse.

Vitamins Protective chemicals required in small amounts in the diet to maintain good health.

Index